Dialogicality in Development

Edited by
INGRID E. JOSEPHS

Advances in Child Development
Within Culturally Structured Environments
JAAN VALSINER, *Series Editor*

Westport, Connecticut
London

Library of Congress Cataloging-in-Publication Data

Dialogicality in development / edited by Ingrid E. Josephs.
     p. cm.—(Advances in child development within culturally structured
environments)
  Includes bibliographical references and index.
  ISBN 1–56750–576–7 (alk. paper)
  1. Developmental psychology. 2. Developmental psychology—Social aspects.
I. Josephs. Ingrid E., 1961– II. Series.
BF713.D53   2003
155—dc21   2003046308

British Library Cataloguing in Publication Data is available.

Library of Congress Catalog Card Number: 2003046308
ISBN: 1–56750–576–7

First published in 2003

Praeger Publishers, 88 Post Road West, Westport, CT 06881
An imprint of Greenwood Publishing Group, Inc.
www.praeger.com

Printed in the United States of America

The paper used in this book complies with the
Permanent Paper Standard issued by the National
Information Standards Organization (Z39.48–1984).

10 9 8 7 6 5 4 3 2 1

Contents

Varieties of Dialogue:
Instead of an Introduction

Ingrid E. Josephs

In this chapter I will neither praise nor "sell" the notion of dialogue and dialogicality. This might be unusual for an introduction to a book about dialogue and dialogicality, edited by myself. What I prefer to do here is to put the notion of dialogue to a critical test—acting more as the devil's advocate than as a "member of the club." After a critical inspection of the multiplicity of meanings of dialogue and dialogicality, I will propose a conceptual analysis of the constituents of (among potential others) a dialogical approach. Thus, I *introduce* this book through an explicit *non-introduction*, which perfectly fits with the dialogical model outlined below, in which opposites play a major role in the construction of psychological phenomena.

THE TRIPLE FACE OF DIALOGUE

Dialogue is a confusing term, resulting from its inherent "multivoicedness" and "polyphony": It can refer to (1) *concrete phenomena* (for instance, interpersonal or intrapersonal conversations); (2) *formal models* of mapping psychological and non-psychological (e.g., linguistic) phenomena (known as *dialogicality* or *dialogism*); or (3) *metaphorical analogies* to frame psychological phenomena, with the two latter versions often being intermingled. All three ways to conceptualize dialogue, however, are far from consistent in themselves.

Researchers from various disciplines who deal with dialogue as a phenomenon do not agree whether (and if so, how) "dialogue" refers to anything different than related terms, such as verbal exchange, talk, discourse, conversation, communication, or interaction, among others. And furthermore: Can conflict-talk, authoritative talk, love-talk, suppressive talk, supportive talk, educative talk, small talk, and even mutual silence (peaceful or not) all be subsumed under the big conceptual umbrella of dialogue (see, e.g., Hasselberg, Martienssen, & Radtke, 1996)? Is dialogue everywhere and everything, then? Or, alternatively, should the term "dialogue" better be reserved only for Plato's *Socratic Dialogues* as a structured process to find the truth?

Likewise, it is questioned whether dialogue should include non-verbal variants as well, or strictly imply language use. Moreover, it is asked whether self-talk and talk with "imaginal others" qualify as dialogue. In a similar vein it is discussed whether one's interaction with material/symbolic aspects of culture (e.g., texts, art) are productively captured by the concept of dialogue. We are certainly not surprised that the answers given to these questions are heterogeneous and contradictory.

The same conceptual cacophony can be found in the area of understanding *dialogue as a model*: For instance, dialogue is used as a model of man (as in Buber's dialogical philosophy of the *I and Thou* [Buber, 1923/1958]), a model of self (as in Hermans' *Dialogical Self* [e.g., Hermans & Kempen, 1993]), a model of the sign (as in Bakhtin's [1981] dialogicality of the "word"), and a model of meaning-making (e.g., Josephs & Valsiner, 1998; Josephs, Valsiner, & Surgan, 1999; Meinong, 1983). As a model, dialogue (or dialogicality) at times merely refers to an explicit acknowledgment (and even celebration) of multiplicity (of "voices," of parts of a system), without working out the system's qualities, whereas in other approaches multiplicity is taken for granted as a starting point, while the focus is on the elaboration of the relation between "parts" (structure). Here, very often the boundaries between dialogue as a formal model and dialogue as a guiding, *metaphorical analogy* become blurred. New psychological "movements" often start productively under the guidance of broad and fuzzy metaphors. The latter can function like flashlights, directing one's attention to previously overlooked phenomena. Yet celebrating this step as an endpoint of one's endeavors does certainly not fit with a scientific (dialogical) approach.

DIALOGUE AS A VALUE-LADEN CONCEPT

In science and in everyday life, dialogue (dialogicality) is an appealing term, as it is most often associated with harmonious "transactions" of different kinds in which the respective "partners" (real partners or constituents of a supposed model or system) are both "voiced." Suppression of voices, contest, fight, and war, are usually not strongly associated with the notion of dialogue (but with its absence). In pragmatic linguistics, thus, *understanding* (versus misunderstanding) is the taken-for-granted default outcome of real dialogues—whereas misunderstandings are supposed to be "repaired" (e.g., Schegloff, 1992) as quickly as possible. *Monologue*, a similarly value-laden (this time negative, though) concept is regarded as the opposite of dialogue—associated with dominance, power, and suppression of the other (whoever or whatever "the other" is). Monologue is said to mark the absence of dialogue, and vice versa. This aspect is worth mentioning, because if one strips both concepts from their values, and uses them in a descriptive sense, monologue (or "almost monologue") can also be regarded as a possible outcome of dialogue— for the better or worse (see the elaboration of a dialogical model below). Another opposite of dialogue, *dualism*—an explicit, exclusive separation between parts, voices, or whatever—is associated with a similarly negative flavor. However, there is a slight, yet interesting inconsistency here: Almost all dialogical researchers are opposed to dualism, but appreciate (even praise) the concepts of multivoicedness and polyphony, though the latter do only one thing: They draw our attention to many-ness (multiplicity) versus one-ness, without making any claims about the structural qualities of this "many-ness." Thus, as long as alternatives are not worked out, dualism is one possible (and legitimate) variant within multiplicity. Anti-dualistic credos alone will certainly not do the job to get rid of dualistic notions. Dialectics is for many (though not all) a variant of dialogue (dialogicality), specifying the parts as thesis and antithesis, and the novel outcome of this relationship as synthesis. Thus, dialogicality includes dialectics as one sub-form.

The fuzziness of the umbrella term "dialogue," together with its association of beauty and poetics, supports its metaphorical use in all possible contexts. Dialogue carries the cozy notion of "togetherness," which especially in "anti-individual" psychologies (e.g., certain branches of socio-cultural or social constructionist approaches) is celebrated— while subjectivity is easily given up for intersubjectivity, the mind for the social, the "I" for "the other" (or the "we"), and so on. Togetherness is in some sense the new "hero," though a quite monolithic (monological?), "fused" hero (exactly like the *average* in mainstream psychology; see below), *if* it is not specified *how* this togetherness (in a multivoiced self, in intersubjectivity) actually comes about and operates further. Due to the flavor of togetherness and sharing, notions of dialogue and dialogicality easily feed into an emancipatory psychology, a psychology of liberation and empowerment—a non-neutral psychology with the goal to change society, for the better or worse.

DIALOGUE IN PSYCHOLOGY

Psychology at large (academic mainstream psychology, as represented in the "top journals") continues its business remarkably independently from dialogical movements: There is only little, if any dialogue between different streams of psychology, while each stream (main and other streams) proclaims—in a quasi-religious fashion—to know "the truth." Whereas new dialogical streams celebrate (and at times even productively *face*) complexity, mainstream psychology is characterized by an urge to get rid of it as soon as possible. Along these lines, it often purposefully blocks itself from understanding phenomena in terms of dialogue/dialogicality. For instance, in my field, personality psychology, researchers have for decades forced their subjects to articulate a *monological*, straightforward voice in personality questionnaires. Give it a yes *or* a no answer! Ambivalence, ambiguity, multivoicedness, dialogue—a yes *and* a no, for instance—are not allowed! Average your experience as well as possible (even if it is impossible for you), but give a clear answer! What is curiously happening here is that a "scientific" method *creates* a potentially artificial phenomenon, without leaving traces of irritation in the respective researchers, or questions what the "real" phenomenon might have looked like. Likewise, in attachment theory (with a few exceptions, though) a person is basically *either* securely attached *or not*, but *not both at the same time*. Period! It seems that complexity of psychological phenomena is so threatening that it is immediately turned into an artificial simplicity. Thus, to celebrate the average as the main protagonist, and turn variance into the annoying black box of "error," is a purposeful attempt (or a Freudian defense mechanism) to avoid any notion of multiplicity, let alone dialogicality (of a yet to be specified kind). In other terms, despite the conceptual confusion of the various notions of dialogue, it seems that a strong resistance against dialogicality (and its elaboration) is counterproductive for constructing knowledge about psychology's very subject matter: the psyche.

BASICS OF A DIALOGICAL-DEVELOPMENTAL MODEL: A CONCEPTUAL ATTEMPT

How, then, can we make productive use of the concepts of dialogue and dialogicality—fuzzy and ill-defined as they are, creating an immediate *as-if* understanding among researchers, preventing them (us) from becoming more explicit? For psychologists, conceptual fuzziness is generally no surprise, but everyday business. Furthermore, fuzziness is not necessarily negative, as fuzzy concepts can even enhance communication and collaboration between scientists (Löwy, 1992). Yet at some moment, the work of "becoming precise" has to start.

Thus, in this paragraph, I will try to outline the basic assumptions of a dialogical model or approach. I define the dialogical model as a developmental model, thus the terms are interchangeable here. Development can lead to both transformation (with an openness for transformation toward novelty) and active maintenance of temporary stability. Both outcomes have to be captured by the dialogical-developmental model.

The dialogical approach formally denies the Aristotelian/Boolean notion of identity. In contrast, dialogical models rely on a *duality of patterning of mutually related, co-present opposites* (see Chapter 1, this volume), in general and formal terms: {A & non-A}. The term "opposite" or oppositionality is understood here in a broad sense, including contrariety, contradiction, contrast, and negation (see Chapter 2, this volume). In more (yet not sufficiently) concrete terms, a figure is a figure only *in relation* to a co-present ground, a self is a self only *in relation* to a co-present other (as in Buber's philosophy; see Chapter 5, this volume), a mind is a mind only *in relation* to the co-present culture (see Chapters 7 and 8, this volume), a meaning is a meaning only *in relation* to a co-present countermeaning (see Chapter 9, this volume), a speaker is a speaker only *in relation* to a co-present listener—be that in auto- or heterodialogue—and a concept is a concept only *in relation* to the co-presence of what it is not. In terms of cultural psychologist Boesch:

There is no reality without its alternatives: Could I conceive of a circle without the experience of angular forms? . . . Every action forecloses, negates, or at least provisionally eliminates other actions. . . . Reality appears always to be qualified by non-realized alternatives. (Boesch, 1991, p. 77f.)

These points are certainly not new: They borrow from dialectical philosophical systems (Rychlak, 1995, and Chapter 5, this volume) and from the traditions of the Prague Linguistic School (Marková, 1992, and Chapter 1, this volume). Furthermore, we can trace back the origin of conceptualizing phenomena in terms of constructed opposites to the philosophical approach to assumptions by Alexius Meinong, an Austrian philosopher who established the foundations of Gestalt thought in Graz in the 1880s (Meinong, 1983). Roots can also be found within the theory of co-genetic logic (Herbst, 1995) which formalizes the inevitability of looking jointly at a form and its immediately (co-genetically) implied context.

The notion of dualities is non-dualistic in nature, as the parts are not exclusively separated, but, just contrary to that, only exist in and through their relating. On the other hand, to give up the notion of parts altogether, *fusion* (for instance, to fuse mind and culture, or individual speakers into a "joint and shared project" of discourse, or subjectivities immediately into intersubjectivities)—would not only make it impossible to analyze the structure of the whole (the duality), as there is no longer any structure without parts, but also to describe and explain any dynamic transformation (including transformation in the direction of novelty) of the whole, the latter resulting from the co-acting of its parts. From this perspective, fusion is nothing but a type of monologicality, in which the parts are lumped together in a miraculous way (*Monologicality I*). Here we are certainly not far from mainstream psychology's favored averaging. Similarly, denying the very fact of duality in favor of an explicitly monological model (*Monologicality II*, which, by the way, is identical with a dualistic model) renders it impossible to conceptualize transformation. If the phenomenon under investigation, for instance, the "mind," is regarded as an entified and thus monological unit, on which separate other entified and monological units (e.g., "culture") are said to have an influence (qua their status as independent variables), the question of the process of change is only answered statistically, yet not psychologically, as it remains a mystery how this influence is operating psychologically (that is, beyond ANOVA-type of mathematical analyses).

The mere assumption of a duality of patterning, however, does not solve the question how development occurs. *Relation* of the parts (versus mere multiplicity) is one prerequisite. Not specifying a relation is not far from a monological model (*Monologicality II*), in which the parts are simply existing next to each other—as little monads or little homunculi (e.g., sub-selves). A *non-additive* relationship is the second requirement to allow for transformation, as is well-known at least since Gestalt theory's basic insights. Additive relations are *non-dynamic* in nature, that is, they cannot result in potentially qualitatively new outcomes. In a model elaborated elsewhere (Josephs & Valsiner, 1998; Josephs, Valsiner, & Surgan, 1999), we assumed that *tensional* relations between the parts make the duality open for further transformation, in other terms, for development, whereas *non-tensional* relations lead to temporary stability. Tensional relationships, thus, might lead to various outcomes, with emergence of novelty as one possibility (for an overview of a horizon of potential other outcomes, see Valsiner, 2002).

Emotional-Semiotic Mediators as Catalysts of Psychological Processes

The notion of tension does not only historically lead back (which is in contemporary psychology very often a "lead-forward") to psychological models of the person's *life-space* à la Kurt Lewin, but also to chemical and biological theorizing, especially to models of *enzymatic catalysis* (see Valsiner, 2002)—a process "under tension." In the latter models, it is due to the temporary binding role of a catalyst that synthesis of substances (parts) becomes possible, whereas direct and unmediated synthesis is not possible.

Psychological catalysts operate in the form of emotional-semiotic mediators, as can be illustrated with the help of an extension of Fritz Heider's (1958) balance theory: If I generally hate warts on the face, yet the man

I fall in love with happens to have a permanent, hairy (and thus particularly disgusting) exemplar right on his chin, unavoidably tension is built up. Yet soon, if not immediately, I may find myself in a position to like, even tenderly touch this originally disgusting body mark, and see in it something extraordinary (in a positive sense), which belongs to my beloved one (and thus to me). There is neither mystery nor pathology in this process (I am sure that everybody has experienced situations like this in one or the other way, though I want to stress that this example does not come from my personal life-space). It is the powerful emotional-semiotic catalyst (my *felt* notion of love, and the *value* I attach [and I learned *should* be attached] to my partner) which radically transforms my relation to the world (here to a drastic exemplar of a wart) through an immediate overgeneralization of this value orientation. In other terms, there is no rational decision behind my new attitude toward this wart (a meaning-reversal in its extreme from disgusting ugliness to even beauty), and no conscious effort to begin to like it step by step. What happened is an emotionally triggered transformation of my meaning-system due to a strong and felt value orientation—a higher-level regulator (the catalyst) which leads to a new, generalized quality of the meaning-system (dominating and temporarily "de-voicing" my previous disgust): This is no longer "a" wart I hate, but a part of a man I deeply love. I may find myself in a state of actively stabilizing and maintaining my new almost monological voice then—I stress and defend to like the wart (in auto- and hetero-dialogue, here understood as a phenomenon), even if my friend cautiously asks whether I could not try to convince my partner to get rid of it. Enforced stabilizing and maintenance of meaning can also lead to *fossilization*—a meaning becomes a generalized value orientation in itself, stripped from its history of emergence, and can act as a catalyst at any time (for instance, immediately devaluing men with a perfect face, or immediately hating people who react negatively to my partner's wart—to stay in the example).

Often, however, stability is temporary in nature: My dislike of warts in general, and this exemplar in particular, is only temporarily backgrounded, it is still present as a potentiality (see the notion of duality of patterning elaborated above); hence I prefer to use the term "almost monologicality," which I derived from Lewis' (2002) notion of "almost dialogues." The fact that dialogicality is not overruled by "almost monologicality" becomes obvious in this example (and in many more examples) in case relationships fail eventually. The old disgust is suddenly and immediately present again (due to a lack of the general value orientation, and the potential introduction of a new value orientation as catalyst), and the fact that we once liked what we now feel to be disgusting often comes as a personal miracle (if not catastrophe).

Emotional-semiotic-mediators are so powerful that they even can block any building up of tension and thus function as *feed-forward regulators*. For instance, we might even not become aware of peculiarities of our partner, which in other people we would immediately consider as annoying, if not disgusting, or immediately circumvent the building up of tension by creating a countermeaning. Again, when the relationship begins to fail, the temporarily backgrounded, even hidden, meaning is foregrounded again.

There are myriads of other examples which illustrate the powerful role of emotional-semiotic catalysts: If I eat some very tasty food in a foreign country, and I suddenly become aware that I ate a cat, I might immediately escape to the bathroom (example from Valsiner, 2001). The emotional-semiotic catalyst here is a strong value orientation of considering cats as non-food (and not even allowing me to think of them as tasty), whose entrance in my here-and-now system immediately leads to radical change (from considering something, the *objectively same thing*, as tasty to an immediate feeling of unbearable disgust toward this thing). Even my physiological system is strongly affected—which only proves the remarkable power of the catalyst. Another convincing example is the regulation of one's feelings while cleaning the shower's sink from hair: it makes a difference (at least for many people) whether this hair, clean and perfectly identical, belongs to oneself (or close others)—neutral feelings—or to strangers—potential disgust or its avoidance through wearing gloves (distancing through action versus psychological distancing). Here the catalyst transports the powerful value orientation of what is considered to be dirt and non-dirt, with anything belonging to one's body (or bodies one is close with) mostly falling to the second category. Thus, psychological catalysts work extremely powerfully and quickly (and thus "economically"), and they can only do so through their emotional grounding.

The productivity of the supposed model, which can only be roughly outlined here, still needs to be demonstrated within empirical studies. Already now, however, it draws our attention to everyday phenomena, which are otherwise easily overlooked: the miraculous "switch" between love and hate, disgust and pleasure, and the phenomenon of "almost monological" meanings as outcomes of dialogical processes. Furthermore, this model is useful to handle the remarkable quickness with which we as human beings do construct and reconstruct the world or ourselves—basically on the spot. This quickness is due to the guidance of strong emotions, which are an integral part (rather than a separate or separable side aspect) of human reasoning or the mind.

Dialogicality in Development: An Overview

The present volume, truly international in nature, captures a mixture of "language games" with regard to the respective notion of dialogue.

Dialogue is regarded (and worked out!) as a concrete phenomenon, a model, or a productive metaphor by the authors, coming from different sub-disciplines of psychology. All authors try to link dialogue to development—whether in microgenesis, ontogenesis, or phylogenesis—hence the title: *Dialogicality in Development*.

The volume is divided in three Parts: In Part I, the basic concepts of a dialogical approach are introduced in the areas of the human mind and language. This part allows the reader to place the dialogical approach in its historical, philosophical, and linguistic traditions. Dialogicality is a key concept in the linguistic analysis of language. Thus, in Chapter 1, Marková elaborates the concept of dialogicality in linguistics and semiotics, with a special focus on the history of the Prague School of Linguistics until today. In Chapter 2, Rychlak focuses on one of the most important concepts of a dialogical model: oppositionality. He gives a historical overview of the concept of oppositionality, and shows within the framework of his *Logical Learning Theory* how human reasoning is only understandable through the notion of oppositionality.

Part II focuses on dialogicality and the development of the self. In Chapter 3, Lyra and Souza trace dynamic processes in early communication between mother and infant along Bakhtin's notion of dialogism. With the help of microgenetic analyses, they can show how in playful "giving-and-taking" exchanges dialogical patterns of quasi-stability are established. These patterns emerge out of the dyad's history of previous exchanges, and are at the same time open for the future, for the emergence of novel variants. Furthermore, these dialogical patterns, which are unique for each dyad, build the basis from which individual selves emerge. In Chapter 4, Abbey and Davis turn our attention to processes of identity construction in young adults. Also applying a microgenetic framework, they demonstrate how identity construction is semiotically mediated in the young adult's feeling and thinking when confronted with rap music. With its explicit and derogatory lyrics on the one hand, and its inviting beat on the other hand, the authors were able to trigger conversations within people—autodialogue—in which the latter evaluate the roots of their own opinions and beliefs. In Chapter 5, Watkins reminds us of the fact that any end goal in any area of development is not an empirically given fact, but stipulated by the researcher (or the research tradition). For Watkins, the preferred end goal or telos is liberation. Thus, her psychology of the self is emancipatory in nature, with the goal to empower people, to encourage the unvoiced to voice themselves. She demonstrates that dialogue—both inter- and intrapersonal— is an important means to reach this goal. In Chapter 6, Hermans and Josephs outline a developmental perspective on the dialogical self from infancy to adulthood. Their specific focus is on reconciling the notions of constructive innovation and mechanistic routines of the self, which are both necessary for normal functioning.

In Part III, the relationships between culture and person are elaborated from a dialogical point of view. In Chapter 7, Toomela follows Vygotsky in arguing that the emergence and evolution of the human mind is possible only with the emergence and evolution of culture. Culture and individual constitute each other in a dialogue where they have qualitatively different, complementary, roles. Culture is responsible for the differentiation of human minds from other animals. Only humans are capable of semiotically mediated thought. Following Vygotsky, Toomela also suggests that it is possible to differentiate hierarchical levels in the evolution of culture and elaborates this argument. In Chapter 8, Jahoda critically comments on Toomela's approach. Though he generally appreciates Toomela's way of reasoning, he argues against his notion of hierarchy of more or less developed cultures (and the more or less developed thinking of the respective people "in" these cultures) and his evolutionary approach. In Chapter 9, Gupta and Valsiner analyze, with the help of a concrete example, how cultural, macroscopic semiotic complexes—here a myth-story—create a basis for personal, internalized self-regulation. Myths only fulfill their guiding function when becoming dialogically related to the individual's experiential sphere. How the structure of the myth-story as such adds to this function is demonstrated in the chapter. In Chapter 10, Bhatia criticizes Berry's well-known model of "acculturation strategies." Alternatively, he elaborates a model in which power and difference play a role, and acculturation is seen as a process (rather than a state) full of conflict, contest, dialogue, and negotiation, especially for immigrants from diasporic communities. Like Watkins, he makes us aware that any postulated end goal of acculturation (e.g., "integration" in Berry's sense) is stipulated by a researcher rather than representing empirical reality. The stipulation of *different* end goals, or teloi, and *different* means to reach them, might be more productive from the perspective of immigrants from diasporic communities than the means and ends proposed by the acculturation model.

In general, the chapters of this volume invite the reader to enter into dialogue with different concepts of dialogicality, and different concepts of development. It is my hope and even more so, my conviction, that new ideas and inspirations will emerge from this dialogue.

REFERENCES

Bakhtin, M. (1981). *The dialogic imagination*. Austin: University of Texas Press.

Boesch, E. E. (1991). *Symbolic action theory and cultural psychology*. New York: Springer.

Buber, M. (1923/1958). *I and Thou*. New York: Scribner's.

Hasselberg, E., Martienssen, L., & Radtke, F. (Eds.). (1996). *Der Dialogbegriff am Ende des 20. Jahrhunderts*. [The concept of dialogue at the end of the twentieth century.] Berlin: Hegel Institut.

Heider, F. (1958). *The psychology of interpersonal relations*. New York: Wiley.

Herbst, D. P. (1995). What happens when we make a distinction: An elementary introduction to co-genetic logic. In T. Kindermann & J. Valsiner (Eds.), *Development of person-context relations* (pp. 67–79). Hillsdale, NJ: Erlbaum.

Hermans, H.J.M., & Kempen, H.J.G. (1993). *The dialogical self: Meaning as movement*. San Diego, CA: Academic Press.

Josephs, I. E., & Valsiner, J. (1998). How does autodialogue work? *Social Psychology Quarterly, 61*, 68–83.

Josephs, I. E., Valsiner, J., & Surgan, S. E. (1999). The process of meaning construction: Dissecting the flow of semiotic activity. In J. Brandstädter & R. M. Lerner (Eds.), *Action & self-development* (pp. 257–282). Thousand Oaks, CA: Sage.

Lewis, M. D. (2002). The dialogical brain. *Theory & Psychology, 12*, 175–190.

Löwy, L. (1992). The strength of loose concepts. *History of Science, 50*, 376–396.

Marková, I. (1992). On structure and dialogicality in Prague semiotics. In A. H. Wold (Ed.), *The dialogical alternative* (pp. 45–63). Oslo: Scandinavian University Press.

Meinong, A. (1983). *On assumptions*. Berkeley: University of California Press.

Rychlak, J. F. (1995). A teleological critique of modern cognitivism. *Theory & Psychology, 5*, 511–531.

Schegloff, E. A. (1992). Repair after next turn: The last structurally provided defense of intersubjectivity in conversation. *American Journal of Sociology, 97*, 1295–1345.

Valsiner, J. (2001). *Comparative study of human cultural development*. Madrid: Fundación Infancia y Aprendizaje.

Valsiner, J. (2002). Forms of dialogical relations and semiotic autoregulation within the self. *Theory & Psychology, 12*, 251–265.

Part I

Basic Theoretical Concepts

Chapter 1

Dialogicality in the Prague School of Linguistics: A Theoretical Retrospect

Ivana Marková

The 1920s and 1930s, the period between the two world wars, brimmed with new ideas attempting to liberate the human mind in every aspect of life, art, and science. It was the period of the world destitute and crippled in the aftermath of the First World War, of persecution, migration and uncertainty in many European countries, and the threat of Nazism already looming. Communism, established in the Soviet Union, promised paradise to some and hell to others. It was also the period of the pursuit of the sense of magic, a period galvanized by daring artistic and anti-artistic movements and revolutionary scientific theories. The social sciences and the humanities were polarized by diverse approaches such as positivism on the one hand and dialogicality on the other. This is the broad political, social, historical, and cultural spectrum in which the theoretical achievements of the Prague School of Linguistics must be understood and interpreted.

I propose to discuss here certain aspects of dialogicality as it was adopted and developed by some, though by no means by all members of the Prague School of Linguistics. To my mind, the essential characteristic of dialogicality as an ontology and epistemology of the social sciences and humanities is that it provides conceptual means for the study of the dynamic interdependence between thought and language by semiotic means. Some aspects of this dynamic interdependence were outlined, if not fully theoretically developed, by the Prague School. This is why, today, the dialogical ideas of the Prague School of Linguistics deserve further pursuit and theoretical development, not only in linguistics but in all disciplines in which the study of the interdependence between thought and language are primary goals, such as developmental and social psychology.

While conceptually dialogism has a long history, it seems that the terms "dialogicality" and "dialogism" were first used by the neo-Kantian philosophers of the 1920s, for whom the "dialogical principle" was involved in the interdependence and the mutual acknowledgment between the I–you. The neo-Kantian philosophers assumed that in the process of this dialogical relationship the self becomes a reflexive and a self-conscious object of its own thought. The self develops the ability to comprehend the effect of its own communication (i.e., of speech and otherwise) both on the self and on others.

THE PRAGUE SCHOOL OF LINGUISTICS AND THE ISSUE OF DIALOGICALITY

It would be a mistake to think of the Prague School of Linguistics as a unified school of thought exposing dialogicality as a coherent, conceptual system. The movement known as the Prague School of Linguistics and the history during which its theories developed became more sophisticated and diversified.

The Prague School of Linguistics, and more generally, the Prague semiotic movement, established itself as a leading scientific, artistic, and humanistic approach in Czechoslovakia in the early years of the twentieth century. Although originally it was concerned primarily, though not exclusively, with the study of language, in the late 1920s and in the 1930s it grew into a broadly based interdisciplinary and multidisciplinary semiotic orientation. It interpenetrated many spheres of cultural life, such as the arts, literature, ethnography, aesthetics, film, theater, the social sciences, and humanities.

The main classical period of the Prague School of Linguistics and semiotics is usually placed between the years 1926, when the Prague School Circle was established, and 1939, when Czechoslovak universities were closed by the Nazis (Vachek, 1964). The Circle was founded in 1926 by Vilém Mathesius according to the model of the Moscow Linguistic Circle. The theoretical aims were formulated and developed into the program of the Circle in the *Théses* (1929), presented to the First International Congress of Slavonic Languages in Prague in 1929. The *Théses* dealt with a variety of issues concerning theoretical, methodological, and pedagogical problems of Slavonic languages. One of the main aims of the program was the study of the relationship between synchrony (i.e., the study of language as a static system at a particular time, without regard to its change) and diachrony (i.e., the study of language as a system in change and development). The *Théses*—from the very beginning—included the position that in contrast to the claims of the Saussure school, one should not make a strict separation between the synchronic and diachronic approaches to the study of language. The *Théses* emphasized, instead, that in order to examine the system of language in terms of its functions, it was necessary to study how it develops. One should not presuppose that linguistic changes are destructive elements without any purpose. Rather, the study of linguistic changes facilitates the understanding of the stability of language and of its functions. Moreover, the study of the synchronic system would be incomplete without an investigation of its evolution because the language system as it exists in its present form not only contains its disappearing elements, but it already anticipates its future developments.

Saussure's relevance for the Prague School was still profound. Some of Saussure's students (e.g. Karcevskij and Trubetzkoy) were members of the Prague School or lived in Prague. For a while Saussure's ideas were brought to Prague directly through them. Yet, exactly what Saussure's influence on the Prague School in the 1920s and 1930s was is more difficult to assess. As others (e.g., Fontaine, 1974) pointed out, this impact manifested itself to a great extent as an inspiration for disputes and controversies rather than simply as an acceptance of Saussure's ideas. Much of what Saussure thought about and what was published as his posthumous *Cours de Linguistique Générale* (1915/1959) had already been part of the conceptual framework within which Czechs worked. This was partly due to the fact that Czech linguistic thinking was inspired by similar sources as those of Saussure, for example, the influence of neo-Grammarians, Whitley's linguistics, and more generally by the scientific thema of relativity which had been important both in the study of language and in physical sciences and mathematics since the 1870s.

From the beginning, the Prague School was characterized by its functional approach (the notion "functional" is today replaced by "pragmatic") in the study of language. The Prague functionalism was built on the position that both the linguistic system and discourse processes, comprising the speaker, listener, and situation, represent the proper object of linguistics (Mathesius, 1929). However, the details of this pragmatic approach in terms of, say, the interdependence between sentence and utterance, language and speaking, and so on, were not clearly developed at the beginning of the Prague School approach. Even later, in many respects, Prague theories remained in outlines rather than being spelled out in their entirety.

Many members of the Prague School were oriented toward the study of the use of language. This is perhaps why the concept of interdependence between language and its context was applied to all, or to almost all, linguistic issues. These were all considered in their communicative, extra-linguistic, and cultural contexts, in other words, *as if* in a dialogue (i.e., as if in a person-to-person symbolic communication using a system

of signs). Thus the dialogue-like approach surfaced in the study of phonology, morphology, and syntax, just like in the studies of dialogue
proper, in the semiotics of arts, the ways of thinking and representing,
and in general, in the study of social and cultural phenomena.

For many members of the Prague School, from Mathesius to Jakobson,
proper linguistics should be always oriented toward communication and
to the change of grammatical forms of concrete speech acts in given
situations. It is to be recognized, though, that this orientation was often
only an outline of ideas rather than a proper theory and a complete
linguistic analysis. Probably the most fully developed theoretical analyses are to be found in Jakobson's work. For example, his theory of shifters (Jakobson, 1957/1971) shows how the switch in meanings between
the "I" and "you" is achieved grammatically. The interdependence between shifters (i.e., grammatical categories, such as tense, mood, and
person on the one hand, and concrete communication situations on the
other) makes it clear that he considered the relationship between the
statics and dynamics, form and meaning, grammar and communication,
as interrelated and inseparable. He also showed that, in contrast to a
person without a communication problem, a person with aphasia totally
loses his or her ability to use shifters. Not being able to take the perspective of the other, such a person no longer communicates dialogically;
in fact, one can say that he or she is completely deprived of the "why"
of communication.

Finally, there were considerable theoretical and conceptual differences
between various members of the Prague School. For example, some
members were more inclined to adopt a static approach of Saussurean
synchrony rather than the synchrony/diachrony approach. There were
also differences among the members with respect to the ways the relation
between *langue* and *parole* was conceived (cf. Fontaine, 1974; Toman,
1995). Some members, like Jakobson, focused primarily on the theoretical
development of linguistics and of other language-based disciplines while
others, like Mathesius, emphasized practical issues in the study and the
use of language (cf. Daneš, 1998).

Although during the Second World War and the Nazi occupation the
work of the Prague Circle was not totally disrupted, it was significantly
reduced. This was due not only to the direct restriction of activities by
the Nazis, but also to death (e.g., Trubetzskoj) and emigration of some
essential figures (e.g., Jakobson, Wellek) of the movement, caused by the
Nazi regime.

Immediately after the Second World War, the Circle again increased
its activities. Unfortunately, these were soon quashed, this time by the
communist ideology, which became a dominating force in all aspects of
intellectual life. With the communist takeover in 1948, the Circle ceased
to exist. Thus, more than twenty years of regular scholarly meetings, at

which, in addition to the members of the Prague School, many significant international guests presented their ideas (such as Tesnière, Jespersen, Carnap, Husserl, Benveniste, Hjelmslev, Tynjanov among others), were finally brought to an end. In the late 1950s and in the 1960s the activities of the Prague School were gradually renewed although, having been always controlled by totalitarian and post-totalitarian ideology until 1989, they never reached the pre-war originality, its creative spirit, and the same international reputation.

Dialogical Thinking in the Conception of Synchrony and Diachrony

Viewing synchrony and diachrony either as parallel and independent phenomena for the study of language (as the Saussureans did), or as interdependent phenomena (as Jakobson did) divided the Prague School between those who adopted and who did not adopt dialogical thinking. Of course, as is always the case, other members of the Prague School fell between the two positions.

If dialogicality is an ontology and epistemology of the social sciences and humanities then, clearly, it must lay bare all aspects of thought and language relevant to the themes in question. My focus here on synchrony and diachrony is underlined by theoretical and by historical reasons. Theoretically, the opposing conceptions of synchrony and diachrony expose tendencies in thinking (1) either toward universals and stability or toward social change, (2) of oppositions being treated as either independent and parallel or as interdependent, (3) of oppositions as linear and contingent rather than as co-present and in tension with one another, (4) of structures as self-contained rather than as situated in and interdependent with their communicative contexts.

The second main reason for the importance of this theme lies in history. The view of language as being situated in culture and revitalized by speaking has a long tradition in the Czech thought. The Czech language was, during the Habsburg era from the sixteenth to nineteenth centuries, close to extinction and the wake-up of the nation in the eighteenth century meant the renaissance of language through common speech. The view that speech cultivates culture and culture is enriched by speech was an important theme in building up the notion of national identity.

The Distinction between Language Statics and Dynamics

Although the distinction between the relatively stable (cultural) and the relatively variable (individual) features of language was already anticipated by Humboldt, the relationship between statics and dynamics became a scientific theme, both in mathematics and in linguistics, around 1870 (Jakobson, 1972/1985, pp. 81ff.). At that time, in these two fields the questions of invariance and variation, of symmetry and asymmetry and of breaking the symmetry, assumed much attention. Einstein pointed out that when Maxwell's electrodynamic laws for bodies at rest are applied to phenomena in movement, asymmetries will immediately come into focus. They are not inherent in the phenomena themselves but in their relationships with other phenomena (Holton, 1978, pp. 380–381).

Analyzing Einstein's ideas about mathematics and linguistics, Jakobson (1972/1985, pp. 81ff.) refers to Einstein's adolescent years when he became acquainted with the work of Jost Winteler, a pioneer of the idea of asymmetry/symmetry in linguistics. Einstein never forgot to acknowledge the influence of Winteler upon his own thinking. Einstein's ideas on relativity go back to his adolescent years when, having failed the entrance examination to the Federal Institute of Technology in Zurich, he studied for a year in Aarau. He became there a boarder in Winteler's home, who at that time wrote a dissertation, in 1876, in which he made a distinction between "accidental features" in language (variability) and "essential properties" (invariance). Young Einstein was influenced by this idea to the extent that he himself acknowledged later on, on various occasions, that "the germ of relativity theory" was already contained in the paradoxical reflections which first inspired him during the Aarau year (Jakobson, 1979/1988, p. 259).

Unfortunately, because Winteler's ideas were too progressive for his time, the conservative Germanic environment was wholly unresponsive to them. It was only in the 1930s that a member of the Prague School, Trubetzkoy, rediscovered the novelty of Winteler's ideas when asymmetry/symmetry and polarities became an essential theme both in the Moscow and in the Prague Linguistic Circles. It was then that the concept of invariance in linguistics was reevaluated, having become conceived as a reverse to change in terms of the relativity theory.

Many years later, when Jakobson fully developed his dialogically based linguistic theories, he (1979/1988, p. 19) reminded us that since the 1870s, in the work of Winteler and Baudoin, sound patterns of diverse languages had appeared to invoke the principle of relativity of sound categories. As in physics at that time, invariance and relativity were viewed as complementary concepts, "the reverse side of invariance . . . is called relativity."

At about the time when Winteler worked on his theory of language, the distinction between statics and dynamics in philosophy and sociology was made by Comte and Brentano. It appears that the Czech philosopher T. G. Masaryk had considerable influence on the conception of language of the Prague School in terms of the distinction between statics and dynamics.

Masaryk's approach to language and his knowledge of linguistics was influenced by the work of Whitney, Delbruck, Steinthal, Paul, and Marty, while his interest in the problems of scientific method was influenced by Brentano. For him, speech was both the means of communication of inner life, of emotions and thoughts, as well as the most suitable means of communication of our inner life (Masaryk, 1885), and a representation of the object-world, the means of communication about objects (see also Jakobson, 1930/1931, p. 40). It is this latter point which, according to Daneš (1990), makes Masaryk's conception of language surprisingly modern. The distinction between statics and dynamics Masaryk (1885) took from Comte. He was also influenced by Brentano's work, in which he differentiated between descriptive and genetic psychology. To me, this particular connection between the father of positivism and Masaryk's views on linguistics is interesting not only as a historical evidence, but also because it provides a nice example of the theory-ladenness of our understanding.

I interpret Masaryk's views as emphasizing both historical and static approaches in science. As he pointed out, where there is development, there must always be something which develops. In the case of language it was necessary to understand its essence both in abstract and in concrete terms. Language must be studied together with its development in speech, that is, in terms of maintaining stability and creating new essences. In contrast, Toman (1995) interprets Masaryk's views as anti-evolutionary, realistic, and influencing Mathesius to amplify his already a-historic approach to language. Thus Toman claims that for Mathesius, the a-historical variant of Masaryk's linguistic realism became the guiding principle for his work (ibid., pp. 77, 84). Moreover, he comments that for the majority of Czechs language was not fundamentally different from signaling on railways. True, one can find a quotation of this kind in Mathesius, just as one can find quotations which express a totally opposite point of view.

There are two comments one can make. First, and as already pointed out, the theory of the Prague School developed and changed over years. Second, there remained unresolved tensions between some members of the Prague School, concerning the concepts of synchrony and diachrony and of langue and parole. These tensions often remained theoretically implicit and, as a result, they expressed different tendencies, sometimes leaning to a Saussurean point of view, sometimes to a dialogical point of view. It seems to me that the Mathesius work reveals these unresolved tensions.

Relations between Synchrony and Diachrony: from Mathesius to Jakobson

Vilém Mathesius, the founder of the Prague Linguistic Circle, in his still underestimated paper *On the Potentiality of the Phenomena of Language* (1911/1964), presented in 1911 to the Royal Bohemian Learned Society, argued for the synchronistic approach to the study of linguistics. Mathesius made a distinction between static and dynamic (synchronistic and diachronistic) linguistic issues. He introduced the notion of potentiality in language, which refers to a *static oscillation*, as opposed to a *dynamic change*. By static oscillation he meant instability within various aspects of language at a given period of time. Thus, there are idiosyncratic kinds of oscillation in speech amongst individuals speaking a particular language. In addition, there is an oscillation in the semantic characteristics of speech, with words having semantic potentialities rather than strictly rigid meanings. In view of these ideas, Mathesius defined linguistics as

a science whose task is to analyse, in a static [= synchronistic] manner, the language materials used by a language community at a given time, and, in a dynamic [= diachronistic] manner, its historical changes. (Mathesius, 1911/1964, p. 22)

Mathesius argued that linguistics should examine speech of individual speakers in order to reveal "the full extent of the potentiality of the concerned language." Mathesius maintained that his own theory was not entirely new and that some of the ideas he presented had been already suggested by other thinkers. It is here that Mathesius declared that the distinction between statics and dynamics was "first clearly envisaged by the present writer when he was reading, during his university studies, T.G. Masaryk's remarks on linguistics" in 1885.

As he pointed out himself later on, Mathesius had made this distinction several years before Saussure's (1915/1959) *Cours de Linguistique Générale* was published. Unfortunately, Mathesius' important paper, which he read in 1911 to the Royal Bohemian Learned Society, was ignored and not a single question was asked by those present (Wellek, 1976). Mathesius, like Jost Winteler before him, was ahead of his time. Jakobson himself became aware of this paper only in the mid-1920s, and it was then that he declared that had Mathesius delivered his lecture "not in Prague but in Moscow, it would have caused there a veritable revolution in linguistics" (Vachek, 1964).

However, although Mathesius advocated both synchronistic and diachronic approaches to the study of language, it is not clear how, in concrete terms, the two approaches might intertwine. In contrast, for

Saussure synchronic and diachronic approaches were clearly independent from one another. As he says, there are two sciences of language, one dealing with static linguistics, (i.e., synchronic linguistics) and the other dealing with evolutionary linguistics, diachronic linguistics (1915/1959). Language, a system of signs as it was developed in a society, is purely social and independent of the individual. On the other hand, speaking is the actuality of the speaker and it is speaking which causes language to develop and change. Language and speaking are therefore interdependent, language being the instrument and the product of speaking. However, "their interdependence does not prevent their being two absolutely distinct things" and "I shall try never to erase the boundaries that separate the two domains" (Saussure, 1915/1959, pp. 19–20). All language changes take place at the level of parole, having a particular and accidental character. These changes can be analyzed, synchronically, at each stage of the evolution of language. However, synchrony and diachrony are irreducible into one other.

I have already noted that the idea that both synchronic and diachronic approaches in the study of language should be applied was spelled out in the *Théses* (1929), although some members of the Prague School were not in full agreement with that position (Fontaine, 1974). However, those who, like Jakobson, were oriented toward the theoretical development of dialogicality based on the idea of interdependent oppositions expressed their criticism of a pure synchronic approach very clearly. For Tynjanov and Jakobson (1928/1981), pure synchronism was only an illusion because every synchronic system has its past and its future. Every system exists only as evolution and, on the other hand, evolution is inescapably of a systematic nature:

The opposition between synchrony and diachrony was an opposition between the concept of the system and the concept of evolution; thus it loses its importance in principle as soon as we recognize that every system necessarily exists as evolution, whereas, on the other hand, evolution is inescapably of a systemic nature. (Tynjanov and Jakobson, 1928/1981, p. 79)

Why Is It So Difficult to Conceptualize Change?

The difficulty involved in the conceptualization of synchrony and diachrony is not just an example of tensions and conflicts in the Prague School. This difficulty is an expression of a deeper theoretical problem, which has troubled the social sciences and humanities for centuries. The problem is the following: How does one conceptualize social change and the processes related to social change? One can see that both Mathesius and Saussure struggled with this problem. On the one hand, they both conceived of language as a social phenomenon, as a social institution, which changes and develops through the actions of individuals. Yet, the conceptualization of social change as an interdependence between the social and individual or the cultural and individual was and indeed still remains a theoretical and empirical problem if one tries to accomplish this conceptualization using pre-dialectic or pre-dialogical theories.

Like Descartes, Saussure's ideal of science, in this case of synchronic linguistics, was the study in a static manner of the logical and psychological relations existing in the collective mind of speakers. Like Kant, Saussure was aware of the tension between oppositions that he so postulated: between static and dynamic, social and individual, cultural and individual. For him, the fact that language changes appears to have been a sheer nuisance from a scientific point of view. Changes mess up the language system because it changes somewhat all the time and in spite of everything. In true science, one must therefore disregard these arbitrary and accidental changes of little importance. Since Saussure considered synchrony and diachrony as dualities irreducible into one another, the only way to study social change in the thought and language was to study change as a succession of static states.

In reflecting on these issues, one cannot resist from asking the same question again: Why is it so difficult to conceptualize social change despite the fact that we all experience changes all the time? Our needs, whether personal or social, our wishes, hopes, and fears express themselves through the tensions we experience, through intentions by means of which we try to change our existence, through failures and disappointment which magnify the discrepancy between reality and our desired ideal. Yet, much of our research in the social sciences is like the Saussurean study of change in language: the study of the system synchronically at each stage of development.

I propose, therefore, to turn attention to this more general difficulty to conceptualize change which, to my mind, has something to do with the difficulty to adopt the dialogical ontology and epistemology of oppositions and triads.

Thinking in Oppositions and in Triads

Generally speaking, the idea that we think in polarities and that word meanings imply, implicitly or explicitly, their opposites seems to be beyond any doubt. If one attempts to press the point, he or she is likely to be accused of "bringing wood into the forest," as the Czech saying describes the kinds of activities which are absolutely unnecessary. However, despite the danger of this accusation I shall press this point further.

Thinking in Oppositions

The assumption of the oppositional nature of thought and language has a very long history in various human societies and cultures. Indeed, one can say that thinking and expressing meaning in terms of polarities or oppositions is probably as old as human thinking and speaking. This very old idea highlights the point of view that concepts and linguistic expressions make sense only in relation to something else. For example, one can understand what freedom is only in relating it to what one considers that freedom is not; what is synchrony in relation to diachrony; what is static in relation to dynamic; and so on. Conceptually, there are different ways of how oppositions have been treated in the history as well as how they are treated today. One can identify different kinds of oppositions ranging from dualities, dualisms, complementarities, analogies, polarities, and so on.

The oppositional nature of human psychological processes was noticed and commented upon as early as in ancient Greece and in ancient China. Ancient Greek philosophy was preoccupied with different kinds of oppositions and polarities in various areas of daily life and of sciences, ranging from cosmology, mythology, and medicine to rhetoric and dialogue. However, apart from the oppositional thought of Heracleitus, ancient Greek philosophy did not treat oppositions as interdependent and co-existent and therefore, in our sense, as dialogical. Ancient Chinese thought, in contrast, treated oppositions as interdependent and complementary, as in a wave-like motion, one opposition balancing the effect on the other. Therefore, in these two civilizations scientific and mythological theories conceptualized the oppositions and polarities differently, leading to diverse scientific systems and to different speculations about the nature of change and of coming-to-be (Lloyd, 1990, 1994).

The roots of dialectical oppositions in modern European thinking can be detected in the writings of the seventeenth-century scholar and speculative mystic Jacob Bohme, who apparently influenced Hegel in developing dialectic. Another source of dialogical oppositional thinking can be traced through the work of Giambatista Vico (Hermans & Kempen, 1993) and the German romanticists and expressivists (for the term "expressivism," see Berlin, 1976) such as Hamann, Herder, Humboldt, and Hegel. Hegel's dialectic was influential in the Moscow Linguistic Circle in the 1920s. When Jakobson emigrated to the United States, Peirce was for him, as he himself pointed out, the most powerful source of inspiration (Jakobson, 1971, p. v). This affinity of thought is probably due to the underlying alliance with Hegel's dialectic both in Peirce and in Jakobson. Peirce expresses this association as follows: "My philosophy resuscitates Hegel, though in a strange costume" (1.41). Jakobson's Hegelianism has been commented on by many (see e.g., Holenstein, 1987). Such claims of course could mean many different things in different contexts. What I mean here by Hegelianism is the theoretical adoption of the notion of interdependent oppositions and the resolution of their tension in triads, the emphasis of the holistic approach and of dynamism in the structure of thought and language.

BAKHTIN'S DIALOGICALITY

For Bakhtin, any coherent complex of signs, any text, a work of art, a piece of music, a historical interpretation, all have dialogical properties. When such a coherent complex of signs is experienced by humans, it turns into "the reflection of a reflection" (Bakhtin, 1979/1986, p. 113). Bakhtin refers to dialogism (rather than monologism) as an epistemology of the human sciences, human cognition, and communication. In his sense, dialogism is an epistemology concerned with the knowledge of social objects, rather than with the knowledge of natural or physical objects. Such dialogical knowledge, or to use Bakhtin's preferred term, "understanding," is fundamentally reflexive because it is an understanding of the self and the other.

Dialogism and Dialectics

At different stages of his career, Bakhtin emphatically made two kinds of distinctions: First, dialogism is to be distinguished from dialectics; second, dialogism is to be distinguished from semiotics. Bakhtin argued that dialectic was born of dialogue, but that in Hegel's treatment it became an abstract consciousness deprived of the heterogeneity and polyphony of different voices. Therefore, it became empty and deprived of life.

Bakhtin characterized Hegel's dialectic as monologism. He argued that in the study of the natural sciences human cognition stands in opposition only to a physical object, to a voiceless thing of the natural world, which is to be cognized. In contrast, human cognition in the social and human sciences always stands in opposition to another human cognition. Wherever there are two (or more) thoughts in oppositional tension, there is a dialogue, something to be negotiated, constructed, and created. This is why dialogicality is an epistemology of the social sciences and humanities.

Although one might have some reservations with respect to this kind of a distinction between dialogicality and dialectic, one can accept, in principle, that dialogicality is an ontology and epistemology of the disciplines requiring mutual acknowledgment of two or more consciousnesses, for example, a text and its interpreter, human subjects in interpersonal interaction, person and society, and so on. One could say that while dialectical principles apply to the natural sciences as well as to the social sciences and humanities, dialogism in the sense of Bakthin makes sense only with respect to the latter.

By using the terms "dialogism" or "dialogicality" rather than "dialectic" in this chapter I wish to underline my concern with the nature of knowledge in the social sciences and humanities rather than with that of the natural sciences. By doing this I ally with neo-Kantians and with Bakhtin rather than with Marx and Engels. In certain contexts, however, "dialectic" and "dialogicality" are acceptable as interchangeable notions. On a more general note, one can observe that today, even if they do not use the term "dialogism" or "dialectic," many twentieth-century humanistic and social science approaches are infiltrated by some features of dialogical and/or dialectic epistemologies. This applies, for example, to certain kinds of semiotics, pragmatism, phenomenology, and sociocultural theories of the mind. Moreover, if either of these terms is used, the terminological preferences for either "dialogicality" or "dialectic" are often underlined by the authors' political and ideological choices. It may be more difficult to justify such preferences on conceptual grounds.

DIALOGISM AND SEMIOTICS

In discussing Bakhtin's distinction between dialogism and semiotics, it is essential that we consider it from a historical perspective. Bakhtin associated semiotics primarily with what he called the Saussurean ready-made codes and their transmission. As such, he objected to semiotics. Moreover, he associated semiotics with an object-related rather than a person-related approach to the study of language, and therefore, with monologism. In contrast, dialogism, to him, meant the self–other relatedness in the polyphony of voices, which are in conflict, which contain hidden and displayed polemics, which are harmonized and orchestrated at several levels of communication at the same time. Summarizing, for Bakhtin semiotics was a static view of language while dialogism was dynamic.

Clearly, the term "dialogicality," like most terms used in the period of clashes of ideas and conceptual struggles, obtains different meanings and may even be associated with different underlying concepts. Therefore, while in general terms it is likely that many scholars will conceive of dialogicality as an ontology and epistemology of the social sciences and humanities, it is unlikely that for all of them dialogicality will be characterized in the same manner. Moreover, the importance of particular characteristics of dialogicality might be partly determined by the specificity of issues to which dialogicality, as the theory of knowledge, refers. For example, a dialogical theory of knowledge referring to personality may foreground internalization and inner mental structures. In contrast, a socio-cultural theory of mind might emphasize specific culture/individual features. In this chapter, dialogicality will refer primarily to the dynamic interdependence, using semiotic means, between thought and language on the one hand and thinking and speaking on the other (Marková, 1994), and this, again, will necessarily foreground certain issues and de-emphasize others.

With these preliminaries, dialogicality will be ontologically character-ized as follows: (1) Dialogicality conceives of social phenomena as being in change rather than presupposes that social phenomena are based on invariant universals. (2) Dialogicality conceives of social phenomena as having a dyadic or oppositional nature. This means that each phenom-enon is defined by both what it is and what it is not, like figure and ground. Examples of such oppositions are individual/environment, in-dividual/collective, dialogue/monologue, langue/parole, voiced/un-voiced phonemes, and so on. (3) Dialogicality conceives of such oppositions as mutually interdependent and always co-present, whether implicitly or explicitly. (4) Dialogicality conceives of interdependence be-tween oppositional components as being in tension and creating tension and conflict. As a result, these dyadic components reciprocally co-develop or co-change. (5) Dialogicality conceives of reciprocity with re-spect to dyadic interdependence as being asymmetrically distributed within and between these oppositional components. Therefore, some components co-develop more slowly and become stabilized, while others continue to change. (6) Dialogicality conceives of oppositional phenom-ena as situated in and interdependent with their external contexts, rather than being self-contained systems. This interdependence, too, creates ten-sion and conflict. Therefore, in studying social phenomena, we are al-ways faced with structures of structures in their dynamic development.

Dialogicality will be epistemologically characterized as follows: (1) The human knower understands, creates, and constructs his or her social reality by means of signs and representations rather than to adopt them as ready-made codes. (2) Semiotic relationship is a triadic relationship involving the two (at least) interlocutors and a sign or a representation of an object. Therefore, epistemologically the basic unit of the construc-tion of knowledge is a triad or a three-step semiotic process of com-munication. (3) The construction of knowledge proceeds through interdependence between culturally and collectively transmitted signs which are re-constructed, given new meanings, and are changed in the experience of individuals.

It is apparent that the terms "ontology" and "epistemology" as used in this chapter do not have their traditional metaphysical and philo-sophical contents. Rather, they are used here as some specific assump-tions concerning the structure of social reality, of thought and language, and of the ways these are semiotically co-constructed, symbolically rep-resented, and communicated. Moreover, I make no sharp distinctions here between the terms ontology and epistemology. Ontology is used when referring to the structure of social reality, of thought, and of lan-guage; epistemology refers to the knowers' symbolic representation, se-miotic mediation, and communication of those dynamic structures of social reality and of their changes. I consider this conception of dialogicality to be in broad agreement with that of Valsiner (1998; Valsiner & Van der Veer, 1999), Hermans (1996), Hermans & Kempen (1993), Linell (1998), and Wertsch (1991).

Dyadic and Triadic Semiotics

Concepts like *dyad, dyadic process, triad*, and *triadic process* are all part and parcel of the dialogical ontology and epistemology and the respective notions are used in the dialogically based semiotics. Ontologically speaking, the tension of interdependent oppositions which underlie the structure of thought and language leads to co-change and co-development of both components of the oppositions by means of three-step processes (e.g., Hermans & Kempen, 1993; Marková, 1990).

Concerning epistemology, the dialogical theory of knowledge cannot be postulated without communication. In other words, the representation of objects and communication process form triads (e.g., Bühler, 1982; Moscovici, 1984; Mukarovsky, 1940/1977; Peirce, 1931–1934). This, however, is not always understood. Consider, for example, the following quotation:

There are two versions of semiotics: pragmatist (American) and Saussurean (European). The two approaches differ in some basic ways, although there is no scholarly agreement concerning the nature of these differences. . . . It is widely agreed, however, that American semiotics is "triadic" (based on the sign, interpretant, and object) and European is "dyadic" (based on the signifier and signified). (Willey, 1994, p. vii)

While there could be "a wide agreement" about such differences, they are based on a fundamental misunderstanding of the underlying philosophies of those two kinds of semiotics. The so-called American triadic semiotics refers to Peirce's theory of the sign. Yet, this theory involves the conception of interdependent opposition, which was fundamental as the constructive principle in language and thought. It is Peirce's logic and his conception of natural classification, which is dyadic and his ontological position with respect to oppositions is clear. Natural classification takes place by dichotomies (1.438). A dual relative term, such as "lover" always signifies a pair of objects which are in a converse relationship. Thus the converse of "lover" is "loved" (3.328ff.). For Peirce, dyads are brought to oneness, which is a fundamental assumption for the study of signs. Moreover, among various kinds of relational dyads, it is opposition which manifests *the ontology of being*, and the problem of science is to understand the conception of being by means of opposition (1.457). However, since for Peirce semiotics is the theory of knowledge, it must involve the human knower, the sign-giver and the sign-receiver (like for Bühler). Therefore, the semiotic triadic movement proceeds through mediation, representation, and communication.

It is Peirce's conception of the sign and his theory of the growth of knowledge that is triadic. His main purpose is to explain communication and the growth of knowledge by means of signs. Knowledge cannot be instantaneous and intuitive. All intuitions are determined by previous ideas and there is no exception to this claim. Peirce's interests lie primarily in the growth of knowledge in the sense of logic rather than of psychology. He uses the concept of sign in two senses. First, in a broad sense a sign is a triadic relation between the object, the interpretant, and a sign proper (representation). The second sense of sign is therefore the sign proper (representation). It only refers to the representative function. In conclusion, while his semiotic approach is normally characterized as triadic, it is (normally) ignored that Peirce's dynamic triadic model of semiotic relations stems from his firm insistence on interdependent oppositions which, as he puts it, manifest the ontology of being. In other words, and as already emphasized, both oppositional and triadic thinking are part of dialogical ontology and epistemology.

The so-called European "dyadic" semiotics refers to Saussure's semiotics or in his terms, *semiology* (Saussure, 1915/1959, p. 16). It was already noted that the nature of Saussure's sign was arbitrary and there is no intrinsic link between signifier and signified because their relation too was of an arbitrary nature. Saussure's oppositions, while interdependent, were ontologically and epistemologically part of the static (i.e., pre-dialogical conceptual framework).

In the Prague School of Linguistics one finds frequent references to Karl Bühler. His anti-Cartesianism and the emphasis of the social matrix of language over the individual-related speech act theory were very similar in kind to the Prague School spirit. Bühler echoed Humboldt's conception of language as an interdependence between *ergon* and *energeia*, the product and the process of language, rather than their strict separation and viewing them as parallel phenomena. Bühler's criticism that "separation into aspects can never be accomplished in the concrete with a dismembering instrument such as the butcher's knife" (Bühler, 1982, p. 103) reminds us of Humboldt's (1836/1971) insistence that language cannot be studied like a dead body by an anatomist.

In addition, Bühler's conviction that language should never be regarded as a self-contained system but as a system which interrelates with and re-presents an extra-linguistic reality, was, in general, shared by the Prague School. He argued that although language communities have their "inner language forms" (Bühler, 1982, p. 152), it is also essential to recognize that language is not a Kantian thing-in-itself, but that the language of each community represents the world in its own manner. This again is a point of view which Humboldt expressed more than a hundred years earlier. It is often referred to as linguistic relativism. How-ever, one needs to distinguish between two concepts: relativism and re-lationism. Relativism is associated with an idea that the world may appear in one way to one language and in other ways to another lan-guage. According to my understanding, Bühler's point of view refers to relationism rather than to relativism. Relationism considers a particular "world" (or culture) and language as a dyad. In such a dyad the two components, world and language, are mutually interdependent. They are in the relation of a simultaneous tension—one shaping the other, one affecting the other, in a process in which they mutually co-change. It is because of the representational function of language that each language thematizes social reality in its specific manner (Bühler, 1990). All signs are related to the field of praxis in which they are relevant. Saussure's concept of the arbitrariness of symbols really does not fit Bühler's ap-proach: "every symbol needs a field and every field needs symbols if serviceable representations are to be possible" (ibid., p. 210; on this point, see also Valsiner, 1998, p. 268f.). This idea of viewing symbol and ref-erent as interdependent was also endorsed by Jakobson.

In his *organon model* of linguistic sign, the concept of linguistic repre-sentation is Bühler's most important axiom. As it is for Peirce, also for Bühler it is a sign or a representation which mediates certain content between the object and the interacting partners. However, Bühler's con-cept of representation does not refer to the mind mirroring the external world. The conception of mirroring would imply, again, separation be-tween the object and the mind, a kind of Kantian thing-in-itself and its cognitive re-presentation. Rather, re-presentation in Bühler's sense means the ability to imagine, to fantasize, to create something new from the interdependence between the symbol and the field. Indeed, when dealing with the expressive and the appellative function of language, Bühler uses the notion of "transposition" of the self's own perceptual space into a space of fantasy.

Therefore, neither does Peirce make American semiotics triadic nor Saussure make European semiotics dyadic. Instead, Peircean semiotics is both dyadic and triadic and so is European dialogicality (though not Sausserean semiotics, which is merely dyadic).

Yet, despite the general recognition of the importance of oppositions in scientific thinking, it has rarely become part of the conceptual frame-work within which science operates. As Jakobson pointed out not so long ago:

Yet the entire symmetry-asymmetry complex in linguistic research, both in its ontological commitment and in the role of a pure formal device, must be seen to belong more to the victories of tomorrow rather than to the solutions of yes-terday and today. However, we may perhaps console ourselves on that point with a thought that Einstein wrote down only four weeks before his death: For us the distinction between past, present and future is only an illusion, albeit a stubborn one. (Jakobson, 1979/1985, p. 264)

Jakobson argued that whatever level one considers in the study of the structure of language (e.g., phonemes, grammar and semantics), it is always underlined by oppositions (Jakobson, 1975/1985, 1982/1988). Referring to linguists such as Baudouin de Courteney (Jakobson, 1958/1971, p. 461) and Kruszewski (ibid., p. 517) who actually introduced the ideas of oppositional character into the linguistic analysis, Jakobson pointed out that Saussure apparently took the idea of oppositions from them. However, Jakobson's conception of opposition is dialogical while that of Saussure is pre-dialogical.

MUKAROVSKY'S MODEL OF DIALOGUE

Bühler's organon model of language and Peirce's triadic model of the construction of knowledge are both built on the components of I, you, re-presentation. However, both Bühler and Peirce applied their triadic models to single utterances or single language signs. Yet, although single utterances and signs are dialogical in the sense as being directed to another interlocutor, I shall now focus on Mukarovsky's (1940/1977) triadic semiotic approach to dialogue, which was originally published as *Two Studies of Dialogue*. However, he applied the same semiotic approach in the study of poetics and art (Marková, 1992). In his important eassy, "Art as a Semiotic Fact," Mukarovsky (1936) refers to Saussure's and Bühler's study of the sign. He emphasizes that the research of the Prague School contributes to semiotics because all the elements of the linguistic system, whether they are sounds, words, utterances and so on, are viewed from a semiotic perspective. The semiotic perspective was then extended to the arts and humanities, which, too, all have more or less a semiotic character. So conceived, Mukarovsky's concept of representation as a cultural/individual opposition, which is filled with tension on the one hand and a constructive and creative ability on the other, bears a certain similarity to Moscovici's (1984, 1992; Moscovici & Marková 1998; Moscovici & Vignaux, 1994) concept of social representation. In contrast, they both differ from many current social constructionist and social constructivist approaches which seem to fall into two extremes. First, they differ from those which attempt to construct everything from the here-and-now (e.g., Gergen, 1994), ignoring the relatively stable contexts in which the here-and-now is embedded. Second, they also differ from those approaches, which question the limits of construction, and therefore implicitly assume some kind of the Kantian thing-in-itself which the mind attempts to capture.

Whatever aspect of Mukarovsky's work one touches, his thinking in oppositions and in triads is always foregrounded in one way or other. For Mukarovsky (1940/1977), dialogue is a linguistic phenomenon which has three aspects, all of dyadic, that is, oppositional nature. The first is the relation between the two dialogical participants, "I" and "you." He emphasizes polarity between the two, with the role of the speaker and the listener being constantly alternating, and the interrelation between "I" and "you" being felt as a tension, not bound to either of them, but actually existing "between" them. The second aspect is the relation between the two participants on the one hand, and the real situation, in which the dialogue takes place, on the other. The situation can penetrate the dialogue either directly or indirectly. In the former case the situation affects the direction of the dialogue by changes of the topic as a result of events, which attract the speakers' attention (e.g., a cat, a sudden noise). In the latter case, the material situation itself becomes a theme of dialogue (e.g., business talk). The third aspect is constituted by the specific character of the semantic structure of the dialogue. This pertains to what Mukarovsky calls different dialogical contextures, that is, phonological, semantic, and other aspects. These are, again, oppositional in nature, mutually interpenetrating each other and resulting in a polyphony of meanings. Perhaps one could say, using the language of Bakhtin, that Mukarovsky implies here an interplay of different voices in dialogue. Although, to be sure, dialogue must have its unity, each participant contributes specific contextures, which interpenetrate and even contradict one another, collide, and contain sharp semantic reversals. As Mukarovsky points out, the more vivid the dialogue, and the shorter individual replies are, the more distinct is the collision of the contextures.

Mukarovsky's studies of dialogue are no more than an outline to be theoretically developed. The Bakhtinian echo of the dialogical nature of an utterance expressing itself in multivoicedness, saturating the entire speech from the changes of gesture, of voice, to facial expression, are all part of this outline. It is not a single speech act with a single function but a metacommunicative spectrum signaled through semantic reversals, asymmetries, conflicts, continuities, and discontinuities. It is multivoicedness and metacommunication that make a true dialogue: "The more 'dialogical' the dialogue is, the more densely it is saturated with semantic reversals regardless of the boundaries of the replies" (Mukarovsky, 1940/1977, p. 109). These ideas, however, need to be theoretically developed and then applied to the study of real dialogue.

TWO KINDS OF TWO-SIDEDNESS

For Saussure, the linguistic sign was a two-sided entity, with the two elements, concept and sound image, being intimately united. Similarly,

Bakhtin (Volosinov, 1929/1973, p. 86) described a word as a two-sided act. It is instructive to consider what the two-sidedness means to these two scholars. For Saussure, the two-sidedness of a sign is a psychological entity. Two-sidedness in language and in signs is a Janus-like face: "thought is the front and the sound the back; one cannot cut the front without cutting the back at the same time . . . one cannot divide sound from thought nor thought from sound" (Saussure, 1915/1959, p. 113). Yet the bond between concept and sound is arbitrary and the linguistic sign, likewise, is arbitrary. Saussure's duality cannot resolve itself in a change because it represents a static point of view. This is despite the fact that the oppositions with which Saussure was concerned were considered to be interdependent. As in the Gestalt pictures of the figure-and-ground, Saussure's oppositions were static, although inseparable.

For Bakhtin, a sign, too, is two-sided; it is a Janus-like face. However, rather than being an entity, a word is an act between the speaker and the listener; it is a bridge between the two interlocutors. Yet, interaction, crossing the bridge, for Bakhtin, is not something peaceful. It is filled with tension, with the opposing points of view, with different belief systems, different intentions (Bakhtin, 1981, p. 314). Analyzing Dostoyevsky's poetics in language, Bakhtin (1973) brings to the extreme the dynamics involved in the plurality of voices which triumph in Dostoyevsky's novels. Dostoyevsky's "hetero-directed double-voiced word" reflects all the hidden polemics, hidden dialogue in which nothing at all is objectified or predetermined, in which no struggles are ever decided beforehand.

CO-EXISTENT AND SUCCESSIVE OPPOSITIONS

Only co-existent opposites, which not only are intimately interconnected in such a way that the appearance of one inevitably elicits the other, but which also are in the relation of tension, form the basis of dialogicality. It is such dialogical oppositions which form the structure of language and of thinking. While in general terms both Jakobson and Karcevskij adopted many of Saussure's concepts, the basis of their criticism of Saussure is directed toward his a-dialogical approach to oppositions.

Jakobson maintains that Saussure's idea of opposition was seminal (Jakobson, 1979/1988, p. 22). However, he argued against the "unfortunate confusion between opposition and contingency" in linguistics. The Saussurean point of view was based on oppositions as contingent or linear, isolated, rather than as co-present. In order to clarify the difference between Jakobson and Saussure in their approach to oppositions, let us consider it at the level of phonemes. Jakobson (1979/1988, p. 23) argued that the Saussurean analysis viewed sense-discriminative con-

stituents in language as successive segments of the sound sequence, as-
cribing merely linearity to the sounds of language which were
measurable in one temporal dimension. However, so conceived succes-
sivity disregards co-existence, simultaneity. In a concrete example, he
pointed out that the kind of Saussure question as to what is the opposite
of the English [m] makes no sense because there is no unique opposite
to a phoneme. A phoneme, in this case, [m] carries the whole range of
phonological differences, which must be systematically examined in
terms of "distinctive features" to identify proper oppositions. Distinctive
features are phonological oppositions, for example, markedness versus
unmarkedness, or voicedness versus unvoicedness. These distinctive features are usually asymmetrical yet it is essential that they are co-present,
that is, the occurrence of either of them is possible. Different kinds of
phonological oppositions are mutually related which means they either
can co-occur or their co-occurrence is impossible. What is important from
the point of view of a dialogical perspective is that phonological change
is not simply a replacement of particular phonemes but a change in the
total pattern of distinctive features composed of interdependent oppositions. This is because

every single constituent of any linguistic system is built on an opposition of two
logical contradictories: the presence of an attribute ("markedness") in contrapo-
sition to its absence ("unmarkedness"). The entire network of language displays
a hierarchical arrangement that within each level of the system follows the same
dichotomous principle of marked terms superimposed on the corresponding un-
marked terms. And second, the continual, all-embracing, purposeful interplay of
invariants and variations proves to be essential, innermost property of language
at each of its levels. (Jakobson, 1972/1985, p. 85)

In other words, for Jakobson, the dialogical approach to oppositions
involves uniting two entities, which are distinct but at the same time
bound and co-present and in competition with another, whether explicitly or implicitly. Saussure's notion of linearity of signs, in Jakobson's
view, is confusing. Rather than viewing oppositions as co-present, they
are in a line, allowing for associative chains but not for tensions and
contradictions leading to the generation of co-change.

HOMONYMY AND SYNONYMY

Linguistic antinomies also play an essential role in the work of Karcevskij, one of the founding members of the Prague Linguistic Circle.
Having been well familiar with Saussure's work as his student, he was
critical of his view, which tended to separate the components in opposition to one another. Thus he argued against Saussure that pure and

single opposition necessarily leads to chaos. It is not simply that a tree is a tree because it is neither a house nor a horse nor a river. Oppositions are in a unique contradictory relationship and not in an arbitrary relationship with respect to one another. This is precisely the same point, which Jakobson also made when he referred to Saussure's conception of phonemes. Karcevskij argued that true differentiation as a feature of dialogicality is based on both a simultaneous resemblance and difference: "linguistic values exist only by virtue of their opposition to one another" (Karcevskij, 1929, p. 51).

In the same essay on asymmetric dualism, Karcevskij drew attention to the changes in language meanings due to the continuous discrepancy between two characteristics of the sign, that is, homonymity and synonymity. Homonymity means referring to particular phenomena by different signs. For example, the word "democracy" can be associated with the government of people, rule of majority, elections, freedom, the mafia. These words function both as homonyms and as synonyms. Each of these homonyms, say, "freedom," may be associated with different things. It may mean rights, democracy, free speech, and so on. At the same time, "freedom" has a number of synonyms which could equally express the characteristics with which "freedom" is identified (e.g., independence, liberty, choice, emancipation). Therefore, each sign can be expressed as an intersection between these two conceptual series, homonymity and synonymity, these two belonging simultaneously to a series of transposed values of the same sign and to a series of values which are analogous but which are expressed by different signs. There is always a tension between the two. Homonymity and synonymity, according to Karcevskij, constitute the most important relational coordinates of language because they keep it in tension and in dynamism. It is through this tension that the meaning develops and changes. Every use of a sign is a new mapping of the relations between elements of the code and what they designate; the code and designated reality are the two relational axes of Karcevskij's system or, as he calls them, the coordinates of which every linguistic sign is an intersection. Thus Karcevskij deals with oscillation of linguistic signs between two poles, the stable and variable, social and individual. The form of a verbal sign gravitates to homonymy, while its function to synonymy—and it is this interplay that constitutes the life of language.

In the dialogical perspective, therefore, an opposition is considered as something which is alive and capable of co-development and co-change. Such a point of view was expressed by Hegel when he characterized logical contradictions: "Something is therefore alive only in so far as it contains contradiction within it, and moreover is this power to hold and endure the contradiction within it" (Hegel, 1812–1816/1976, p. 440). Jakobson (1963) expressed this idea in a similar manner: "The opposition is alive when both opposites are able to occur in the same context, given, that is, the identity of concurrent and adjacent features" (p. 27). This is why so dynamically conceived oppositions in tension, conflict, and asymmetries also provide conditions for a triadic dialectic or dialogical movement.

LINGUISTIC ORGANIZATION OF DIALOGUE

The linguistic organization of each of the aspects of dialogue is oppositional. First, the opposition between "I" and "you" has its linguistic correlates in the semantic opposition between personal and possessive pronouns of the first and the second person. There are also semantic oppositions between the first and the second person of the verb, the imperative, vocative, affirmation of the negation, the syntactic relations between sentences (e.g., but, however), and so on. Second, the material situation in relation to the speaking subjects, too, is expressed in linguistic terms. This is reflected in different spatial and temporal deixis of "here and now," for example, "this," "that," "here," "there," "now," "in the morning," "in the evening," and in the verbal tenses (e.g., the present in opposition to the past, versus the future). Finally, the semantic structure expresses itself in the already mentioned polyphony of contextures, and specifically, in what Mukarovsky calls semantic reversals. Semantic reversals are oppositions signaling shifts in meanings through changes in intonation, in lexical ambiguities, lexical contrasts, and in various kinds of unexpected paradoxes. Semantic reversals make demands not only on the participants' comprehension of such reversals, but also on their ability to control expressions of such reversals. Such discourses, Mukarovsky maintains, contribute to the development of communicative culture and to the subtlety of expression.

Although each of these aspects must be present in a dialogue, specific focus on each of these aspects will bring out a different type of dialogue. If the specific focus is on the opposition between "I" and "you," then a range of different kinds of relationships could be foregrounded, ranging from those expressed as a dispute to those expressed as bargaining. On the other hand, focus could be on the relation between speaking persons and the actual situation, for example, on those relations which may manifest themselves in business talk. Finally, the focus could be on semantic reversals, which is largely independent of the external situation, but instead is characterized by talk for the purpose of talking, (i.e., a conversation).

THE PRAGUE SCHOOL THEORY OF DIALOGUE TODAY

During the 1960s and 1970s, dialogue, as a subject of specific study, was reintroduced into Prague linguistics. This renaissance was due to several factors: first, to the influence of new approaches that were developed abroad in the study of conversation, dialogue, and discourse, both in Western and in Russian linguistics; second, to a limited ideological relaxation in post-totalitarian European regimes at that time; third, to technological advancements, which led to relatively easy audio-recording and video-recording of authentic speech, enabling new ways of analyzing dialogue (Müllerová & Hoffmannová, 1994). All these changes were significant not only because they facilitated research in general terms, but because, after several decades, they fulfilled an old aim (Skalicka, 1948): the establishment of *parole linguistics* as a scientific discipline.

Due to these conditions, work on dialogue has been rapidly growing and has attached itself eclectically to a variety of approaches which at the time dominated, and some of them still dominate, international fashions. These include conversation analysis, various brands of discourse analyses, computational linguistics, and so on. In addition, however, new developments occurred which stem from the Prague School dialogicality. These to my mind are very promising both theoretically and empirically. They are based on thematic analysis and they follow directly from the ideas of Mathesius, Mukarovský, and Daneš.

Thematic Analysis

According to Mathesius (1942), by forming an utterance, the speaker responds to some kind of reality, usually to a certain communication situation. In order to communicate something or, in the then terminology of the Prague School, to fulfill their communicative functions or pragmatic roles, utterances must be equipped with certain devices enabling them to express the speakers' patterns of thought. For example, speakers express their communicative intentions by intonation or their thoughts are arranged in a particular word order. Mathesius was particularly preoccupied with the word order in utterances and sentences and their relationship to the given (i.e., old knowledge and to the new knowledge). He made a distinction between the *theme* of a sentence (i.e., the foundation, something that is being spoken about in the sentence) and the *rheme* (i.e., the core, something that the speaker says about that theme). The conception based on the distinction between theme and rheme is translated into English as "the functional sentence perspective." As Mathesius himself emphasized, his analysis of utterances in terms of the functional sentence perspective is of a totally different kind than a formal analysis of sentences. This is particularly important in the study of dialogue, where an utterance is a speaker's response to another utterance and where a text is viewed as an organized whole. The functional sentence perspective is based on the analysis of the contextual arrangement of utterances in their relationship to the underlying sentence patterns.

Mathesius also suggested that theme and rheme have different communicative functions thus affecting in different ways the direction of communication. This idea of Mathesius was further developed by Firbas (1992). He introduced the notion of the "communicative dynamism," which means the extent to which the sentence element contributes to the development of communication. This states that theme, being the given knowledge or the known information, carries in the sentence the lowest communicative dynamism while rheme pushes communication forward.

The Mathesius distinction between theme and rheme forms the basis of Daneš' (1968, 1974) conception of the thematic progression in text. Specifically, he develops connections between the functional sentence perspective and the structure of professional and scientific text. According to his position, text is organized along some principles of thematic progression. By this he means the choice and the ordering of utterance themes, their mutual connections and hierarchical arrangements, and their relationships to the hyperthemes of some higher-order units (e.g., paragraphs, chapters, the whole text). Although the criteria for distinguishing between theme and rheme are complex, they are usually based on word order and intonation, and on grammar and lexical means (cf. Daneš, 1968).

In this approach, the traditional linguistic distinction between sentence as a syntactic structure and utterance as an attitude of the speaker is not tenable. As Daneš maintains, a sentence and an utterance are not, in principle, two different formations but a single formation with different aspects and components (ibid., 1968). This position, again, reflects the dialogical point of view, which does not sustain langue and parole as parallel and independent formations but which, instead, draws attention to their interdependence in terms of the analysis of language.

The basis of progressive thematic analysis of text consists in the identification of different patterns of the thematization of themes and rhemes, that is, of given and new knowledge and of their derivations, recurrence or otherwise, in the progression of text. While these are clearly pragmatic characteristics of the text, they are also reflected in the grammatical structure of sentences/utterances—the idea already implied in Mathesius.

Thematic analysis applied to the study of dialogue (Müllerová, 1976; 1979) opens up the possibility of exploring the dynamics and progression of interactions in a polyphonic and semiotic perspective. In accordance with dialogical principles, there is a fundamental presupposition of this approach. Each dialogue is no more than a slice of an ongoing discourse between the participants, which started in the past, which takes place at present, and which will continue in the future. Themes, whether explicit or implicit, derived and recurrent, are determined by what the participants understood, represented, and what they jointly constructed previously. Therefore, in a studied corpus of dialogical data, one proceeds systematically, in a hermeneutic manner, from the whole to specific aspects of the dialogue and back to the whole. Although each dialogue has its own structure and its linguistic style, there is a pragmatic, grammatical, lexical, and interactional interdependence between the local situation and the whole context. Therefore, each dialogue displays the dynamics of the unique and the general, of the continuous and the discontinuous. In other words, each dialogue has features which are common to all these repeated dialogues, for example, each interlocutor has its individual characteristics manifesting themselves on each or on most occasions and he or she responds to the other interlocutor in a similar manner. At the same time, each communication situation has its own specific characteristics, such as, the change in the interlocutor's mood, some external circumstances, and so on. If the researcher does not analyze the whole corpus and selects, instead, only specific dialogues or specific situations, he or she cannot well understand the nature of themes, the content, language style, linguistic characteristics and other phenomena displayed by the discourse (Müllerová, Hoffmannová, & Marková, in press).

The Present Significance of the Prague School

One might raise the question as to why, in addition to historical interest, one should discuss, today, the dialogical theory of the Prague School. As Jakobson (1963) maintained, there is no doubt that the label "Prague School" became, in the 1920s and 1930s, a significant constituent of the international scientific efforts toward the development of modern linguistics. He points out that it is relatively easy to identify the specific features of various schools of linguistics flourishing simultaneously at that time, including the Prague School (i.e., the Czechs with their collaborators from Germany and Russia), the schools of linguistics in Holland, France, Norway, Rumania, and others. He observes, however, that considering the richness of the ideas constituting those theories, it would be difficult to find the features which would distinguish the Prague School as a whole from other schools. I would argue, though, that validity and justification of such claims requires a longer time perspective. The present may hide what can only become apparent in the future.

It is my view that the dialogicality of the Prague School, both in its outline and in its theoretical development, has much to offer not only to linguistics and semiotics but to social, cognitive, and socio-developmental psychology. It remains the task of a future historian to explain the following puzzle. Why is it that despite the fact that human beings create and sustain their social reality primarily through symbolic representations, language, and communication, the "mainstream" cognitive, social, and developmental psychology has largely neglected the study of language and communication? This is the question which has been repeatedly asked for several decades by some leading psychologists like Moscovici, Rommetveit, Nelson Giles, and others. In current textbooks of social psychology, the subject of language and communication is still largely relegated to a chapter in a textbook rather than treated as a phenomenon constituting the main presuppositions of human activities. More than eighty years ago, Saussure (1915/1959, p. 16) defined semiotics (or semiology, in his case) as a science which, studying "the life of signs within society . . . would be part of social psychology and consequently of general psychology." As he pointed out, that science was nonexistent at the time and nobody could say whether it would ever exist. Today, many years after the publication of his *Cours*, a special issue on "Semiotics and Psychology," published in *Theory & Psychology* (1998) draws attention to the omission of the study of signs in psychology, and it is proposed that dialogue between semiotics and psychology be initiated. Many decades after Saussure, the authors in this special issue acknowledge that both fields are concerned "with the understanding of the functions of the mind, the organization and representation of knowledge, the mechanics and pragmatics of human communication, and the constitutive role of signs in cultural life" (Smythe & Jorna, 1998, p. 729).

The study of social change still remains a theoretical and empirical challenge for psychology as well as for other social sciences. It can be argued that psychology, better than other social sciences, might be able to cope with this challenge by studying activities of the individual as being socially and culturally embedded. Specifically, the study of the mind of the individual, in the dialogical perspective, involves the study of the dynamic interdependence between the thinking and speaking of the individual on the one hand, and the collectively and culturally shared thought and language on the other (Marková, 1994). Dyadic and triadic ontology and epistemology emphasizing co-occurrence of complements in tension and polyphony of different levels of communication goes some way to respond to this challenge.

These issues, which were raised and discussed in the Prague School of Linguistics, are also issues in the center of attention of the theory of social representations, co-constructivism, and the socio-developmental theories of the mind. For example, the analysis of *themata* proposed by Moscovici in the context of the theory of social representations and thematic analysis based on linguistic insights of Daneš and Müllerová and Hoffmannová promise mutual cross-fertilization between social psychology, linguistics, and semiotics.

Dialogicality provides an essential body of knowledge, which people express through language, thought, emotions, sentiments, dreams, images, and symbols. These are issues which social psychology of today cannot ignore, if it has any ambition to raise its status among other human and social sciences. This is also why social psychology should treat the Prague School of Linguistics not only as a theoretical retrospect but, above all, as a fundamental theoretical prospect.

ACKNOWLEDGMENT

I am grateful to Serge Moscovici for discussing with me the ideas developed in this chapter and for his inspiring comments, criticism, and suggestions on an earlier version. I also thank Frantisek Daneš for discussing with me the Prague School of Linguistics and drawing my attention to some relevant references. Responsibility for any errors in interpretation of these issues, of course, is my own.

REFERENCES

Bakhtin, M. (1973). *Problems of Dostoevsky's poetics*, 2nd. ed. (R. W. Rotsel, Trans.). Ann Arbor, MI: Ardis.

Bakhtin, M. (1979/1986). *Estetika slovesnovo tvorchestva*. Moskva: Bocharov. [Edited by C. Emerson & M. Holquist as *Speech genres and other late essays*. Austin: University of Texas Press.]

Bakhtin, M. (1981). *The dialogic imagination: Four essays by M. Bakhtin* (M. Holquist, Ed.). Austin: University of Texas Press.

Berlin, I. (1976). *Vico and Herder: Two studies in the history of ideas*. London: The Hogarth Press.

Bühler, K. (1982). The axiomatization of the language sciences. In R. E. Innis (Ed.), *Karl Bühler, semiotic foundations of language theory*. New York: Plenum Press.

Bühler, K. (1990). *Theory of Language: The representational function of language*. Amsterdam: John Benjamins Publishing Co.

Daneš, F. (1968). Typy tematickych posloupnosti v textu. *Slovo a Slovesnost, 29,* 125–141.

Daneš, F. (1974). Functional sentence perspective and the organization of the text. In F. Daneš (Ed.), *Papers on functional sentence perspective* (pp. 106–128). The Hague: Mouton.

Daneš, F. (1990). T. G. Masaryk a jazykoveda. *Slovo a Slovesnost, 51,* 185–191.

Daneš, F. (1998). Analýza zdrojü prazského lingvistického funkcionalismu. Unpublished manuscript.

Firbas, J. (1992). *Functional sentence perspective in written and spoken communication*. Cambridge: Cambridge University Press.

Fontaine, J. (1974). Le cercle linguistique de Prague. *Bibliotheque Reperes*. Tours: Mame.

Gergen, K. J. (1994). *Realities and relationships: Soundings in social construction*. Cambridge, MA: Harvard University Press.

Hegel, G.W.F. (1812–1816/1976). *Science of logic*. London: Humanities Press.

Hermans, H.J.M. (1996). Opposites in a dialogical self: Constructs as characters. *Journal of Constructivist Psychology, 9,* 1–26.

Hermans, H.J.M., & Kempen, H.J.G. (1993). *The dialogical self*. San Diego, CA: Academic Press.

Holenstein, E. (1987). Jakobson's and Trubetzkoj's philosophical background. In K. Pomorska, E. Codakowska, H. McLean, & B. Vine (Eds.), *Language, poetry and poetics* (pp. 15–31). Berlin: Mouton.

Holton, G. (1978). *The scientific imagination: Case studies*. Cambridge: Cambridge University Press.

Humboldt, W. von. (1836/1971). *Linguistic variability and intellectual development*. Coral Gables, FL: University of Miami Press.

Isatchenko, A. V. (1948). Obsah a hranice synchronickej jazykovedy. *Slovo a Slovesnost, 10*, 201–208.

Jakobson, R. (1930/1931). Jazykové problémy v Masarykové díle. In Masarykuv sborník, *Svazek páty* (pp. 396–414). Praha.

Jakobson, R. (1957/1971). Shifters, verbal categories and the Russian verb. In *Roman Jakobson selected writings* (Vol. 2, pp. 130–147). The Hague: Mouton.

Jakobson, R. (1958/1971). The Kazan school of Polish linguistics and its place in the international development of phonology. In *Roman Jakobson selected writings* (Vol. 2, pp. 394–428). The Hague: Mouton.

Jakobson, R. (1963). Efforts toward a means-ends model of language in interwar continental linguistics. In *Trends in European and American linguistics 1930–1960*. Utrecht.

Jakobson, R. (1971). Acknowledgement and dedication. In *Roman Jakobson selected writings* (Vol. 2 pp. v–viii). The Hague: Mouton.

Jakobson, R. (1972/1985). Verbal communication. In S. Rudy (Ed.), *Roman Jakobson selected writings* (Vol. 7, pp. 81–92). Berlin: Mouton.

Jakobson, R. (1975/1985). A few remarks on Peirce, pathfinder in the science of language. In S. Rudy (Ed.), *Roman Jakobson selected writings* (Vol. 7, pp. 248–253). Berlin: Mouton.

Jakobson, R. (1979/1988). Einstein and the science of language. In S. Rudy (Ed.), *Roman Jakobson selected writings* (Vol. 7, pp. 254–264). Berlin: Mouton.

Jakobson, R. (1982/1988). La théorie Saussurienne en rétrospection. In S. Rudy (Ed.), *Roman Jakobson selected writings* (Vol. 8, pp. 391–435). Berlin: Mouton.

Karcevskij, S. (1929). Du dualisme asymetrique du sign linguistique. *Travaux du Cercle Linguistique de Prague, 1*, 33–38. [Reprinted as The asymmetric dualism of the linguistic sign. In F. Steiner (Ed.), *The Prague School: Selected writings, 1919–1946* (pp. 47–54). Austin: University of Texas Press, 1982.]

Linell, P. (1998). *Approaching dialogue: Talk, interaction and contexts in dialogical perspectives*. Amsterdam: John Benjamins Publishing Company.

Lloyd, G.E.R. (1990). *Demystifying mentalities*. Cambridge: Cambridge University Press.

Lloyd, G.E.R. (1994). New perspectives on ancient science. *European Review, 2*, 1–98.

Marková, I. (1990). Introduction. In I. Marková & K. Foppa (Eds.), *The dynamics of dialogue* (pp. 1–22). London: Harvester Wheatsheaf.

Marková, I. (1992). On structure and dialogicity. In A. Wold (Ed.), *Language, thought and human communication* (pp. 45–63). Oslo: Scandinavian University Press and Oxford University Press.

Marková, I. (1994). Sociogenesis of language: Perspectives on dialogism and on activity theory. In W. De Graaf & R. Maier (Eds.), *Sociogenesis reexamined* (pp. 27–46). New York: Springer.

Masaryk, T. G. (1885). *Základy konkrétné Logik*. Praha.

Mathesius, V. (1911/1964). O potenciálnosti jevu jazykovych. [Reprinted in J. Vachek (Ed.), *A Prague School reader in linguistics*. Bloomington: Indiana University Press.]

Mathesius, V. (1929/1971). Die funktionale Linguistik. In E. Beneš & J. Vachek (Eds.), *Stilistik und Soziolinguistik* (pp. 1–18). Berlin: List.

Mathesius, V. (1942). Rec a sloh. In B. Havranek & J. Mukarovsky (Eds.), *Cteni o juazyce a poesii*. Praha: Druzstevni prace.

Mestchaninov, I. I. (1949). Nove uceni o jazyku v SSSR v jeho soucasne vyvojove fazi. *Slovo a Slovesnost, 11*, 1–7.

Mestchaninov, I. I. (1950). Uloha N.Ja. Marra ve vyvoji sovetske jazykovedy. *Slovo a Slovesnost, 12*, 1–9.

Moscovici, S. (1984). The Phenomenon of social representations. In R. M. Farr & S. Moscovici (Eds.), *Social representations* (pp. 3–69). Cambridge: Cambridge University Press.

Moscovici, S. (1992). *Communication introductive à la première conférence internationale sur les représentations sociales*. Italy: Ravello.

Moscovici, S., & Marková, I. (1998). Presenting social representation: A conversation. *Culture & Psychology, 4*, 371–410.

Moscovici, S., & Vignaux, G. (1994). Le concept de thêmata. In C. Guimelli (Ed.), *Structures et transformations des représentations sociales*. Neuchâtel: Delachaux et Niestlé.

Mukarovsky, J. (1930/1931). Masaryk jako stylista. In Masarykuv sborník. Praha: Svazek páty. [Reprinted in S. Cmejrkova & F. Daneš (Eds.), *O Capkovych Hovorech s T.G. Masarykem* (pp. 163–183). Praha: Academia, 1994.]

Mukarovsky, J. (1936). L'art comme fait sémiologique. *Actes du VIIIe Congrés international de philosophie à Prague, 2–7 septembre 1934*. Praha.

Mukarovsky, J. (1940/1977). Two Studies of Dialogue. In J. Burbank & P. Steiner (Eds.), *The word and verbal art: Selected essays by Jan Mukarovsky* (pp. 81–133). New Haven, CT: Yale University Press.

Müllerová, O. (1976). K tematicke vystavbe nepripravenych mluvenych dialogickych projevu. *Slovo a Slovesnost, 37*, 308–316.

Müllerová, O. (1979/1997). *Komunikativni slozky vystavby dialogickeho textu*. München: Otto Sagner.

Müllerová, O., & Hoffmannová, J. (1994). *Kapitoly O Dialogu*. Pansofia.

Müllerová, O., Hoffmannová, J., & Marková, I. (in press). Od teorie dialogu k institucionálni komunikaci. *Slovo a Slovesnost*.

Peirce, C. S. (1931–1934). *Collected papers of Charles Sanders Peirce* (edited by C. Hartshorne & P. Weiss). Cambridge, MA: The Belknap Press of Harvard University Press.

Saussure, F. de. (1915/1959). *Cours de Linguistique Générale* [Course in general linguistics.] Glasgow: William Collins.

Skalicka, V. (1948). The need for a linguistics of "la parole." *RLB, 1*, 21–38.

Smythe, W., & Jorna, R. J. (1998). The signs we live by: The relationship between semiotics and psychology. *Theory & Psychology, 8*, 723–730.

Théses présentées au Premier Congrés des philologues slaves. (1929). *TCLP, 1,* 5–29.

Thomas, L. L. (1957). *The linguistic theories of N. Ja. Marr.* Berkeley: University of California Press.

Toman, J. (1995). *The magic of a common language (Jakobson, Mathesius, Trubetzkoy, and the Prague Linguistic Circle).* Cambridge, MA: The MIT Press.

Tynjanov, J., & Jakobson, R. (1928/1981). Problems in the study of literature and language. In S. Rudy (Ed.), *Roman Jakobson selected writings* (Vol. 8, pp. 3–6). The Hague: Mouton.

Vachek, J. (1964). *The linguistic school of Prague.* Bloomington: Indiana University Press.

Valsiner, J. (1998). *The guided mind: A sociogenetic approach to personality.* Cambridge, MA: Harvard University Press.

Valsiner, J., & Van der Veer, R. (1999). *The social mind.* New York: Cambridge University Press.

Volosinov, V. N. (1929/1973). *Marxism and the philosophy of language.* New York: Seminar Press.

Wallon, H. (1945). *Les origines de la pensée chez l'enfant.* Paris: Presses Universitaire de France.

Wellek, R. (1976). Vilem Mathesius (1882–1945). Founder of the Prague Linguistic Circle. In L. Matejka (Ed.), *Sound, sign and meaning* (pp. 6–14). Michigan Slavic Contributions, 6. Ann Arbor: Department of Slavic Language and Literature, The University of Michigan.

Wertsch, J. V. (1991). *Voices of the mind.* Cambridge, MA: Harvard University Press.

Willey, N. (1994). *The semiotic self.* Chicago: University of Chicago Press.

Chapter 2

The Logic of Oppositionality
in Intrapersonal Dialogue

Joseph F. Rychlak

A BRIEF HISTORICAL OVERVIEW OF OPPOSITIONALITY

For forty years now I have been arguing that oppositionality is a basic feature of human reasoning, and that psychology must adapt its theories of human action and development to accommodate this fact. Initially, I called this "dialectical reasoning," based on my sequential study of first Marx, then Hegel, leading to Socrates/Plato, and finally, Aristotle. I soon learned that dialectical themes were prominent in recorded history earlier than the Greeks. We find, for instance, dialectical formulations in the writings of the ancient Upanishadic philosophies of the Vedic literature in India. Both Hindu and Buddhistic formulations are heavily dialectical, as is the Chinese yin-yang principle found in the Tao Te Ching, recorded in 600 B.C. (see Nakamura, 1964).

I decided that Aristotle had the best formulation of dialectic for my purposes. I was seeking an understanding of the intrapersonal reasoning process rather than the dynamics of interpersonal dialogue as employed by Socrates and others. In this connection, I should point out that the term "dialogical" is heavily weighted with the meaning of interpersonal relations. Also, apparently there is not always an oppositionality intended in the use of this concept (see, e.g., Hermans, Kempen, & van Loon, 1992, p. 29). So, it might be that I am somewhat out of step with other contributors to this volume on dialogicality in development. I find oppositionality to be essential to an understanding of human reasoning—which does, of course, invariably reflect itself in interpersonal relations. Intrapersonal dialogue goes on in both solitary and social situations.

Aristotle believed that humans were predicating organisms, that they always reasoned from what he termed a beginning major premise. Today we could legitimately call this framing premise a "constructed" point of view. Aristotle said that when we take on such major premises based on solid, "primary and true" factual evidence, with only one position therefore possible for affirmation, we carry out a *demonstrative line of reasoning*. On the other hand, if we come to our major premise based on selecting one side or the other of an opinion (rather than on a rock-hard certainty) we carry out a *dialectical line of reasoning* (Aristotle, 1952c, p. 143). In either case, no matter how we begin, we then follow a syllo-gistic progression, moving logically from our major-premise assumption to our minor premise(s), and thus arriving at a newly generated, con-cluding belief. Aristotle emphasized that humans rely on both demon-strative and dialectical reasoning strategies depending on circumstances. Aristotle argued that when Socrates put his initiating question to a stu-dent or opponent in his interpersonal dialectical method he was asking that a position be taken within a range of opinions. If the student took position A as opposed to its contradiction (non-A), Socrates defended the latter stance in the discourse to follow. If the student took non-A, Socrates would defend the opposing A position. It was all the same to Socrates, who believed that knowledge was bound together (many into one) by way of oppositionality (wrongs into rights and vice versa). As Heracleitus had said before him, we humans would not know what jus-tice signified unless we also knew the meaning of injustice. Although the Socratic oppositionality occurred interpersonally (dialogically?), Plato later showed how such question-answer cognition goes on within the same individual as a kind of intrapersonal dialogue.

Plato also clarified the nature of predication, which, as we shall see, plays an equally important role in my theory. In the Sophist dialogue, Plato (1952) explains how we use words (nouns, verbs, etc.) to frame predications and thereby further or create new meanings out of already known meanings. The assemblage of word-meanings per se we call a sentence. The subject of the sentence is predicated by the combination of verb and object—the "complete" predicate. Thus in the sentence "Soc-rates is wise" we have the first word under predication by the latter two words. Plato also states that we can "predicate many names of the same thing" (p. 569). We can say: "Socrates is wise and tenacious." Predicating meanings form into a context of assumptive (constructed) knowledge that interlaces complexly, moving ever from a broader to a narrower focus of meaning. Aristotle (1952a) believed that predication could be seen in all meaningful associations. Thus, he said: "Why does one thing attach [associate] to another? . . . We are inquiring, then, why something is predicable of something . . . the inquiry is about the predication of one thing [wisdom] of another [Socrates]" (p. 565).

Even so, Aristotle was critical of the Socratic approach to knowledge in which it was held that we can begin in error but come to know truth entirely through rational discourse, verbally stripping the husk of error to find the kernel of truth. Since Socrates sets out with a question of the sort, "What is justice?", the student must predicate "justice" by certain meanings which seem plausible to him, and which in turn reflect the student's even broader predicating assumptions (constructions) forming into an extensive context of knowledge that enables the student to lend meaning to experience. Aristotle essentially argued that if a line of such reasoning did not begin with primary and true meanings (e. g., empirically demonstrated facts), it could never extricate itself from mere verbal speculation. And, in a case like this, we have the inevitability of talky-talk "garbage in, garbage out." Aristotle is one of the fathers of scientific method, which follows a demonstrative strategy based on observation, rigorous definition, and valid evidence. The talky-talk ends and hard evidence intrudes by predicting to a criterion which cannot be verbally modified once the research is underway.

Ironically, it was this very scientific method of proving things that Aristotle favored—and literally got underway in his empirical study and recording of natural events—that was to one day short-circuit the teleological human image that he favored. The rise of empirical science in the seventeenth century was accomplished by placing great emphasis on demonstration. This was fine so far as the method of proof was concerned, in which "control and prediction" of variables was highlighted. The causal manipulation here was what Aristotle (1952b) had called an *efficient cause*, a kind of a billiard-ball thrust that moved events along mechanically, without benefit of intrinsic purpose or intention. The latter concepts are reflections of what Aristotle termed *formal* and *final causes*. Teleological theories spring from the latter interpretations of causation.

As it turned out, the seventeenth century witnessed the decline of formal and final causation in scientific description. Whereas Aristotle would have said that leaves are for the purpose of shading the fruit on trees, critics during this century claimed that since we cannot "see" a purpose there is no point in assigning such descriptions to natural objects or events. Francis Bacon (1952, p. 450) helped initiate such criticism, and long before a host of scientists who were to some extent in reaction to the repression placed on science during the Inquisition (which held Galileo under house arrest, etc.) began to call for the abolishment of formal-final causal description in "natural" science altogether. Intentional and purposive descriptions invited a first-person or introspective account, one in which there is an effort to see things through the eyes of the deity (God's "ends"), for example, but also through the eyes of a person interpersonally dialoguing with us. This resulted in formal-final cause explanations of the universe that were later satirized by Voltaire (1930) when he had the "metaphysicotheologo-cosmolo-nigologist" Pangloss teach his young charge, Candide, that "everything is made for an end [telos] . . . noses were made to wear spectacles; and so we have spectacles" (p. 14). Rejecting such intentional explanations, natural science took a strictly third-person or extraspective view of things, accounting for them entirely on the basis of material and efficient causation.

By the time modern psychology was established late in the nineteenth century, the discipline of science was completely Newtonian, which means it was extra-spective, efficiently causal, and demonstrative in tone. The possible functioning of a dialectical capacity in human reasoning was never seriously entertained in the closing decades of the nineteenth century nor was it posited over the first half of the twentieth century. Behavioristic formulations of psychologists like Watson, Tolman, Hull, and Skinner held sway over this period. And now, over the last half of the twentieth century we have had a similarly demonstrative, mechanistic conception of human behavior in the so-called "Cognitive Revolution" of that period—which is no real revolution at all, but merely a shift in the demonstrative terminology from mediated stimuli and responses to mediated inputs and outputs. Dialectic is still the rejected stepchild of psychology.

LOGICAL LEARNING THEORY

I turn now to an overview of my logical learning theory (LLT). It is "logical" because to explain human behavior it relies on the *Logos* realm of interlacing patterns of meaning—what the ancients called the "one and many"—rather than on the reductive *Bios* or *Physikos* realms (Rychlak, 1993). It recognizes a contribution to human behavior from the *Socius* realm, but does not begin on the assumption that people are unidirectionally shaped by collective social forces such as language or class level—a strategy that we find in the traditional Marxian formulation as well as in the postmodern social constructionist theories of today (see Rosenau, 1992).

My first theoretical maneuver was to find a substitute for the efficient-cause concept of stimulus-response, or, as used today in computing models, input-output. Such language biases us in the direction of extraspective, mechanistic formulations. I therefore coined the term *telosponse* for this purpose. People are active telosponders, not passive responders. This means that they behave for the sake of an intended end, one that is most often conscious but can also be unconscious (Rychlak, 1997). Such ends can vary from the immediate, as in deciding to reach for a pencil, to the long term, such as working to earn an advanced academic degree. To understand behavior we must see things through the introspectively framed (phenomenal) assumptions of the individual. In fact, merely saying, writing, or even thinking of something reflects an end or reason in the meaning under formulation. Thus, when I say "Good morning" to another person I am making a purposeful effort ("intending") to be civil and/or friendly. Telosponsivity thus involves behaving for the sake of something like the major premise that Aristotle had in mind. Logical learning theory pictures the behaving organism as a construer, an affirmer of reasons entering into purposes and intentions (i.e., final causes). I was, in effect, taking a Kantian position here as opposed to the traditional Lockean style of theorizing that we see in psychology (Kant, 1952, p. 14; Locke, 1952, p. 413). But there was a problem in the theoretical development to this point. The telosponse construct was not fleshed out enough. In time I came to see that it was essentially a logical process, the same sort of process that Aristotle's syllogism captured. But this process was only important to the person because of the meanings that it conveyed. In other words, there was a process-versus-content issue here. A process is a discernible, repeatable course of action on the basis of which some items under description are believed to be meaningfully patterned. The items under processing in telosponsivity were those verbal and pictorial experiences that the person construed in (phenomenal) perception. Following Kant, I am suggesting that although there may well be an independent, nominal realm of experience, this realm is always patterned into meaning by the telosponsive framing of the person. In fact, we always find meaning in order, and vice versa. This patterning is what Aristotle meant by formal causation.

A content is an ingredient that is produced, conveyed, or otherwise employed by a process. Traditional learning theories have such contents "shaped" into the S-R mechanism by the environment (Socius), the genetic makeup of the person (Bios), or some combination of both. The behaving organism on these views was not said to be the originating source of these contents (cues, signals, etc.), patterning them into existence. The organism merely moved such contents along once under stimulation or upon receiving a certain input signal. The basic process in such mechanistic accounts is mediation, in which something that is produced elsewhere and taken in comes to play a role in the process that was not initially a part of or intrinsic to it. According to this model, people say and/or think what they do because they have been repeatedly shaped to contiguously align certain verbal or pictorial cues together entirely without purpose or intention. The formal-cause patterning of cognition is on this view totally demonstrative, an efficiently caused outcome of shaping without purpose or intention. There are no dialectical dualities in which one meaning (e.g., injustice) delimits the very definition of its opposite (justice), as Heracleitus had suggested. There is no intrinsic capacity to negate an input as it is entering cognition. To negate today's input we must have yesterday's input, functioning now as a mediator, unidirectionally influencing cognition in efficient-cause fashion (see Hebb, 1974, for an example of this sort of theorizing).

In place of mediation, LLT proposed the concept of predication. Predication is the logical process of affirming, denying, or qualifying precedently broader patterns of meaning in sequacious extension to narrower or targeted patterns of meaning. The target is the point, aim, or end of the meaning-extension. Instead of the stimulus-response or input-output thrust of efficient causation, LLT was substituting an intentional meaning-extension flowing from a broader realm of meaning to a narrower, targeted realm. This broader realm is the precedent; that is, a meaning coming before another in logical order—which is not the same thing as spatial order. For example, in the sentence "Socrates is wise," the word wise is a precedent predication of the word Socrates even though it follows the latter in the sentence format. We might picture this as two Euler circles, one engulfing the other. The broader circle with the larger diameter (representing wisdom) thus extends its meaning to the smaller, engulfed circle (representing Socrates). This meaning extends sequaciously, which means in a slavishly compliant or logically necessary manner.

Now, up to about this point I had been speaking globally about dialectical reasoning, equating it with oppositionality in reasoning. But how was I to picture dialectical reasoning in terms of a predicational process? Well, the traditional "thesis versus antithesis" alignment was oppositional, resulting—but not always!—in a synthesis (e.g., Hegel occasionally left the two sides unjoined). How could one picture this contrast on the predicational model? What if we thought of the inside of the larger Euler circle as a thesis (A) and its outside (non-A) as an antithesis? When we predicate "Socrates is wise" (A) as our thesis, we would necessarily imply that "Socrates is not wise" (non-A). Drawing the broader Euler circle need not be thought of as cognitively dismissing the non-encircled realm of meaning. The sequacious extension of "wisdom" to the target (i.e., Socrates) would pan passu involve the extension of "non-wisdom" as well. It is then up to the reasoning individual to evaluate and thereby align Socrates on some kind of oppositional evaluation of "wise versus not-wise," akin to the "A versus not-A" strategy of the interpersonal Socratic method. The eventual synthesis (or, synopsis as the Greeks called it) would then be up to the evaluative decision of the individual reasoner—to arrive at one alternative, the other, or some combination qualifying the meaningful statement (wise sometimes, not so wise other times, etc.).

This is the course I took, and as a result began to speak of oppositionality as an aspect of predication rather than of dialectical reasoning per se. There is no difference, really, but I had a motive for downplaying the use of "dialectic." That is, there is so much historical baggage that is lugged into the discussion when one uses this term that it is almost impossible to convey anything new. Everyone seems to hear the word "dialectic" and immediately begins to predicate the resulting discussion with their unique recollections and typically irrelevant understandings of Hegel, Marx, Socrates, and so on. Fortunately, the word "oppositionality" was hardly used at all in learning-theory accounts. Oppositionality enters into four distinctive logical relations: contrariety (All is A. None is A); contradiction (All is A. At least one is not A); contrast (A leans in "this" direction. Non-A leans in "that" reverse direction); and negation (All is A. A does not exist, is wrong, is irrelevant, etc.). Contrariety appears to be the fundamental logical pattern in oppositionality, with the other three forms being variations on this basic theme. When I began shifting from dialectics to oppositionality the latter word was not even to be found in the literature-search programs, but I have since put out enough empirical data on this topic to bring it in.

The concept of lending meaning to experience via predication, or meaning-extension as it is referred to in LLT, is a crucial notion. How is it possible for meanings to be extended from a predicate to a target, and does this not imply that humans must be born with "innate ideas" to get the initial meaning-extensions underway? Logical learning theory relies on the principle of tautology to explain how a telosponder can bring forward a predication of the sort "Socrates is wise." Tautology can be defined as a patterned relation of identity occurring between meaningful referents. This patterning is not dependent on time's passage; just as soon as the meanings are aligned predicationally, there is an immediate (not mediate!) tautological extension from the broader to the narrower realm of meaning. Once affirmed, the meaning symbolized by the word "wisdom" engulfs our understanding of Socrates. This tautological aspect of the predicational process is how learning always takes place. We learn by extending meanings we know to what we are trying to know (or "learn") in light of such precedents. Not all tautologies are carried out like the Gertrude Stein example of "a rose is a rose is a rose," implying 100% identity from predicate to target. Usually, the meaning-extension from predicate to target is analogical. Analogies are, in effect, partial tautologies encompassing both an identity and a non-identity in the predicating meaning under extension. The same is true of similes, metaphors, allegories, and so on.

In order to address the question of innate ideas it is necessary to first point out that oppositionality has relevance for both process and content. In LLT, we speak of a generic and a delimiting oppositionality—with the former referring to process and the latter to content. Generic oppositionality is intrinsic to the predicational process, where specific targets ("Socrates") fall either under or beyond the meaning being extended by the framing predicate ("wisdom"). This relating of broader-to-narrower realms must not be thought of as "in" the words used (e.g., as due to the predicate [wisdom] being more abstract in meaning than the target [Socrates]). We can express the simile "A person is like a tree" or, using the same words, express "A tree is like a person." In both cases, the target or subject word takes on meaning under extension from its predicate, even though the resultant meaning changes across sentences. If the intrinsic oppositionality here would be brought into play by the reasoner, it would probably occur as a negation. For example, the opposite of the simile "A person is like a tree" (thesis) would be "A person is not like a tree" (antithesis). Anyone framing the former meaning with true understanding would necessarily grasp the latter meaning (as a negating possibility). The final position taken by a reasoner would be on one side or the other; it might even encompass the third step of dialectical reasoning to suggest that "both" similes contained truth as well as error (synthesis).

Not all words have opposites, but many do—as in the example of Heracleitus in which justice delimits (sets the boundary line of meaning) for injustice, or vice versa. Images have opposite meanings as well. We bring together symbols of life and death into one pictorial image, as in a work of art or possibly a dream. The human/lion image of the sphynx is a perfect example of bringing together opposite (human versus nonhuman) images into a single figure. This capacity that certain content-meanings have to imply their opposites is what LLT means by delimiting oppositionality. Linguists have pointed to the important role played by opposition in all extant language systems. Indeed, Trier (1931) essentially defined delimiting oppositionality when he observed that every antonymic word that is uttered implicitly suggests its opposite meaning to both the speaker and hearer. Lyons (1977) has said that "opposition is one of the most important principles governing the structure of language" (p. 271), and Richards (1967) has singled out opposition as one of the essential principles through which language works. Delimiting oppositionality is very important in the drawing of implications. For example, to say that "John is not reliable" implies that he "is" unreliable (even though this may not be precisely what is meant).

It is the principle of tautology in telosponsive conceptualization that enables LLT to account for how infants from the outset of cognitive life begin predicating experience without the aid of an initiating "inborn idea." Logical learning theory holds that the very first contents of the predicational process are items tautologized of themselves, establishing thereby a sense of identity for the item in question by the infant learner. The infant, in the first hours of life, conceptualizes "a nipple is a nipple" or some such notion (actual words are learned later, of course). If we were to express this as a statement, "nipple" would be located in both the subject (target) and predicate location. Obviously, such a syntactic array does not make sense at this point, because the infant is cognizing in idiosyncratic images, feelings, sucking tensions, bodily sensations, tastes, and so forth. The initial tautologizing of a psychological content with itself might be called recognition. The infant comes to recognize the targeted item in question, for example, its mother's nipple. Now we have our first precedent taking shape, a distinctively recognized identity that is "known" so that further knowing is possible (doubtless several such initiating points of awareness occur, as in the tautologizing of a bodily orifice like the ear with itself, etc.). Initially serving as a target, the maternal nipple can now act as a predicating frame of reference to items presumed to be nipples or nipple-like in the course of ongoing meaning extension. Partial tautologizing now also takes place. For example, over the early months of life, the infant begins sucking any other items that, like the nipple, are capable of being sucked. Some of these items neither look, feel, nor taste like mother's nipple.

Just as with our Euler circle model we necessarily find both an inside and an outside under meaning-extension, so too when a tautology is extended from nipple(ness) to nipple(ness), the child cognizes an immediate sense of nonnippleness. Generic oppositionality of the predicational process makes this possible. The resulting sense of contrast allows the infant to learn that some things are like a nipple, but not exactly, which is what LLT interprets as a partial tautology. As the child matures, delimiting oppositionality greatly enhances the experiential contents being processed cognitively through both imagery and language. To the extent that such ongoing telosponsivity proves useful—for example, the baby learns to avoid sucking certain things because they are uncomfortably bitter, cold, or grainy—we can say that learning takes place. Indeed, for the rest of a person's life he or she will manifest learning when a point is reached where a previous target is sufficiently known so that it can now be used as a predicate. People thus learn by way of extending what they now know to what they can come to know. What is learned need not be objectively "true," of course. People do learn error, and come to order their lives based on such distortions and misunderstandings.

Emotions are important in learning, but we know from considerable research that emotions are themselves framed by predicational contexts, the situation that people find themselves in, and so on (Rychlak, 1994). Thus, in one context a person might sense a "righteous" anger that was perfectly appropriate yet in another feel ashamed over losing his or her temper. Logical learning theory relies upon delimiting oppositionality to account for such evaluations of emotions. An emotion is understood as a pattern of physiological sensations that is targeted by the predications of the person feeling these sensations. The situational contexts in which the sensations are experienced plays a crucial role in identifying the predicated meaning of the emotion experienced. Emotion is often confused with what LLT terms "affection" or "affective assessment." An affective assessment is a form of predication in which the person immediately judges the meanings under cognitive processing, including emotional feeling-tones, framing them within the oppositional contrast of what is "liked" (preferred, good, positive, etc.) by the person versus what is "disliked" (rejected, bad, negative, etc.).

Affective assessments therefore have to do with meaningfulness, or the extent of significance that a given meaning has for the person concerned. People render such affective assessments for the targets they are predicating even as this meaning-extension is taking place. The student learns a subject matter in school, and concurrently renders an affective evaluation (e. g., liking history, disliking mathematics, etc.). Affection can also change over time. The beginning jogger may find the exercise boring, but in time come to look forward to this break from daily routine. People like certain things and dislike others even though they may not actually "say so" to themselves at the time. Logical learning theory holds that, in principle, it may be possible to avoid rendering such an evaluation. A person might say "I really have no attitude about this, one way or another," but in practice this is usually reflective of a lack of interest in the issue at hand—which in turn suggests that a mild negativity is at play in the conceptualizations of the person.

The final concepts I would like to mention as basic to LLT are the related notions of transcendence and self-reflexivity. Transcendence is the capacity all humans have to rise above their ongoing predications and put them to question or examination by reasoning from the opposite point of view (i.e., the outside of the larger Euler circle). When people do indeed transcend what is ongoing in cognition to see alternative possibilities like this, we can speak of self-reflexivity taking place. Reflexivity always leads to the appreciation that the meanings presently under affirmation in telosponsivity could be otherwise. It is this capacity to see beyond the given affirmation that provides humans with the capacity for conscious free will (see Rychlak, 1997).

A word should be said concerning LLT's view of human development. In LLT, development is viewed as a series of increasingly important, challenging levels of behavior calling for higher and more complex manifestations of learning. The same predicational process that I have described in the learning of an infant is presumed to be carried on throughout life. It is the content which gradually develops into increasingly complex formulations. New conceptualizations will be taught to the person over time, thanks to modeling and interpersonal dialogues of one form or another (with parents, teachers, friends, employers, etc.). Theories which rely on physical changes to account for development taking place, such as biologically moving through uniform stages of maturation, would not be in accord with LLT.

RESEARCH SUPPORT AND GENERAL CONCLUSION

Much of the early work in LLT was done on affective assessment (Rychlak, 1994). We measured this via ratings of like/dislike, so that subjects might first rate a series of words or consonant-vowel-consonant trigrams (e. g., HIB, LAT, PIQ) for likeability. We carefully equated such learnable items for other possible influences on learning such as familiarity, frequency in language contents, pronounceability, judgments of easy versus hard to learn, and so on. It was then found repeatedly that "normals," people with self-confidence, and who liked to participate in the experiment, learned words or trigrams that they personally liked more readily than those they disliked. On the other hand, people who were abnormal, who were diagnosed as mentally ill, alcoholic, having weak self-images, and who disliked taking the experimental task, did not show this preference for liked items in learning facility. In fact, they often learned their disliked materials significantly faster than their liked materials.

We attributed this difference in affective learning style to the framing predication that affection made possible, so that the tautological meaning-extension moved readily from "liked" to "liked" when the learner actually had some such positive affirmation in the task at the outset, in contest to a learner who began from a "disliked" affirmation of self and task. Negative self-evaluators actually could be seen to extend meaning more readily along a negative than a positive course in life, bringing about a self-fulfilling prophecy of expected disappointment and misery. Negativity can indeed breed negativity. A criticism which arose, one that actually had some bearing on human development, held that differences to be noted in affective assessment were actually the result of ongoing conditioning in behavior. From earliest years, the fact that we are shaped through positive and negative reinforcements determines the observed differences in performance that LLT research was reporting. To answer this criticism a study was conducted in which 169 children across the first six grades of elementary school were given a recognition task for pictures of designs and paintings, projected onto a screen before them (Rychlak, 1975). The first time these materials were presented the children rated them for affective assessment on our like/dislike scale. The pictures were then presented a second time, in a different randomized order, mixed in with other pictures that had not been presented initially. The task for the children was to indicate whether they had seen a design or painting previously. If the criticism holding that the affective-assessment effects were due to conditioning is sound, it would follow that children from the higher grades would be more likely to manifest these contrasting differences than children from the lower grades. The former children would have had more time to be "shaped" by positive and negative conditioning than the latter children. Logical learning theory contends that affective assessment begins at birth. In fact, the claim is made that since infants lack verbal discriminants they are actually relying more on affective than conceptual learning. As we go along in life it becomes possible to surmount affective preferences to a degree, but never to the extent of removing them entirely. Returning to the experiment under discussion, it was found that children at all grade levels recognized more of their liked than their disliked materials. More importantly, a significant statistical interaction between grade level and affective recognition established that first graders had a larger positive affective-assessment effect than did the children in any of the higher grades. It is therefore clear that we cannot explain away affection in learning based on "shaping" through previous conditioning.

As work progressed, we spent more of our time trying to prove that something like predication actually was taking place. One of the first studies along this line involved giving participants a list of sentences of the sort, "An ash tray can be used as a plate." Participants were asked to put these sentences to memory. Later, they were tested for sentence recall by cuing them with either the subject noun (i.e., ash tray) or the predicate noun (i.e., plate). It was found as predicted that predicate cuing led to greater recall than subject cuing. This supports LLT's claim that meaning extends from the framing predicate context "to" the targeted item exactly as depicted in our Euler circle analysis (see above).

To answer critics, who claimed that predicate cuing was due simply to grammatical rules learned in sentence structuring, we designed a "triplet" task in which three words that were not grammatically bound together, but did share a meaning, were presented to subjects. That is, we were moving now from syntax to semantics. An example of a triplet would be "nose, face, eye." Since the word "face" is the broadest in meaning, subsuming both eye and nose, it would most probably be the predicate if these three words were joined together in a meaningful fashion. We therefore predicted that if participants were asked to read over a list of such triplets and then later be cued for recall, the broadest term (i.e., "face") would prove to be the most efficacious cue. This prediction was validated.

Turning to some typical findings on oppositionality per se, we have shown that it is a frequently overlooked form of elaboration in the "depth of processing" research (see Rychlak, 1994). The oppositionality of affective assessment is important enough so that people can recall the affective quality (i.e., like or dislike) of a word's meaning even before they recall the actual word. We have shown how oppositionality can facilitate learning in this manner: Indeed, we have drawn a learning curve for oppositionality. There are many experiments which could be cited at this point if space permitted. A recent tracking of LLT research has located 150 empirical data collections to date.

The vast majority of these experiments has supported LLT's image of the human being as an organism that can reason both demonstratively and dialectically. Computing machines may be said to "think" but if this is true then they do so only in a demonstrative manner. There is no oppositionality in the binary units of the computer, there is only demonstratively framed opposition (i.e., side by side). Modern psychology has yet to confront the fact that humans are not limited to the mediating, unidirectional form of efficient-cause cognition and behavior that current learning theories uncritically embrace. We need a more comprehensive understanding of the human being, one that captures the full range of human reasoning. Oppositionality is the key that can open the doors to such an image of the human being. This proper understanding of what it means to be human can only enhance our grasp of dialogicality in development.

REFERENCES

Aristotle. (1952a). Metaphysics. In R. M. Hutchins (Ed.), *Great books of the western world* (Vol. 8, pp. 495–626). Chicago: Encyclopedia Britannica.

Aristotle. (1952b). Physics. In R. M. Hutchins (Ed.), *Great books of the western world* (Vol. 8, pp. 253–355). Chicago: Encyclopedia Britannica.

Aristotle. (1952c). Topics. In R. M. Hutchins (Ed.), *Great books of the western world* (Vol. 8, pp. 143–223). Chicago: Encyclopedia Britannica.

Bacon, F. (1952). Advancement in learning. In R. M. Hutchins (Ed.), *Great books of the western world* (Vol. 30, pp. 1–101). Chicago: Encyclopedia Britannica. (Original work published 1605.)

Hebb, D. O. (1974). What psychology is about. *American Psychologist, 29,* 71–79.

Hermans, H.J.M., Kempen, H.J.G., & van Loon, R.J.P. (1992). The dialogical self: Beyond individualism and rationalism. *American Psychologist, 47,* 23–33.

Kant, I. (1952). The critique of pure reason. In R. M. Hutchins (Ed.), *Great books of the western world* (Vol. 42, pp. 1–250). Chicago: Encyclopedia Britannica. (Original work published 1781.)

Locke, J. (1952). An essay concerning human understanding. In R. M. Hutchins (Ed.), *Great books of the western world* (Vol. 35, pp. 85–395). Chicago: Encyclopedia Britannica. (Original work published 1690.)

Lyons, J. (1977). *Semantics* (Vol. 1). Cambridge: Cambridge University Press.

Nakamura, H. (1964). *Ways of thinking of Eastern peoples.* Honolulu: East-West Center Press.

Plato. (1952). Sophist. In R. M. Hutchins (Ed.), *Great books of the western world* (Vol. 7, pp. 551–579). Chicago: Encyclopedia Britannica.

Raju, P. T. (1967). Metaphysical theories in Indian philosophy. In C. A. Moore (Ed.), *The Indian mind: Essentials of Indian philosophy and culture* (pp. 19–40). Honolulu: University of Hawaii Press.

Richards, I. A. (1967). Introduction. In C. K. Ogden (Ed.), *Opposition: A linguistic and psychological analysis* (pp. 7–13). Bloomington: Indiana University Press.

Rosenau, P. M. (1992). *Post-modernism and the social sciences: Insights, inroads, and intrusions.* Princeton, NJ: Princeton University Press.

Rychlak, J. F. (1975). Affective assessment in the recognition of designs and paintings by elementary school children. *Child Development, 46,* 62–70.

Rychlak, J. F. (1977). *The psychology of rigorous humanism.* New York: Wiley-Interscience.

Rychlak, J. F. (1993). A suggested principle of complementarity for psychology: In theory, not method. *American Psychologist, 48,* 933–942.

Rychlak, J. F. (1994). *Logical learning theory: A human teleology and its empirical support.* Lincoln: University of Nebraska Press.

Rychlak, J. F. (1997). *In defense of human consciousness.* Washington, DC: APA Books.

Trier, J. (1931). Der deutsche Wortschatz im Sinnbezirk des Verstandes. [A glossary of German terms relevant to the subject matter of understanding.] Heidelberg, Germany: Winter.

Voltaire, F.M.A. (1930). *Candide.* New York: J. J. Little & Ives.

Part II

Dialogicality and the Development of Self

Chapter 3

Dynamics of Dialogue and Emergence of Self in Early Communication

Maria C.D.P. Lyra and Micheline Souza

The study of early communication has been the focus of interest to different research orientations in recent years. Our focus here will be centered on the study of dynamic processes of early communication. More specifically, we aim to propose a model of communicative development based on historical and dynamic properties of the system of communication and on dialogism as developed by Mikhail Bakhtin. This focus allows us to explore the phenomenon of *abbreviation* as it defines periods of quasi-stability within early communication and illustrates a new form of communication which emerges through its development. Our goal is to understand the emergent characteristics of a dialogical self, conceived as an author that exists within a relational simultaneity of different positions, particularly at the moment of facing novelty.

Two main directions in the study of early communication can be found in contemporary psychology. First, there has been research on the antecedents of language mastery. Second, particularly during the late 1970s and 1980s, the study of the infant's pre-adapted characteristics to interact with the social world became popular. Researchers within the latter tradition have, in general, assumed that the communicative partners develop as independent actors, and that the process of communication—the relationship—is an add-on quality to their individual characteristics.

In both perspectives—those of language mastery and development of relationships—the transformative power of communication as a dynamic process remains hidden. A different conception has emerged more recently. In this new approach, the dynamics or processual nature of communication are highlighted.

TWO CONVERGING PERSPECTIVES: DYNAMIC SYSTEMS AND DIALOGISM

Two major perspectives have contributed to this new approach: the notion of dynamic systems and the attempt to elaborate dialogicality in human development. These two perspectives share some common aspects: First, they concentrate on the history of systemic relationships and on the dynamic nature of development. Second, they understand development as a process of emergence of novel forms. The focus on the systemic-relational and creative nature of development as a process of emergence of new forms is well stated by Paul van Geert (1998, p. 144):

Development is a process that incorporates and transforms a host of processes and influences that each have their unique sources, laws and forms and integrates them into a phenomenon that is more than just the sum of its parts. That is, development integrates the biological condition of growth and change with external sociocultural influences, support and education, with the subject's own activity, motives and goals, with the formal, structural and historical properties of the contents and skills that become part of the subject's mental and behavioral equipment.

One of the challenges that both approaches face is precisely to map or to grasp this process of emergence of new forms. We propose that it is at the realm of the *microgenetic* developmental changes that this search can be accomplished.

Dynamic Systems

The dynamic systems perspective offers conceptual tools for understanding the dynamic aspects of the history of communication. For instance, instead of searching for the linear-causal features of developmental change, this approach focuses on the dynamic aspects of the system that develops in irreversible time. It is the dynamic cooperation of the elements involved in that particular system that allows for the emergence of new forms (Fogel & Thelen, 1987; Thelen & Smith, 1998). From that perspective, the process of communication between the adult and the infant is conceived as a dynamic developing system that exhibits periods of quasi-stability and periods of instability that emerge from the self-organization of the elements of the system under investigation. The identification of those self-organizing characteristics allows the comprehension of both the process of change and the emergent developmental features of communication (Fogel, 1993).

However, when applied to the process of early communication as setting the conditions for the emergence of individualities, the dynamic systems perspective fails to consider the emergence of the intrasubjective nature of the developing subjects who are embedded and involved in the relational process of communication. The notion of an individual, a self, or a subject requires the conceptualization of the specific nature of these intrasubjective processes that allows for conceiving the agentive nature of these subjects. The dynamic nature of the communication process conceived as dialogue allows us to approach both the interdependent characteristics of the communicative partners and this intrasubjective dimension of emergent selves.

Dialogism

The dialogical perspective—or dialogism—is based on different ontological and epistemological assumptions (Hermans, 1996, 1997; Hermans & Kempen, 1995; Marková, 1990, 1997) from that of the dynamic systems approach. Dialogism is conceived as a conceptual framework for the study of social sciences and humanities. Dialogism as an ontological and epistemological position relies on the semiotic functioning of human beings. It is basically through language that dialogicality assumes its full expression. With regard to the area of developmental psychology, language and semiotic functioning make it possible to fulfill two major interdependent requirements of dialogism: (1) the reflexive, intrasubjective activity—that allows the existence of selves as individualities through the functioning of a mediating device, and (2) the intersubjective exchanges—that permit this reflexive, intrasubjective activity to take place in conjunction with intersubjective exchanges (Holquist, 1990; Marková, 1997).

Using dialogue as the central metaphor we can analyze its historical process in order to explore the functioning of individuals that are at the same time related and distinguished from each other while embedded in dialogue. According to the dialogical perspective, historicity implies both the broader cultural-historical background that is inherent in the semiotic functioning of dialogue and the particular historical unfolding constructed by partners through dialogue (Hermans & Kempen, 1995; Marková, 1997). Our focus here, however, will be on the historical unfolding from a microgenetic point of view, as it permits us to study the emergence and the constitution of individual subjects as co-authors of particular histories. The notion of dialogue can be used in different ways. If the dialogical perspective is used as a new label for describing the interaction between ontologically conceived, separated partners, that label will not add much to the understanding of the emergence of relational individualities involved in the process of communication. Therefore, it is necessary to clarify the principles that underlie the assumption of the dialogical perspective that, in our view, will offer some tools to help understand the historical construction of individualities emerging in the process of communication. The principles that underlie the assumption of the dialogical perspective in this chapter will be taken from some of the ideas developed by Mikhail Bakhtin (1973, 1986, 1993).

When we talk about the ways in which dialogue occurs in early infancy, we face the problem of tracing the process through which the infant emerges as an individual or self. At this period of development we cannot rely on semiotic functioning or linguistic mediating devices as a way of describing and comprehending the intrasubjective functioning of individuals. We try to show, in this chapter, that some Bakhtinian ideas are very helpful for mapping the emergence of dialogical selves. This will be accomplished through the analysis of the microgenetic dynamics of the early mother–infant exchanges through time. These dynamics, conceived as dialogical processes, help us to explore the emergence of new organizational levels of communication, which allow us to identify the emergence of relational individualities.

In order to trace the microgenetic changes of communicative systems in early life, which make up the roots of dialogical selves, we first present a model of communicative development that describes periods of quasi-stability of the mother–infant communication system. We show how the dynamics of this system move toward the creation of a new organizational pattern of communication—abbreviation—illustrating simultaneity of different positions, which is the seed of individualities as authorship.

A MODEL OF THE DYNAMICS OF COMMUNICATION IN EARLY LIFE

We propose a model of communicative development that guides the understanding of the process of change and construction of new levels of communicative exchanges at the beginning of life. In this chapter we will concentrate on mother–object–infant exchanges. This type of dyadic exchange requires the object as mediating the communication between the mother and the infant.

Two basic assumptions set the stage for this model. First, the system in consideration is conceived as composed by the mother–infant dialogical exchanges. In this work, we particularly refer to the first eight months of the infant's life. Second, the development of dialogical communication is assumed to be constructed through the historical unfolding of the microgenetic transformations of the partners' exchanges. The historical examination of the development of the systemic relations allows us to identify periods of quasi-stability of the developing system of communicative exchanges, which indicate the emergence of novel qualities within the process of development.

Three periods of quasi-stability make up the process of development of this system: *establishment, extension,* and *abbreviation.* They are conceived as dialogical processes, and their historical construction allows us to understand and explain the developmental mechanisms of transformations and emergence of novel forms at the microgenetic level of analysis.

In order to conceptualize establishment, extension, and abbreviation, we start by identifying four dimensions that compose the fields of action focused upon in this model: (1) time spent in order to initiate partners' exchanges; (2) number and quality of the turn-takings; (3) quality of partners' adjustment; (4) degree and quality of the mutual knowledge.

Establishment Period

Considering mother–object–infant dialogical exchanges, more specifically the construction of the give-and-take game, the establishment period shows the following characteristics: (1) The exchanges are not immediately established. The partners spend some time initiating exchanges. (2) There is a small number of turn-takings that focus on the establishment of a first element to be shared by the dyad (partners' joint attention toward the object). (3) The mutual adjustment between the partners is irregular and rough (not smooth). (4) Mutual knowledge becomes constructed through highlighting a particular element of the partners' exchanges in order to reach a minimum degree of shared communication (partners' joint attention toward the object). This element becomes a *figure* against the *background* of other possible elements of the partners' flow of dyadic exchanges (e.g., infant's leg movements).

Extension Period

During the extension period, the dialogical exchanges exhibit the following characteristics: (1) The exchanges are immediately established (partners' joint attention toward the object). (2) There is a large number of turn-takings that concentrate on the elaboration of elements related to the task of offering and taking the object (offering the object by the mother and taking the object by the infant). (3) The smooth quality of the partners' exchanges—mutual adjustment—starts by the end of the extension period but only for separated elements (or a group of elements) of the exchanges, each one at a time (for instance, the infant's arm movements toward the object separated or together with the open movement of the hands). (4) Mutual knowledge develops on the background of the previously constructed minimum shared communicative knowledge (i.e., the partners' joint attention toward the object)—highlighting the separated elements (or a group of elements) as the figure of the partners' exchanges (e.g., the infant's arm movements toward the object separated or together with the open movement of the hands).

Abbreviation Period

Abbreviated dialogical exchanges exhibit the following characteristics: (1) We find immediately established exchanges. In other words, the partners show an instantaneous joint attention toward the object. (2) A small number of turns and/or turns that demonstrate a condensed nature characterize this period. In this last condition, elements of antecedent separated exchanges appear mixed and/or integrated as composing a single turn (for instance, the movement of directing the arm, opening the hand, grasping and taking the object by the infant is coordinated in a fast and compact way). (3) The smooth quality of partners' exchanges becomes visible in the adjusted and fast unfolding of communicative turn-taking. It is possible to suppose that each partner starts to know his or her partner's position (or role) and his or her own position (or role) in relation to the other partner regarding this type of exchanges (the mother offers and the infant takes the object). (4) The partners' mutual knowledge can be identified in the abbreviated exchanges. It represents a subsequent level of the smooth quality of the exchanges. In the present case, it is required that each partner knows his or her partner's position (or role) and his or her own position (or role) in relation with the other partner, but *now* regarding the group of integrated elements that compose the mother–object–infant type of dialogical exchanges (the mother offers and the infant takes the object). The partners share a holistic group—like a Gestalt—composed by the partner's actions and the subject's own actions. However, this does not exactly correspond to the successive elements of the turn-takings because it includes the uncertainty that each actualized turn-taking carries. This means that variability within the limits of this shared knowledge (for instance, the mother can delay in leaving the object in the infant's hand) is a characteristic of the abbreviated period.

Another characteristic of the abbreviated period regarding partners' mutual knowledge is the "explosion toward novelty creation." After a first period in which the organization of the system of communication exhibits abbreviated exchanges as described above, we find a new development of the abbreviated dialogical exchanges. This process is characterized in two non-exclusive ways: (1) new combinations of the antecedent elements that compose this holistic group (the mother offers the object and the infant takes it) and/or (2) the introduction of completely new elements into these exchanges. Following the "explosion toward novelty creation" a new period of extension takes place.

Our claim in this chapter is that the concept of abbreviation and its aspect of "explosion toward novelty creation" exhibit the possibility of exploring the emergence of dialogical selves, characterized by the simultaneity of different positions, which allows us to conceive the relational nature of individualities. Thus, let us summarize some of Bakhtin's ideas regarding his conception of authorship. This core concept offers us theoretical support for extending the notion of abbreviation toward the domain of intrasubjective processes as fundamentally interdependent with the intersubjective activities. In other words: the relational nature of individualities.

DIALOGICAL SELF: CONTRIBUTIONS FROM MIKHAIL BAKHTIN

In Bakhtin's view, the dialogical relationship must be considered as a phenomenon that goes beyond the logic of the semantic of disembodied relations. For Bakhtin (1973), the difference between a word as a linguistic object and a word as an utterance lies in the embodied positioning that a word carries in becoming an utterance. Two exactly equal sentences are never the same in a dialogue. For one partner it can be a declaration, for the other a request for more information, for instance. Therefore, the different individual positionings are necessary conditions for the existence of the relational dynamics of dialogue.

Bakhtin focuses on dialogue as the concrete situation in which different actors dynamically exchange points of view regarding a reality that exists due to the power of these actors. The analysis of Dostoevsky's work (Bakhtin, 1973) shows the creation of a new type of artistic thought, which Bakhtin has called "polyphonic novel." This novelistic form offers a metaphoric tool that can be extended beyond the field of the novelistic genre, as Bakhtin has proposed, becoming helpful for a dialogical conception of human development (for instance, see Hermans, 1996, 1997; Hermans & Kempen, 1995; Marková, 1990, 1997; Wertsch, 1991).

We can emphasize two main points about Dostoevsky's polyphonic novel as a way to the metaphorical comprehension of human functioning. In this novelistic form there is not an absolute reality to be represented by the characters. One cannot find in Dostoevsky's work any description of the external world. On the other hand, the points of view from which the characters see the world are determined by the representation of surrounding reality. Second, the perspectives of the characters are independent and mutually opposing to each other. The characters are no more considered "voiceless slaves" (Bakhtin, 1973, p. 4) acting under the guidance of the author. They can disagree not only between themselves, but with their creator too, even rebelling against him. In this way, the author is only one voice among a number of different characters' voices.

The concept of an author as a co-author embedded in constant dialogues is highlighted in the polyphonic novel. There is a "plurality of independent and unmerged voices and consciousnesses" (Bakhtin, 1973, p. 4), represented by different characters' voices, telling their own history and being involved in dialogical relationships. Different voices take different spatial positions that exist side by side, at the same time. This simultaneity of voices creates the possibility of dialogues between them.

The dialogical approach that emerged from the metaphor of Dostoevsky's polyphonic novel led Bakhtin to reflect about the subject's inner world, and, at the same time, the subject's outer world in the form of interpersonal relationships. The human being, as in Dostoevsky's characters, is always in dialogue. The dialogue can be with real others—interpersonal dialogues—and with imaginary others—internal dialogues. The metaphor of the polyphonic novel offers a dynamic world of individual perspectives involved in constant relational exchanges, progressively composing a historical reality, which can be analyzed and comprehended from the point of view of us as developmental scientists. This metaphor sets the stage for exploring the emergence of a self as a co-author of his or her unique historical development.

Simultaneity of Different Positions and Selfhood as Authorship

For Bakhtin's dialogism (Bakhtin, 1973, 1986, 1993; Holquist, 1990) the "self" means an event in existence—the event of being a self—organized around the categories of space and time. Everything is perceived by the self from a unique position. However, the self never stays alone and is not pre-existent to relationships with others. Because the event of being a self is a relational event, the status of being a self means a co-being reality. The simultaneity of different spaces, occupied by individuals' unique positioning, allows the dialogue to assume a pervasive character in existence.

The world addresses the self and the self cannot choose but to give an answer to the world. In Bakhtin's words, "we have no alibi in existence" (*Estetika*, p. 179, in Holquist, 1990, p. 29). The uniqueness of the place the self occupies in existence gives to the self the characteristic of answerability. From the place I occupy in existence, only I can answer to the world. Even the choice of being completely passive reflects an action of answering, an answerability. This way, Bakhtin highlights the dynamic nature of the dialogical self. Life is activity, a constant dialogue among events addressed to the self and the expression of an answer to those events. Therefore, if the self stops answering, the self is dead, because life is expression.

On the basis of the dialogical, dynamic nature of the self, we can elaborate the conception of selfhood as authorship. Answerability of the self allows us to apprehend the nature of authorship of the self. The self carries the capacity to articulate the different addressed parts of its life experience, creating a pattern of relations organized as a whole. The self-author constructs this kind of wholeness in the form of texts, or even utterances, that reflect a particular point of view. In literary metaphorical terms, these texts constitute a book that belongs to a specific genre. However, this genre does not stay static through time. The text is dynamic with regard to each new dialogue, which the self establishes with the world. Therefore, the text changes through a constant reorganization of the self's point of view.

Through the dialogues with the world, the self writes its own unique text, a text that is then its biography. Thus, the self is an author of its own history. But this biography is only updated in the relationship with others. The self has only access itself through the others' perception, thus becoming an object of its own perception. Consequently, the self's biography is always a history of co-authorship.

DIALOGICAL DYNAMICS AT THE BEGINNING OF LIFE

The dialogical conception proposed by Bakhtin seems to be a helpful conceptual tool to understand the dynamics of self-emergence as authorship. Considering dialogue at the beginning of life, we concentrate on the dynamics of early communicative actions between the infant and his or her partner. Any individual action is, at the same time, an individual-unique action and a co-action that includes the other. Conversely, any joint action, conceived as a simultaneous occurrence, includes different individual positioning and authorship.

The emergence of a dialogical self, characterized by the simultaneity of different positions, is explored through the analysis of the abbreviation period of the mother–object–infant communication. The abbreviated mother–object–infant exchanges reveal shared knowledge among the mother and the infant about the "give-and-take" exchanges. This shared knowledge includes the assumption of different positions, as well as innovations. At the same time, the particular historical unfolding of different mother–infant dyads seems to illustrate the process of co-authorship of unique biographical sketches, through the dynamic of dialogue. Moreover, the "explosion toward novelty creation," which characterizes the abbreviation period, seems to highlight the dialogical condition of self-as-author, in the sense that it points to how each partner introduces innovations in his or her exchanges, without breaking the relational dimension of co-authorship.

Abbreviation in the Mother–Object–Infant Communication System

We will analyze the mother–infant exchanges that include the object from weekly videotaped records (20 minutes each) of two Brazilian mother–infant dyads, interacting at home in natural situations, during the first eight months of the infants' lives. For the purpose of this discussion we will focus on the abbreviated character of the exchanges. We concentrate on the seventh and eighth months of the infant's life because we have observed that during this time, mother–infant–object communication is predominantly characterized by abbreviated exchanges. As we have observed that in the seventh and eighth months the abbreviated character dominates the partners' exchanges regarding mother–infant–object communication (Lyra, 1988, 1999; Lyra & Rossetti-Ferreira, 1995; Lyra & Winegar, 1997; Souza, 1999; Souza, Lyra & Lyra, 1998), we concentrate particularly on the seventh and eighth months of the infant's age.

Our analysis of the microgenetic transformations is based on (1) the examination of the changing character of the minute-by-minute dyadic exchanges in comparison to earlier ones, as well as on (2) the characteristics of the period of quasi-stability of the communicative system as it opens possibilities for the future. In both dyads we can observe the following pattern of "give-and-take" exchanges, which characterizes the abbreviation period of the mother–object–infant communication.

First illustration: (1) The mother gives the object to the baby. (2) The baby takes and holds the object. This pattern of give-and-take exchanges illustrates partners' historically constructed minimum agreement about this abbreviated type of exchange. This agreement refers to the organizational-relational pattern assumed by the dyadic exchanges as a new form of communication. The notion of agreement, in this case, is in the same sense used by Bakhtin (1973; see also Emerson, 1997). Agreement, in this way, is neither a fusion nor a perfect state of concordance but a co-voiced new achievement that, resulting from the dynamics of dialogue, necessarily includes degrees of disagreement.

Another aspect that we can observe during the abbreviation period is a progressive increase of the variation regarding the organizational form of the abbreviated exchanges. These variations are due to the particular dyadic history and to the tendency toward innovation. At the time the abbreviated pattern is maintained, it also allows for variations and innovations based on the history of the dyadic exchanges—like a pushing forward on the basis of the mutual minimum agreement already known (or shared) by the partners. It is exactly this historically well-established minimum agreement among the partners that allows the variability between dyads and the "explosion toward novelty creation" to happen without the danger of "breaking" the mutual knowledge about this pattern of communication. Let us exemplify some possibilities that are not present in the first illustration, which illustrate this variability and openness for novelty among dyads.

Second illustration: (1) The mother can include the object's noise, a touch on the baby's body, before offering the object to the baby, or place it next to the baby. (2) The baby can take the object and explore it, immediately release the object or put it in his/her mouth or even take another object that is close to the object offered by the mother.

Considering all these characteristics of abbreviation concerning the give-and-take dyadic exchanges, this concept seems to be a valuable theoretical tool for understanding the emergence of the dyadic subjects as dialogical selves. In other words, the relationship between the minimum agreement and variability among dyads, along with the "explosion toward novelty creation," which constitute the abbreviated exchanges, allow us to visualize the different positions occupied by each dyadic subject. At the same time, we can comprehend how the dynamics of dialogue create a relational pattern of exchanges organized as a history of co-authorship.

However, it is only through the analysis of the individual dyadic histories that the specific characteristics of this new, abbreviated period of quasi-stability and the emergent quality of simultaneity of different positionings (involved in the dialogical composition of those abbreviated exchanges) can be pursued or narrated. In addition, each new abbreviated negotiation reflects, at a given moment, the past history of the dialogue, and the possibilities created for the immediate future. In this way, each new abbreviation example highlights the process of emergence of authorship—the self's biography—through the dynamic of dialogue.

Let us examine first the characteristic abbreviated way of the give-and-take game in the two dyads, and afterwards the particular history of construction of these abbreviated exchanges. As a further step, we will analyze how a unique dyad can exhibit different organizational forms of abbreviated give-and-take exchanges—"explosion toward novelty creation"—in order to highlight how the possibility of innovation in the abbreviation period remains related to the minimum agreement historically co-constructed by the mother and the infant.

Abbreviated Period as Illustration of Simultaneity of Different Positions and Selfhood as Authorship

The two dyads discussed in this chapter exhibit the characteristic give-and-take game illustrated above (see first illustration). However, each dyad has a characteristic way of abbreviating the exchanges that reflects the co-authorship of their particular historical, constructed minimum agreement. The following examples highlight characteristic abbreviated exchanges regarding the two different dyads—*Dyad A* and *Dyad B*. The first example of abbreviated exchanges is from Dyad A (mother with a female baby, 28 weeks old):

> Mother and baby are sitting on the sofa.
>
> Mother takes the rubber toy and brings it into the baby's visual field.
>
> Baby looks at the rubber toy, stretches her arms, and holds the object offered by her mother, making sounds with her mouth.

The second example of abbreviated exchanges is from Dyad B (mother with a female baby, 29 weeks old):

> Mother is sitting on the bed with the baby on her lap.
>
> Mother takes the rubber toy, brings it near the baby, and squeezes it.
>
> Baby does not look toward the object.
>
> Mother kisses the baby and throws the toy on the bed, out of the baby's reach.
>
> Baby looks toward the toy.
>
> Mother says "Get it!" taking a rattle and throwing it near the rubber toy.
>
> Baby moves her body forward and gets on her hands and knees on the bed and, with the mother's help, crawls toward the objects, stretches her arms, takes the rattle and holds it.

We can observe that in both dyads the abbreviated give-and-take exchanges illustrate the emergence of a new level of agreement—minimum agreement—between the mother and the infant. This minimum agreement necessarily includes a relation of differences, and thus, degrees of disagreement. The mother and the infant constitute a dialogical relation, where each one occupies a different position, and it is exactly these differences that permit the existence of a dialogue. Each participant directs each step further in each abbreviated give-and-take exchange. This constitutes a co-authorship relation, without breaking the minimum agreement historically co-constructed.

In Dyad A, the actions of both the mother and the baby constitute a straightforward kind of abbreviated give-and-take exchange. This means that neither the mother nor the infant realizes intermediary actions between the action of giving the object by the mother, and the action of taking it by the infant. In Dyad B, on the other hand, both the mother and the infant exhibit many intermediary actions between giving and taking. For example, the mother offers the object and the infant "chooses" not to look at this object, only looking at it when the mother throws the object out of the infant's reach. In addition, the mother offers two objects, throwing both out of the infant's reach, while the infant takes only one of them.

The examples of the abbreviated exchanges of the two dyads are characterized by different relational organizations. However, both relational organizations seem to exhibit the emergence of a dialogical self, since they are composed of different individual positionings regarding both the infant and the mother. Each step further in the abbreviated exchange carries a particular direction due to the participation of the unique positioning occupied by each partner. For instance, in Dyad B it is the mother who "decides" to offer two objects and it is the infant who "decides" not to look at the object offered and to "choose" one of the two objects offered by the mother. In Dyad A, the partners had chosen to maintain a kind of prototypical giving-and-taking game in which complementary actions of offering and taking are successively used. It is the different historical development of each dyad's relational construction that is responsible for the emergence of particular positions and individual selves from dialogical relationships.

For Dyad A, the prototypical way of the give-and-take game illustrates that the infant is developing an authorship that includes, for instance, being very sensitive to the partner's delay to respond or to the introduction of new objects before taking the object offered by the mother. The mother is also developing her partnership as an author in this dialogue that includes responding in a very sensitive way to the infant's demonstration of not taking the object offered. For both, disengagement means to break the cadence of this sequence of playing the give-and-take game with the object.

For Dyad B, the infant is developing an authorship that seems to be more sensitive to the mother's actions (to throw the object) than to the mother's gaze to the object and offering it in front of the infant's gaze. Moreover, the infant needs to move in order to grasp and take the object. In this dyad the mother seems to develop a sensitivity to disengagement that is focused on the infant's action of taking an object—not a specific object—requiring the infant's effort of moving toward the object before taking it (she throws two objects out of the infant's reach). This systematic pattern allows the dyad to accept a greater delay within the give-and-take game (the action of offering by the mother and the action of taking the object by the infant).

The Role of History

The uniqueness of abbreviated organization requires a form of analysis and comprehension that is historical and interpretive. In order to understand the characteristic abbreviated dyadic exchanges and the different partners' positioning regarding those mutually adjusted, abbreviated

exchanges, we must rely on each dyad's—and, therefore, each partner's—historical development. In other words, the relational and individual aspects of the development of dialogue can only be revealed
through their historical unfolding. This historical analysis, which will be
exemplified below, represents narratives that connect meaningful pieces
of the process of construction of an emergent system of early communication as a dialogical relation that exhibits selves as co-authors.

The History of Dyad A

This dyad presents, since the establishment of this type of communicative exchange, a dynamic of exchanges characterized by a constant
adjustment between mother and baby, in the sense of exploring the object
together. Thus, the mother tries to catch the baby's gaze with the object,
always manipulating it near the baby, keeping it within her reach, until,
progressively, the baby is able to get the object. Besides this, the mother
always participates in the baby's exploration of the object—vocalizing,
helping the baby to hold the object, and so on. The abbreviated exchanges of giving-and-taking objects emerge in a very direct way. In
other words, the baby takes the object directly from the mother's hand,
without many intermediary actions between the giving and the taking.

The History of Dyad B

Dyad B, differently from Dyad A, builds, with the establishment of
this type of communicative exchange, a dynamic pattern directed toward
an individual effort of exploration of the object by the baby. Thus, as
soon as the mother catches the baby's gaze with the object, the mother
often manipulates the object out of the baby's reach, and the dyad engages in an effort to reach the object on the baby's part and, when she
reaches it, she explores it with little participation from the mother. The
dyad gradually begins to share a type of abbreviated exchange of giving-
and-taking objects, characterized by an effort on the baby's part to try
to reach the object before taking it, and an individual exploration of the
object, after taking it.

In these two histories of constructing abbreviated exchanges, we can
observe that each dyad develops a particular kind of dialogical relationship; therefore, the dynamics of co-construction of the exchanges in these
dyads exhibit different patterns of co-authorship. In other words, Dyad
A has developed a history of co-construction where the positioning of
each partner is very adjusted to the positioning of the other partner.
Thus, the characteristic abbreviated give-and-take exchanges in this dyad
show the emergence of dialogical selves, whose early biographical sketch
is being constructed through smooth and adjusted positions between the
partners, as co-authors. In terms of Dyad B, we can note that the mother
and the infant develop a dialogical history in which the mutual adjust-

ment of the partners relies on two different aspects. On the one hand, the mother requires from the infant a number of motor actions due to the fact that she locates the object out of the infant's reach. On the other hand, this leads to a time delay that enables a greater possibility of different actions from both the mother and the infant that can happen between the action of offering and taking. The dyadic partners start, thus, to write a biographical sketch that relies on more variability of different positioning regarding the give-and-take exchanges. This variability allows the co-authors to develop a kind of diverse mutual adjustment—considering the prototypical give-and-take game—which leads to more freedom of actions.

Innovative Character of the Abbreviated Exchanges

The unique historical nature of the abbreviation is the basis for the mutual and interdependent changing nature of the partners within dialogue. Thus, the innovative character of the dialogue carries the past history of dialogical exchanges while moving the dialogue toward the future. Therefore, we will focus now on an episode that shows an innovative organizational form of the abbreviated give-and-take game in Dyad A. This example illustrates how each new abbreviated negotiation reflects, at a given moment, the past history of the dialogue, and the possibilities of creating a different immediate future. Moreover, this example highlights the process of emergence of the dyadic subjects as co-authors of their biographical sketch through their innovative actions in the dynamic of dialogue. The following example for the innovative form of abbreviation is from Dyad A:

Baby is standing on sofa and her mother is sitting beside her.

Mother takes a rubber lion and brings it into baby's visual field and squeezes it.

Baby looks toward the lion and makes sounds with her mouth.

Mother touches baby with the toy, bringing it near and moving it away from the baby, saying "He's going to get you!"

Baby follows mother's actions with her gaze, stretches her arms toward the object (there are brief periods of eye contact between mother and baby).

She makes sounds with her mouth (they sound like sounds of complaint).

Mother brings the rubber lion toward baby's hand.

Baby takes the toy from mother's hand and puts it to her mouth.

In this example the mother tries to introduce a new strategy of exchange using the object. However, the infant reacts from her own perspective or position, introducing also innovative actions (for instance, sounds of complaint). The infant's perspective or position relies on the history of the construction of joint actions that does not include a "delay before playing." On the other hand, the mother immediately returns to the shared form of abbreviated joint actions, bringing the object toward the infant's hand, allowing the infant to take the object from the mother's hand and put it to her mouth.

Considering the first abbreviation example and history of Dyad A, we can note that this last example is clearly an innovative form of the give-and-take abbreviated exchange. In spite of this novelty, the minimum agreement is not broken and we can identify the occurrence of the action of giving by the mother and the action of taking by the infant. Therefore, this example illustrates the possibility of creating a different immediate future regarding the patterns of the mother and infant dialogue, through the past relational history of the dyad.

Moreover, this example highlights the individuality of each dyadic partner in order to direct each step further in the dynamics of dialogue. It also highlights the role of co-authorship of these partners in the dynamics of construction of new organizational patterns of exchanges, constituting the writing of the selves' dialogical biographies. Therefore, the coordination/integration of the past and the future within a specific present moment occurs exactly because there are individual subjects writing their own biographies, united by a dialogical relationship.

CONCLUSIONS

We have examined the microgenetic dynamics of the early mother–infant communication in order to propose a theoretical reflection and methodological criteria to analyze and comprehend dialogue at the beginning of life. We proposed a model of the dynamics of communication in early life and the use of Bakhtinian ideas in order to understand the emergence of selves. We have made use of the concept of abbreviation, a moment of quasi-stability that exhibits an "explosion toward novelty," as a focal concept to describe the emergence of dialogical selves as co-authors of their relational history. The microanalysis of the abbreviated give-and-take exchanges between the mother and the infant allowed us to illustrate the historical and creative process of emergence of simultaneity of different positionings that characterize the emergent selves. The positioning of each dyadic partner regarding the abbreviated exchanges and in facing novelty reveals the dialogical and relational nature of the individual subjects while writing their biographical sketches. As dialogical selves, the mother and the infant cannot exist prior to each other. They come to existence together, as a dynamic movement of figure and ground. According to Marková (1997), in spite of the mother being part of a historical-cultural system and being engaged in a number of different dialogical relationships with other members of this semiotic system, she becomes a parent only when her baby is born. It is exactly at this moment that the "mother–infant" system comes into existence, constituted by complementary and interdependent parts. The concept of abbreviation—conceived as a new Gestalt—and the concept of "simultaneity of different positionings" allow us to integrate the relational and individual nature of dialogical development in early life.

REFERENCES

Bakhtin, M. (1973). *Problems of Dostoevsky's poetics*, 2nd ed. (R. W. Rotsel, Trans.). Ann Arbor, MI: Ardis.

Bakhtin, M. (1986). *Speech genres and other late essays* (C. Emerson & M. Holquist, Eds.; V. W. McGee, Trans.) Austin: University of Texas Press.

Bakhtin, M. (1993). *Toward a philosophy of the act* (M. Holquist & V. Liapunov, Eds.; V. Liapunov, Trans.). Austin: University of Texas Press.

Emerson, C. (1997). *The first hundred years of Mikhail Bakhtin*. Princeton, NJ: Princeton University Press.

Fogel, A. (1993). *Developing through relationships: Origins of communication, self, and culture*. Chicago: University of Chicago Press.

Fogel, A., & Thelen, E. (1987). Development of early expressive communicative action: Reinterpreting the evidence from a dynamic systems perspective. *Developmental Psychology, 23*, 747–761.

Hermans, H.J.M. (1996). Voicing the self: From information processing to dialogical interchange. *Psychological Bulletin, 1*, 31–50.

Hermans, H.J.M. (1997). Three misunderstandings about dialogicality: The deeply-rooted persistence of Cartesian thinking. *Polish Quarterly of Developmental Psychology, 3*, 109–114.

Hermans, H.J.M., & Kempen, H.J.G. (1995). Body, mind and culture: The dialogical nature of mediated action. *Culture & Psychology, 1*, 103–114.

Holquist, M. (1990). *Dialogism: Bakhtin and his world*. New York: Routledge.

Lyra, M. C., & Rossetti-Ferreira, M. C. (1995). Transformation and construction in social interaction: A new perspective of analysis of the mother–infant dyad. In J. Valsiner (Ed.), *Child Development in Culturally Structured Environments, Vol. 3: Comparative-Cultural and Constructivist Perspectives* (pp. 147–173). Norwood, NJ: Ablex.

Lyra, M. C., & Winegar, L. T. (1997). Processual dynamics of interaction through time: Adult-child interactions and process of development. In A. Fogel, M. Lyra, & J. Valsiner (Eds.), *Dynamics and indeterminism in developmental and social processes* (pp. 93–109). Hillsdale, NJ: Erlbaum.

Lyra, M.C.D.P. (1988). *Transformação e construção na interação social: A díade mãe-bebê*. Unpublished Ph.D. dissertation, Universidade de São Paulo, São Paulo.

Lyra, M.C.D.P. (1999). An excursion into the dynamics of dialogue: Elaborations upon the Dialogical Self. *Culture & Psychology, 5*, 477–489.

Marková, I. (1990). A three-step process as a unit of analysis in dialogue. In I.

Marková & K. Foppa (Eds.), *The dynamics of dialogue* (pp. 147–177). New York: Springer-Verlag.

Marková, I. (1997). Dialogical models and reference. *Polish Quarterly of Developmental Psychology, 3,* 137–144.

Souza, M. (1999). *Desenvolvimento da comunicação mãe-bebê mediada por objetos: Um estudo de dois casos.* Unpublished Master's thesis, Federal University of Pernambuco, Recife, Pernambuco, Brazil.

Souza, M., Lyra, P. L., & Lyra, M.C.D.P. (1998). *Emergence of abbreviation in early mother-infant communication* (Report No. RIE-PS-98-11). Champaign, IL: Resources in Education. (ERIC Document Reproduction Service No. ED 419 585.)

Thelen, E., & Smith, L. B. (1998). Dynamic systems theories. In W. Damon & R. Lerner (Eds.), *Handbook of child psychology,* 5th ed., Vol. 1, *Theoretical models of human development* (pp. 189–232). New York: Wiley.

van Geert, P. (1998). We almost had a great future behind us: The contribution of non-linear dynamics to developmental-science-in-the-making. *Developmental Science, 1,* 143–159.

Wertsch, J. (1991). *Voices of the mind: A sociocultural approach to mediated action.* Cambridge, MA: Harvard University Press.

Chapter 4

Constructing One's Identity through Music

Emily Abbey and Patrick C. Davis

Culture constitutes arenas in which social suggestions have the potential power to guide identity by directing persons as to who and how to be. As an agent within culturally structured environments, a person engages in complex and dynamic processes of communication with the world, as ways to create personally relevant meanings out of socially and cultur-ally situated information. An understanding of what goes into this dia-logical process undertaken by persons to constitute a subjectively meaningful relationship between themselves and their environment is central to any discussions of identity. In this study, we use music as a source of cultural information. Music is encoded with meanings and sug-gestions that are open to personal interpretation, and is therefore well suited to our study of identity-forming practices.

IDENTITY DEVELOPMENT: FOCUS ON PHENOMENA UNDER CHANGE

We are interested in the analysis of the processes which underlie change and maintenance in personal identity claims. As we will show, the dynamic nature of identity and its construction and maintenance makes its study challenging. Traditional quantitative methods are insuf-ficient, as they do not cater to the variations (e.g., individually, culturally, etc.) which shape the form of identity-constructive processes. A simple analysis of stage-wise changes (e.g., "I used to be X, I am now Y") does little to elucidate the processes underlying their emergence. We choose a developmental perspective because it is only through an analysis of phenomena under change, or "in process," that any developmental questions may be posed or answered. By "in process" we refer to our use of the *microgenetic method*, which is tailored to the research of the mechanisms which underlie cognitive and more broadly psychological development. Microgenetic studies examine changes while they are occurring and suggest ideas about the mechanisms that produce the changes. We try to show how a truly process-oriented description of intrapsychological phenomena taps into the ongoing person–environment interaction process, both in theory and in practice.

Meanings of Identity

We view identity as a non-static concept: It is a perpetually developing form that is never final nor consummate. Persons are considered to be involved in an ever-changing, self-modifying relationship between themselves and their environment. Identity is then considered as a dynamic concept representative of a more general process of construction. This means that when individuals make claims about their "identity," they refer directly to a perpetual process of construction and maintenance rather than to a predetermined entity. We claim construction and maintenance to both be part of this process for clearly, persons are oriented toward maintaining some sense of continuity or stability of the self across time. Concrete identity claims such as "I am X" represent stable moments linked to personally salient components of the dynamic identity process. It is the ability of the person to extract such moments from the procedural flow that makes any identity claim possible.

Persons confront periods of change which may support, or challenge, portions of their identity. Oftentimes individuals may construct elaborate, personalized methods for dealing with something that they perceive as representing a challenge to their notion of self. Our work presupposes that identity-constructive processes are cultural-psychological processes— a belief which is reinforced by our general semiotic-constructive perspective on human psychological functions.

In this way, individuals interpret and synthesize information provided by the social domain, reconstruct and thus project their reconstruction back into the social sphere, causing a reconstruction of that domain as well. Such interpretive and reconstructive processes are closely linked to concepts of internalization and externalization (Valsiner, 1987; Vygotsky, 1935). The externalization component of the process extends to include Kurt Lewin's field theory (Lewin, 1951). We create a model of the social construction of self-to-other relationships, which focuses on the identity-constructive process.

Identity Construction within a Field-Theoretic Perspective

Kurt Lewin's field theory (e.g., Lewin, 1951) is a means of discussing orientations of self within an environment. In this chapter, we borrow

Lewin's concepts of *valence*, *forces*, and *life-space* and incorporate them into our model for making identity claims. Life-space comprises the complete experiential, historical, and affective life of the person. It combines thoughts, feelings, and perceptions about the world, both past and present, to create an individually meaningful sphere for living. The life-space is constructed by the individual as she or he moves along many different trajectories throughout his or her life. As individuals episodically enter new experiential fields, they construct the demands from that experience (e.g., signs) in ways which become personal and thus included within the life-space. As experiences occur, knowledge is acquired, and a higher level of differentiation of the person and the life-space is attained. It is essential to focus on the personal and subjective uniqueness of these differentiated life trajectories. In doing so, each life-space is considered equally unique as it is formulated by each individual's constructions of his or her subjective life experience. In and through contact with the external world, the internal world of the person is constantly reconstructed to retain new and personally relevant information.

In the life-space, forces and valences are linked together in an inseparable manner. We can think of forces as inputs from the life-space of the individual. The sum of forces in the life-space can create a valence (or many valences) that motivates the individual to act in some way. Each force results in a valence which constructs one or numerous personal orientations to the environment. It is important to stress that forces within the life-space and/or the active individual can play equal roles in any valence construction. A valence may push the individual in conflicting or compatible directions. For example, a child may want dessert (A) yet is instructed that he or she cannot have it until she or he eats some undesired food item currently on the dinner plate (B). In this life-space, force A is pushing toward the desired food so that dessert can be obtained, while force B pushes away from the child as a behavioral control. The sum of forces A and B creates a valence that moves the child in some direction (either toward the food item or away from it). In summary, valences may be considered as resultant orientations constructed by the person as sense-making tools for inputs from within the life-space.

Semiotic Mediation within the Life-Space

Our socio-cultural look at identity borrows from Vygotsky, who is sensitive to the embeddedness of human psychological functioning in a complex socio-historical system of relevancy. Vygotsky, however, pushed the issue of reconstructive and constructive psychological processes when he incorporated semiotic mediation into all developmental processes. When mediated by semiotic systems, lower psychological functions increase in complexity and in their capacity to function at a higher cognitive level. In this way, subjects do not move simply from stimulus to response.

Vygotsky was also interested in the sign-processes involved in internalization and externalization functions, which are key to the issue of identity construction and the maintenance of self-to-other (sign) relationships. The notion of dialogical intrapsychological process can also be traced to Vygotsky and his understanding of progressively integrated (i.e., internalized) speech as a regulator of psychological functioning. Vygotsky remarks that

the emergence of inner speech is based on external speech. Originally, for a child, the speech represents a means of communication between people, it manifests itself as a social function, it is its social role. But gradually a child learns how to use speech to serve himself, his internal processes. Now speech becomes not just a means of communication with other people, but also a means for the child's own inner thinking processes. (Vygotsky, 1935/1994, p. 353)

Communication as Identity Process: The Theoretical Model

Our process-oriented model of identity construction affords a microgenetic analysis of the processes behind identity maintenance and change. Instead of examining changes from perceived static state to static state (i.e., A to B), developmental changes within the individual are understood as inclusively separated from (i.e., directly part of, yet separated from) environmental demands (Valsiner, 1987; Werner, 1957), social and cultural suggestions, and semiotic systems. We claim that identity construction is a process of self-regulation and maintenance. Within the process, a mutually constructed relationship between person and environment is posited (see Figure 4.1).

In this relationship, the person is privileged with the ability to engage in interpretive projects that allow for the construction and reconstruction of meaningful relationships between the person and socially and culturally constructed information existing in the environment. We argue that such information exists in the form of a sign, which is encountered against a specific socio-cultural background. A sign is anything which can be perceived by the person, either through sensory (i.e., an object, a song, a smell, etc.) or intramental (i.e., an abstract political concept, a social suggestion, a religious belief, etc.) processes. Signs have culturally and personally relevant meanings, within a given environment and to a specific person.

The relationship between the person and her or his environment demands an examination of the intrapsychological processes utilized to navigate and negotiate cultural worlds. These processes that fall under the heading of *autodialogue* are best understood as the synthesis of one

Figure 4.1
Life-Space

LIFE-SPACE

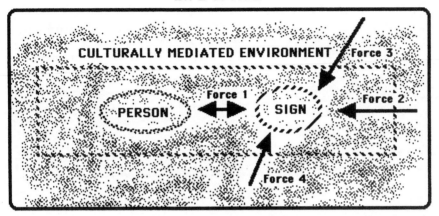

form to another—the process by which individuals create a meaningful relationship between themselves and a sign in their environment.

Autodialogue

Autodialogue is communication within the psychological realm of the person, where the person engages in talk about the world of one's self. The goal of this internal communication is the regulation and mainte-nance of semiotically mediated constructions of meaning by the person (see Josephs & Valsiner, 1998; Josephs, Valsiner, & Surgan, 1999). Thus the process by which the person creates a meaningful relationship be-tween her- or himself and a sign in his or her environment is defined as autodialogical.

In autodialogue, the person comes into contact with something in the environment that he or she constructs as a sign and for whatever reason internalizes it. Through internalization, the sign's social and cultural meanings are contextualized in personal, idiosyncratic ways through the transformation and reconstruction of these meanings (e.g., forces). Forces become personally relevant tools for the regulation of intrapsychological processes and sense making. It is only after the completion of this dia-logue between self and sign that the person externalizes the sign as a novel entity that is now laden with an identity claim (see Figure 4.2).

The autodialogical process thus allows persons to organize and make sense of their world and place within it through the emergence of mean-ings between the individual and her or his environment. In this way, any sign and its related forces can undergo a synthesis from the socially

Figure 4.2
A Model of Autodialogue

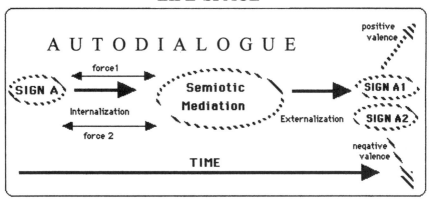

presented form to one that is more personally relevant and thus applicable to all aspects of the individual. This process allows for differentiation amongst each successive life experience on the basis of the other, previously internalized experiences. The life-space becomes an active medium in which the interpretation, reconstruction, and application of complex phenomena, such as conflicting forces, constitute the relationship between environment and person.

With the internalization of sign A (see Figure 4.2), the person engages in a process of synthesis between the personal and cultural meanings of that sign. This dialogue results in the self-to-sign relationship of A1 (and possibly A2, A3, etc., also, where the individual feels more than one way at the same time). Episodically, the individual evaluates him- or herself in relation to sign A, creating (momentarily) his or her identity as sign A1. Given the dynamic and co-constitutive relationship between person and sign A, autodialogue allows the person to relate to sign A1 through processes of externalization. Externalization constructs an arena through which relevant self-to-sign relationships may be expressed and actualized.

Self-to-sign relationships correspond to a set of valences associated with them. Valences can be positive, negative, neutral, and ambivalent. In the diagram, the self-to-sign of identity A1 has a positive valence associated with it, and the self-to-sign relationship of A2 has a negative valence.

Music as a Cultural Vehicle

In this chapter we examined the activity and results of identity-constructive processes in vivo. The local, episodic nature of the stimulus and subjects' responses was crucial for elucidating the phenomena. To do so, careful selection of the music was required.

Music was selected for a few reasons. On a general level, music is a culturally mediated semiotic device with the power to organize social and personal life. The type of music used in this study was rap, because of its prominent nature, both in terms of the imagery presented and the cultural background that frames such imagery. Rap music has found a solid place in the midst of mainstream pop culture in the United States, and is laden with messages of who and how to be. Rap music carries with it a specific set of social and cultural morals and norms which have been stereotypically applied to a sub-set of the population characterized as lower-class, impoverished minorities living in urban areas. As a consequence, rap music listeners are stereotypically thought of as gangsters, drug dealers, criminals, sexist, aggressive, violent, and overtly sexual.

Given the social grounding of music in general and rap music in particular, the study utilized selected rap songs as the episodic stimuli we introduced into the realm of subjects' constructions of self-to-sign relations. It is by virtue of the culturally significant and somewhat scrutinized place of rap music in mainstream pop culture that our study was able to trigger conversations within people, forcing them to evaluate the roots of their own opinions and beliefs.

The songs chosen for use as stimulus in this study were on the cutting edge of the limits that rap pushes upon. Most selections would not have been played on mainstream radio, and were stigmatized as "hard-core." In part, we hoped to differentiate the whole of rap music into its component parts, in order to understand the process through which a woman could enjoy listening to music that often speaks of violent acts of rape, which she is strongly opposed to. Careful emphasis was put upon the choice of subjects, to understand how rap music carries out personally relevant functions differently for many different individuals.

THE STUDY: CONSTRUCTION OF IDENTITY IN RELATION TO RAP MUSIC

Twenty face-to-face interviews were conducted to discuss personal reactions to, and identity-claim-making processes associated with, a specific song. Subjects were both males and females, from varying socio-economic backgrounds: students at a small liberal arts college, and members of the working class in an urban environment. The interview consisted of four main sections described below. After each, the subject was asked the following series of questions: Did any part of this song become personally relevant to you? Would you listen to this song with your parents? Would you listen to this song with a friend? Additionally, if a subject refused to complete a task for any reason, he or she was asked to share the reason.

Upon entering the room, subjects completed two survey-type tasks. The first was a checklist of "pop music knowledge," in which they were asked to select the types of music to which they most commonly listened. In the second survey-type task subjects were asked to complete a selection sheet which gave them the opportunity to signify the particular listening tastes of (1) one parent and (2) one of their "best friends." This task was also done to familiarize us with the subject's, a close friend's, and a parent's taste in music. In this way, we were able to ask the subject to relate any particular stimulus variable presented to either the parent or the friend by asking "Would you do this with/listen to this with X?"

The initial listening task then commenced. The subject was asked to listen to a song for a ten-minute duration. The subject could ask to stop the tape recorder at any time. The song was of an extreme nature, full of strong explicit sexual content, profanity, and direct references to the subjugation of women as sexual "slaves." We were not only interested in the reactions of those subjects who listened to the song for the full ten-minute duration, but also in those who asked to shut off the tape after the first few lines of the song.

In the second listening task we presented the subject with one particular rap song which was sampled both for its relative popularity and particularly salient imagery. We asked the subject to listen to this song for a full three repetitions. We of course allowed her or him to terminate at any time. Subjects were asked to recount for us as best as possible as many of the images, words, or concepts that were salient to them as they listened to the song. After the music ended, the subjects were asked to talk about what it was they heard.

In the third task subjects were asked to complete a recitation exercise. The chosen piece was in fact a transposition of the lyrics contained in the song used for the initial listening task. The recitation was not recorded to ensure enhanced comfort of the subject in completing this task.

In the final task subjects experienced a melange of different yet purposefully selected "snippets" which introduced stimulus material to the subject and acquired immediate episodically linked responses. For example, one snippet of fifteen seconds' duration would be played twice for the subject. At the conclusion of the second play through, the subjects would be immediately asked to relate their impressions, feelings, and perceptions of what they just encountered.

We focus on two of the four sections of the method, the first listening task and the reading task. These two sections seemed to provide the best stimulus for the subjects into the autodialogical process.

The subjects exhibited a range of responses, from the most straightforward to rather complex. The gradations of responses will be looked at, starting from the most simple, and then extending into the more complex.

One subject, a female in the college community, chosen because her narrative represents the basic episodic identity-construction process, asked that the song be turned off, and then proceeded to describe her self-to-sign construction process. The forces that the music afforded for her were those of "strong language." The reference to women as "whores and bitches" was considered by the subject (in relation to her own ideas) as an objectification of women. Based on this mediation, she externalized her self-to-sign relationship in the form of an "offensive" (here classified as a negative) valence. This response provides an illustration of the basic process of autodialogue.

Due to the open-systemic nature of the model, many other variations of this general form are possible. Oftentimes, subjects increased the complexity of the process by constructing valences that were opposite in nature, essentially saying "I like it but I don't like this part of it." Another example of a male subject from the college community is chosen because he gave a response that was more complex than the basic response of a singular self-to-sign orientation. The subject indicated that in general he found the lyrics in the song to be very explicit (and thus presumably unlikable as is evidenced by his use of the word "though" in the following comment). The subject did, however, enjoy the "beat" of the song. Thus, he constructed a self-to-sign relationship with two valences, one that is negative ("the lyrics are explicit") and one that is positive ("though the beat is good"). It is important to note that the opposition of these two valences did not appear troubling to the subject. For many of the subjects this was the case, and they were content with (or at least did not wish to explain further) how it was that they could maintain these two opposite valences. In these cases, the two valences were in no way put into a relationship with one another. Rather, they simply remained separate. In their separateness there was no tension between them (within the individual) for saying what might appear to be two contradictory things.

Semiotically Mediated Autodialogue: Beyond the Basic Process

Building upon the theoretical model of semiotically mediated autodialogue detailed above, it is beneficial to move into an in-depth analysis of responses to both the listening and the reading task. In the following two cases, the subjects attempted to integrate (or create a relationship between) opposing valences. It should be noted that this is a step beyond the second subject discussed in the previous paragraph, who did not create a relationship between his two valences. The initial attempt at a relationship between valences (especially those that are opposing) often created a feeling of hypocrisy for the subjects, as if they had unsuccessfully tried to combine oil and water. Realizing this, the subject entered into an additional stage in the autodialogical process, through creating a personal reconstruction of these opposing valences.

This reconstruction can take on different forms. In some cases the subject employed powerful "circumvention strategies" (Josephs & Valsiner, 1998) that allowed him or her to reconcile the relationship between the valences. Josephs and Valsiner focus on the goal-directed strategies constructed by persons as "semiotic organizers of dialogic (and autodialogic) relations between meaning complexes" (1998, p. 71). Such strategies can be used to make sense of opposing complexes (i.e., I like X because of Y, but I also dislike X because of Z) as well as to overcome others. As a dynamic and episodic tool, circumvention strategies are "constructed instantly to make sense of a situation in the person's continuous 'effort after meaning' " (Josephs & Valsiner, 1998, p. 71). Circumvention is then essential to making sense of meaning-rich phenomena which persons encounter in everyday life.

In other cases the relationship between two opposing valences remained uncircumvented (i.e., the subject is left feeling hypocritical even after an attempted circumvention). In both cases, however, a latter, more detailed reflection by subjects upon the relationship between valences and previously constructed self-to-sign relationships acted as a semiotic regulator of behavior and intrapsychological functioning.

Circumvention Strategies: Analysis of the Listening Section

In the following case, Subject A (a female subject from the college population) was chosen because she gave a good example of a circumvention strategy. Subject A remarked that upon listening to the rap song we played her, she felt hypocritical, in that she said she felt one thing strongly, yet also felt the opposite with equal fervor (I = Interviewer, S = Subject).

1 I: Did it become personal?

2 S: Well yeah it just, there are the things like that . . .

3   that might be representative of attitudes

4   of people that I might meet on the street . . . that I might be

5   passing someone that had this attitude of just

6   raping anything that walks

7 I: Hmmm

8 S: You know, just to think that people might condone those

9   attitudes

10 I: Hmmm

11 S: But then I feel like I'm being hypocritical because I

12   do listen to "Jammin' 94.5" (local radio station that plays

13   rap music) at times . . .

14 I: Well . . .

15 S: And there are some lyrics that may be to a less of a degree . . .

16 I: Is it the degree that matters?

17 S: In a way

18 I: So it does make a difference?

19 S: Because when I listen to music . . . this sounds odd . . . but I

20   don't listen to the lyrics very often

21 I: You listen to the music?

22 S: Yes

23 I: And you separate the lyrics from the music?

24 S: Yeah . . .

Subject A describes (lines 11–14) how she agentively chooses to listen
to the radio station that plays rap music (positive valence) yet she dis-
likes (lines 2–9) the violent depiction of a woman being raped in the
music she has heard (negative valence). Instead of appearing comfortable
with this disagreement, subject A realizes a relationship between the two
valences. She feels the need to rationalize her construction by synthesiz-
ing her two statements into one. Here she successfully employs a circumvention strategy: her comment (lines 19 and 20) that she doesn't
really listen to the words when she hears rap music. In highlighting the
fact that she only listens to the music (and not the words) when she
hears rap music, the subject has created a single, most important self-to-
sign relationship, which becomes the semiotic regulator for the whole
interaction.

The following example of subject B (a female subject from the college
population) was chosen because it provides another example of moving
between two different self-to-sign relationships (each with its own set of
valences) which then become integrated into one final self-to-sign relationship.

1 I: So what were you thinking while you were listening to it?

2 S: Um, I was slightly amused at times

3 I: Amused how?

4 S: Ahh, the words . . . "The world's biggest dick" did give me a little

5   chuckle . . . Umm, I don't know, I expected to be enraged but I

6   really wasn't

 7 I: You expected to be enraged?

 8 S: Yes

 9 I: Why?

10 S: Well because the first part, like when I first heard the song,

11   right with the first line, I thought this is like absolutely

12   disgusting and thought I would get really upset with it, but I didn't

13 I: What seemed disgusting?

14 S: Oh, the references to bitches, whores, rape, etc. really offend me

15 I: Do you have any idea why you didn't get enraged?

16 S: No actually, I guess that is what surprises me, I guess I have

17   just heard this kind of . . . music so much that I just kinda like,

18   nothing surprises me anymore

19 I: You feel desensitized?

20 S: Yeah, I'm completely desensitized because even like, even I am

21   surprised that I'm like not really upset with that right now, and

22   there is a time when I would have been . . . I'm not even

23   surprised by it, like nothing in it shocked me

24 I: So you are basing that desensitization on exposure?

25 S: Well, well, I mean I went to a public high school in Worcester

26   with a lot of different people and was exposed to a lot of

27   different cultures . . . lot of different things, ummm, I don't even

28   listen to rap music that much, but you know, just stuff that

29   I've heard be it like through a friend's CD, you know like when I

30   first heard something with those lyrics if this was my first

31   time hearing something like that I would be absolutely enraged

32   and disgusted but I've become so used to it now that . . . I think

33   it is absolutely disgusting, but I am just not surprised

In this example, subject B almost instantly constructs a self-to-sign relationship as she hears the first line of the song (lines 10–12). Based on this initial impression, she believes that she will have a strictly negative valence resulting from her self-to-sign construction. The subject is able to point out what forces (lines 14 and 15) she believes would contribute to this strictly negative self-to-sign relationship. However, upon constructing this relationship, she realizes that she is also gaining some enjoyment (in the form of humor) from the song (lines 1–5), hence a positive valence is constructed.

In concordance with subject A, subject B feels hypocritical, which causes her to reinterpret her process of internalization, creating circumvention. The subject remarks how she realizes another force the sign has in her personally relevant world: its connection to overexposure in high school (lines 20–28). According to the subject, this overexposure has caused her to become desensitized, and the strictly negative valence that she would have constructed in the past (in relation to one self-to-sign relationship) has now been changed into a positive valence based on her present "desensitized" self-to-sign relationship. At the end of the passage, the subject then successfully (or with less tension) integrates her two opposing self-to-sign relationships and their valences, leading to her final statement, "I think it is absolutely disgusting, but I am just not surprised."

It is interesting to note that both circumvention strategies are different. Subject B has used time to distance herself from one of the opposing valences, thereby diminishing (although not totally deleting) the tension between the two valences. In contrast, subject A defines herself as having a psychophysiological attribute that allows her to distance herself from the negative valence, thereby also reducing the tension.

Analysis of the Reading Task

The reading task confronted the subject with a slightly different activity: Instead of listening to the music, they were asked to read a sheet of lyrics. This sheet of lyrics was taken directly from the listening task analyzed above. It is important to highlight that the nature of the reading task is qualitatively different from the listening task. In the listening task, subjects had the option to passively listen to the music and afterwards to distance themselves from the vulgarity and violence in its lyrics by reminding us that they didn't really enjoy the song, but continued to listen to it because they simply liked the beat (or any other method of circumvention). In the reading task by contrast, subjects were pushed to assume a more agentive role. Their abilities, or inabilities, to participate in this portion of the study is linked with the notion of internalization and externalization. As we asked subjects to read the potentially objectionable lyrics, their meaning had to be internalized and quickly externalized through the subject's performance of them. Without ample time to construct any carefully considered self-to-sign relationships, subjects were forced to spontaneously enable or unable themselves from using their identities as a vehicle for the lyrical messages. This accounts for a much higher refusal rate amongst our subjects.

The following examples are the responses to the reading task of subjects A and B from above. While both A and B were able to listen to the song when played without having to stop, a different sort of response appeared when they were asked to read those same lyrics out loud. We begin our analysis with subject A:

1 I: Why are you thinking about it (whether or not to read the lyrics out

2   loud . . .)

3 S: Because I want to . . . because I am thinking about the way I want to read . . .

4   this to you

5 I: Okay

6 S: Is that okay?

7 I: Yes

8 S: Good

9 S: I don't want to read this to you

10 I: Tell me why

11 S: Because these aren't things that I want to say out loud. I won't because

12   it doesn't fit with me to say this to you

13 I: Tell me more, why, what's your thought process, is it emotional?

14 S: In a way it is . . . it just . . . it just makes me too uncomfortable to think of . . .

15   reading those lyrics to you

16 I: Just me, or everyone in general?

17 S: Oh everyone in general

18 I: So it's particularly personal

19 S: Yes I can liken it to reading poetry

20 I: Un hun

21 S: I can read my poetry and I have a certain reading voice that

22   comes from within and I sort of identify that reading voice with

23   myself . . . with what my voice really is . . . what myself is comfortable with

24   presenting. So that I wouldn't want to allow my reading voice to read . . .

25   this to you

26 I: So you don't identify with the voice that this is?

27 S: No

In this example, the subject took one look at the words before her and made the decision that she would not read them out loud. She justified this refusal by constructing an identity claim about her ability to distance herself from the stimulus by differentiating two different "voices" within the self. The subject said (lines 22–25) that she had a reading voice and this voice was intimately tied to or "identified" with herself. Due to this relationship between voice and self, the subject could not let her voice say the words with which her self was not comfortable.

Subject B seemed to experience a similar sort of resistance to verbally aligning her voice with some of the lyrics that she was asked to read out loud. In her case however, the discomfort was not with the whole piece, but rather with the specific word "nigger." Subject B read through the whole song, but each time she came upon the word "nigger" she simply skipped over it or reminded us that it was the word she would not say. When questioned about this, subject B struggled to explain her rationale:

1 I: Why didn't you say nigger?

2 S: That . . . that word offends me

3 I: Why?

4 S: Just because I don't agree with that word, I know um . . . I

5   have . . . I just do not agree, I don't know

6 I: Think it is okay for black people to say nigger?

7 S: Do I think it is OKAY? Um . . .

8 I: Do you think it is more acceptable for a black man to say nigger to

9   another black man than it is for a white person to say nigger?

10 S: Absolutely

11 I: Why?

12 S: Um, I just kind of think like ummm . . . Just because that's

13   something that has been kind of put on . . . Like that's like

14   . . . All right let me think . . . It's like if someone . . .

15 I: Like if you are part of a group it is okay to make fun of

16   yourself, but it is not okay for someone else to make fun of you?

17 S: YES, yes

18 I: So it is even difficult for you to read it even though you're

19   not taking the person's agentive stance of saying nigger . . . ?

20 S: Right

21 I: You're reading a word

22 S: Right, I said it's not a word, yeah, I mean I have black friends . . .

23   . . . and I just . . .

24 I: That's more offensive to you than "if you got a gang

25   of niggers then the bitch will let you rape her?"

26 S: I don't know . . . Not more offensive, but on . . . just that neither

27   . . . I think that both are absolutely ridiculous, but I am more

28   comfortable reading the word rape

29 I: Do you think you have been socialized not to say the word nigger?

30 S: Um, I don't know if it has been socialized or it is just the way

31   I was brought up, just that was not . . . I think the word rape . . . I
32   mean I think it is terrible, I think they're both equally as
33   disgusting but I think the word rape is not . . . I mean, do you
34   know what I mean, what I am trying to say?
35 I: Yes
36 S: Like you could say that (rape) on the news in a news story
37   but the other word is . . .
38 I: A little more hush-hush?
39 S: Yes, so I mean I think both of the things that I . . . The reason I
40   did not read that word is because I do not agree with that word
41   . . . though I am equally disgusted about the thing, the rape
42   thing, I . . . I can say it even though I am disgusted by something . . . I
43   can say it

The distancing of the word nigger is of specific interest, as the subject also used the same voice which could not say nigger, to recite other explicitly sexual phrases, street jargon, and specifically the word "rape." As with subject A, the issue of subjective discomfort arose, with the subject remarking (lines 27–28) that she was simply more comfortable with the word "rape" than the word "nigger." She reduced the tension she felt between being able to say the word rape but not the word nigger by relying on a societal clause, saying that you can say the word rape in a news story, thus implying that the word nigger cannot be used in such public media.

Ambivalence in Self-to-Sign Relationships

The construction of multiple self-to-sign relationships highlights the necessity of a process-oriented, open-systemic view of identity construction. When the subject reversed her progression in the self-to-sign construction process, she had the freedom to work bilaterally between moments of internalization, sign mediation, and externalization, while all the while progressing through time. By saying "I shouldn't like this, but strangely enough I do," the subject returned to the phase of internalization to reconstruct the perceived sign which had acquired different forces. Models without a process orientation would miss the complex mediations and constructions occurring within the individual.

Additionally, the example of subject B's listening task reinforces the importance of the episodic focus that has been assumed here. In this example, the subject remembered a time and a place where her self-to-sign relationship (i.e., identity) was constructed in a different manner than it seems to be today. Models of identity that assume a static or at least slowly changing identity would have assumed that the subject had always thought the song was both humorous and shocking. However, at a microgenetic level the subject clearly signaled a more differentiated perspective of the song. Further, this example illustrates how identity construction is episodic, so much so that the final statement of "I think it is absolutely disgusting, but I am just not surprised" reflects a possible (though unelaborated) third orientation, all in the course of less than five minutes.

It seems that it is exactly the ability of individuals to simultaneously and episodically construct both positive and negative valences that allows persons to enjoy (according to personally relevant limits) rap music. Subject A enjoyed listening to rap music as a whole, yet strongly objected to the violent raping of women that was depicted in the lyrics. She related to us how she could mediate these two opposing valences because when she listened to the music, she didn't listen to the lyrics.

CONCLUSION

Human identity construction is a process of both change and maintenance. It appears that individuals are constantly forming and reforming some of their personal views, while at the same time reinforcing and carrying on with others. This autodialogical process of construction and continuation may require that conflicting valences be maintained simultaneously. In theoretical discussion the simultaneous nature of both maintenance and change may appear both straightforward and logical. In practice, however, the personal autodialogical strategies required to do such a thing are quite complex in nature.

When subject A (a female with a strong feminist stance) turns on her favorite rap music station, part of her feels horrible because she is listening to music that degrades women. Yet she also feels empowered by the songs. The ability to maintain her feminist beliefs yet at the same time enjoy her rap song require her to reinforce her feminist stance by telling herself that she is aware of the (negative) nature of the lyrics, yet she can at least momentarily modify her identity to accept the other portions of the music that she gains enjoyment from.

If identity were anything but an apparent dualism of constant flux and continual maintenance, situations of ambivalence would be quite problematic. It is because human beings have the ability to see themselves as different people in different self-to-sign relationships that they are able to act in the world. If people could not handle these types of situations, it would be very difficult to do just about anything from eating fattening foods that taste good, to appreciating rain for the garden, and condemning it for the burden of raincoats.

REFERENCES

Josephs, I. E., & Valsiner, J. (1998). How does autodialogue work? Miracles of meaning maintenance and circumvention strategies. *Social Psychology Quarterly, 61,* 68–83.

Josephs, I. E., Valsiner, J., & Surgan, S. E. (1999). The process of meaning construction: Dissecting the flow of semiotic activity. In J. Brandtstädter & R. Lerner (Eds.), *Action and self-development* (pp. 257–282). Thousand Oaks, CA: Sage.

Lewin, K. (1951). *Field theory in social science.* New York: Harper & Brothers.

Valsiner, J. (1987). *Human development and culture: The social nature of personality and its study.* Lexington, MA: D. C. Heath.

Vygotsky, L. S. (1935/1994). The problem of the environment. In R. Van der Veer & J. Valsiner (Eds.), *The Vygotsky reader* (pp. 338–354). Oxford: Blackwell.

Werner, H. (1957). The concept of development from a comparative and organismic point of view. In D. B. Harris (Ed.), *The concept of development* (pp. 125–148). Minneapolis: University of Minnesota Press.

Chapter 5

Dialogue, Development, and Liberation

Mary Watkins

In ancient Hebraic tradition human beings were not distinguished from all other living creatures by virtue of their capacity for reason, but rather by virtue of their engagement in three kinds of dialogues: dialogues with themselves, with neighbors, and with God (Niebuhr, 1955). From this vantage point the unfolding of truly human development has to do with the development of our capacity for dialogue. The capacity for dialogue is a necessary precondition for human liberation: for non-violent, respectful relations between people and groups, and for the liberation of thought itself from rigid, stereotypic, and unidimensional narrowness.

Such a focus redirects our attention from the attainment of the logical, abstract thought that science has lauded to the dramatic and dialogical thought that has largely been discouraged by developmental theorists (see Watkins, 1986). While the former depends on a single, heroic ego engaged in highly elliptical, monological thinking, the latter opens to the polyphony of thought, comprised of multiple voices and perspectives, best mediated by dialogue.

CHARACTERISTICS OF DIALOGICAL THINKING

Buber (1958) describes true dialogue as one where the integrity and autonomy of both self and other are preserved, where one neither identifies with nor incorporates the other. As in Bakhtin's (1981) description of dialogue, neither person loses his or her own standpoint, nor transforms the other into an image to serve one's own purposes. Each can address and be addressed. Such dialogue between an *I* and a *Thou* can be evidenced in speech or in silence. Buber likens such dialogue to the holy converse described in Hasidism, where a "divine spark *lives* in every thing and being, but each spark is enclosed by an isolating shell. Only man can liberate it and re-join it with the Origin: by holding holy converse with the thing and using it in a holy manner" (1970, pp. 5–6).

Development and Liberation

I am indebted to Bernard Kaplan (1983a, 1983b) of Clark University for his approach to developmental issues. He asks us to be explicit about the telos of human development we are working for; to then, with this telos in mind, inquire what an ideal sequence of development would look like, and then to analyze the conditions that would mitigate against this development and those that would encourage it. It is from him that I first heard and understood the possible link between human liberation and the study of human development.

The writings of liberation theologians (Goizueta, 1988), socially engaged Buddhists (Sivaraksa, 1992), and liberation psychologists (Martin-Baro, 1994; Sampson, 1993) have proposed that the term "development" should be replaced by "liberation." With regard to economic and cultural progress, "development" of one group seems often to require an oppression of the other. Further, a dominant culture's idea of development is too often imposed on a culture, depriving it of undertaking its own path of development. The term "liberation" is based on a paradigm of interdependence, where the liberation of one is intimately tied to the liberation of the other. Further, as a holistic term it encourages us to consider economic, political, socio-cultural, spiritual, and psychological liberation together. While the term "self" has been critical to developmental theory, liberation theory emphasizes the importance of "the other."

If we hold liberating dialogue as a telos or endpoint of human development, what mitigates against it and what helps its development? It is clear that adulthood can be reached and traveled through without the development of adequate dialogical capacities. Without such adequate capacities, "the other"—be it part of oneself, be it one's neighbor or enemy, nature—can be silenced, used, abused, destroyed. The liberation of "the other" is dependent on dialogue which allows its nature and desires to come forth, to be listened to with attention and care, to be allowed to bring forth its difference from the self. Through such dialogue, "the other" is released from objectification and projection, and becomes the center of his or her own world, rather than determined by the self's (Goizueta, 1988).

Inner Dialogical Development and Liberation

Liberation theologians have stressed the importance of seeing liberation broadly. Liberation in one domain does not necessarily lead to liberation in other domains. One must work across domains—economic, political, cultural, ecological, interpersonal, intrapsychic—to build toward more comprehensive liberation. As a depth psychologist, I was brought up in a tradition which believed that inner development was the precondition and precursor to other forms of liberation. While this may be so in some cases, it is clear that prolonged preoccupation with inner liberation can also contribute to and/or defend one from oppression on other levels of existence—political, economic, ecological, cultural, interpersonal. Martin-Baro (1994) calls this psychology's critical error: "to change the individual while preserving the social order, or, in the best of cases, generating the illusion that, perhaps, as the individual changes, so will the social order—as if society were a summation of individuals" (p. 37).

Often interior life has become used as part of a veil of privatism, a buffer against cultural, economic, and ecological realities and sufferings. In recent Western culture and its psychology we have lauded the development of the autonomous, highly rationalistic individual, bounded from others and nature, presumably responsible for his/her own fate. The threads of interrelationship between self and other, self and community, self and nature, self and spiritual reality have increasingly been neglected by the enactment of such a paradigm of selfhood. Correspondingly, the "inner" world has been more and more looked to for meaning, relationship, ritual, and spirituality. It is imagined by some as though it were an untouched wilderness, a rich preserve to which one can turn for entertainment, mystery, and nurture.

Yet in the most private of the dialogues in our dreams and fantasies, in the most intimate portions of our conversations with ourselves, we come upon the metabolization of culture, economics, and politics. In the structure of power between ourselves and the other voices of thought, we can see the bounty of democratic form, the imbalances issuing from such things as racism and sexism, the struggle between the single voice of monotheism and the multiple voices of a more ancient polytheism, the efforts of a heroic ego attempting to assert control. While the dialogues of dreams and thought seem able to transcend culture in moments, their dramatis personae and the relations between them more frequently conserve it, reflect it. Is it likely for one to be able to achieve inner liberation while part of an oppressive cultural system? Does not liberation in one's daily context support liberation of thought? Correspondingly, does not the capacity for complex, dialogical thinking support the unfolding of social contexts that open such dialogue into public conversation?

As we listen in our thought to the critiques of ourselves and of others, we hear not only the voice of the mother or the father, but also the voice of the teacher, the voice of the style of pedagogy we were schooled in, and the voice of the values of our workplaces. The intrapsychic or the interior or the imaginal is not an isolated preserve. It is a distillation of history, culture, religion, and nature. If we can hear how the intimate, so-called interior, dialogues of thought and dream represent the public, the cultural, and the economic domain, then can we continue to believe that these dialogues can deeply transform without attention to interpersonal, cultural, ecological, and economic life? For instance, if racism in the culture affects the intrapsychic dialogue of a black child, causing one voice within her or him to derogate the color of her or his skin, should we attend to this through a psychotherapy that elicits and modifies self-talk? Or should there also be opportunities for dialogue at home, in the classroom, in the neighborhood, and in the larger culture which invite the voices that inhabit this child to speak, and which contribute toward an inner alternate voice of valuing, respecting, and cherishing the differences amongst us? Such an alternate voice could engage the voice of derision, question it, see through to its origins, gain insight into its functions for the dominant culture, as well as its functions for the child him- or herself—trying as he or she is to assume a popular position, even to his or her own detriment.

In my work *Invisible Guests: The Development of Imaginal Dialogues* (Watkins, 1986), I have described the dialogical nature of thought, how thought is a mosaic of voices in conversation. The complexity of thought can begin to be grasped as we discern the nature of the various voices that are speaking and become aware of the manner of relation between them and between our "observing ego" and each of them. I argued there that the promoting of dialogue amongst this "inner" multiplicity was crucial to psychological awareness and well-being. Here I would like to add that sustained attention to the nurturing of dialogical capacities across domains promises movement toward more comprehensive liberation.

Dialogical Capacities

Let me be more specific about the kind of dialogical capacities I am referring to: the allowing of the other and the self to freely arise and to be given a chance for expression; to allow the other to exist autonomously from myself; to patiently wait for relation to occur in this open horizon; to move toward difference not with denial or rejection but with tolerance, curiosity, and a clear sense that it is in the encounter with otherness and multiplicity that deeper meanings can emerge. Such dialogue presupposes the capacity to grant the other an interiority different from our own—one that is not diminished or dehumanized in any way. Such dialogue assumes the capacity to de-center and to attempt to take the perspective of the other, to attempt to feel the feelings of the other. It presupposes a capacity to take a third-person perspective on the self, so that one can reflect on how one's actions and attitudes have affected the other and the situation.

As these capacities develop, the self moves from being an unreflective center that finds the other to be either like oneself or as the self needs it to be to serve the self's ends, to a self who is able to step to the side, who is aware of the co-creating nature of the interaction with the other, who knows that the other's experience departs from the self's, often in radical ways. In this chasm, where such departures differentiate self and other, there is a choice available to penetrate it through attempts at dialogue and understanding. This penetration is never only an opening toward the other's experience and reality. It signals a willingness to see and question as assumptions one's most cherished attitudes, the core of our own beliefs, approaches, and commitments. To be able to deeply entertain the difference that the other poses, we must, as well, be able to disidentify from our passionately held beliefs, be able to see what ideologies they are based on, and be able to interrogate the function and effects of these beliefs (Bohm, 1996). Through the grasping of the other's difference from us—be it intrapsychic other or interpersonal other—we come to see more clearly who we are. Jung puts clearly the interpenetration of inner dialogue and outer objectivity:

The present day shows with appalling clarity how little able people are to let the other man's argument count, although this capacity is a fundamental and indispensable condition for any human community. Everyone who proposes to come to terms with himself must reckon with this basic problem. For, to the degree that he does not admit the validity of the other person, he denies the "other" within himself the right to exist—and vice versa. The capacity for inner dialogue is a touchstone for outer objectivity. (Jung, 1969, p. 187)

It is through such dialogue with the other, the stranger, that the liberation and re-joining that Buber speaks of can occur.

This manner of holy converse can describe equally as well relations with others, as it does our relations with ourselves, imaginal others, the beings of nature and earth, and that which we take to be divine. As such dialogue occurs there is a shift from the ego as a monolithic, heroic center, one which struggles to maintain power, to an ego which seeks to mediate the multiplicity of any given situation. Elsewhere I have contrasted the individualistic self of modern Western cultures with the paradigm of the interdependent self (Watkins, 1992) or what Sampson (1988) has called the *ensembled self*. The ensembled self is aware of multiplicity at all levels. It locates power and control in a field of forces that includes but goes beyond the person (Sampson, 1988). Dialogue is a way of working amidst his field, this multiplicity.

Dialogicality and Contemporary Psychology

In our Cartesian psychologies we have carefully sorted self from other, body from mind, the imaginal from the perceptual, the spiritual from the material, the so-called "inner" from the so-called "outer." Experientially these separations are not as neat as our modern categories would suggest. Once made discrete, theoreticians approach how they are related in opposing, often lopsided ways. For instance, either imaginal dialogues are seen to subserve interpersonal dialogues allowing us to rehearse for more of the "real" thing, or interpersonal dialogue is viewed as a diversion from the "more important" unfolding of subjective experience. Which side of the Cartesian seesaw is seen as more valuable, more originative of the other? Do experiences with imaginary playmates harm children—as claimed in the 1950s—because they defend children from "actual" friendship, or does social interaction obscure our listening to the "springs of the self"? Here my hope is to hold these domains together in a more interdependent web. I will do this through a close look at dialogue, as I see I–Thou dialogue as a necessary capacity when we understand the multiplicity we are homed in—on the levels of both psyche and culture.

Dialogue is both a fact of our givenness and a deep potentiality of our being. We are thrown from our beginning into a multiplicity—ancestors, family, trees, rivers, earth, animals, neighbors. As Jung said (1947), "The self comprises infinitely more than the mere ego, as symbols have shown since time immemorial. It is just as much another or others as it is the ego. Individuation does not exclude the world but includes it" (p. 477). We are always selves-in-relation or selves-in-dialogue. What is at stake is the kind of relationship we are in, and the paths from it to a manner of dialogical relationship that liberates being.

When we emphasize this frame, there are a number of developmental theorists whose work speaks to the interpenetration of imaginal, social, cultural, natural, and spiritual domains in terms of the development of dialogical capacity. For example, my own work on the development of imaginal dialogues; the research on the coordination of interpersonal perspectives and resulting peer therapy of Selman and Schultz; the work on adolescent girls' loss of voice of Carol Gilligan and her colleagues; the work with women's ways of knowing that affect both their internal dialogue and their relations to others of Mary Belenky and her colleagues; the large-group dialogue work of David Bohm and Patrick de Mare; and, finally, the liberational pedagogy of Paulo Freire. I will turn to these as exemplars to help us see some of the developmental threads that criss-cross between dialogical domains, and to establish signposts beyond this text for those who wish to pursue the cultivation of dialogue.

THE DEVELOPMENT OF IMAGINAL DIALOGUES

I would like to begin by addressing "dialogues with ourselves," what I have called elsewhere "imaginal dialogues" (Watkins, 1986): conversations between aspects of the self, such as "me" and "I"; or between self and an "imaginal other"; or between two imaginal others with the self as audience. In short, imaginal dialogues are present in a child's play and private speech, in adult and child thought, in spiritual experiences, in the experience of dramatists, novelists, poets. While widely acknowledged in popular culture and in expressive psychotherapy techniques, such imaginal dialogues have had an odd fate within the mainstream of developmental psychology. Often the presence of such dialogue has been seen as a sign of childhood or psychopathology, *and* the absence of such dialogue as a sign of adulthood and mental health (see Watkins, 1986, for detailed treatment of these themes in the work of Piaget, Vygotsky, and Mead).

Piaget versus Vygotsky on Imaginal Dialogues

This curious degrading of imaginal dialogues is largely due to developmental psychology's high valuation of the development of abstract thought and logic, and of its priority given to our increasing capacity to adapt to consensual views of reality. Rather than Piaget following the course of imaginal dialogues from their appearance in what he called the "egocentric speech" of young children to the highly elaborate play scenarios of older children, to the artistic creation of drama, and the sustaining of complex, multiperspectival thought, he sees them as being subsumed either by the development of communicative speech or of abstract thought. For him their appearance is indicative of the child's incapacity to take the other's point of view sufficiently to make him or herself understood. The imaginal dialogues of play he sees as distorting of reality, deforming and subordinating reality to the desires of the self (1951, p. 339). For him this kind of pretend play gives way to the "more mature" play of games with consensual rules. In object relations we see a similar priority given to "objective" reality, by judging self- and object-representations as more highly developed if they closely approximate figures in the external world.

If we look with a different eye—one that values dramatic thought and the capacity to create and transform reality—the early imaginal dialogues found in pretend play are extraordinary practice in beginning to widen the repertoire of the self, in making leaps to other points of view, and in refusing to confine oneself to the dictates of consensual reality. The complex play of older children shows an increasing shift away from replicating reality to creating new worlds of characters, where symbolic power appears to increase as the effort to replicate the given is dropped.

Indeed, Vygotsky speaks to how play is used by the child to satisfy needs that reality cannot. In the imaginary situations which a child creates, unrealizable desires can be fulfilled (1978, p. 93). The ability to play is the power which the child has to make another reality. This power is made possible by the ability of the child to subordinate action to meaning. Play releases the child from the dictatorship of the visual realm and the "incentive supplied by external things" and allows the child, freed from these situational constraints, to act with meanings, to rely on internal tendencies and motives (p. 96). Rather than stressing play's egocentrism, as Piaget does, Vygotsky is impressed with the fruits of such a liberation for a child's continued action in the social domain. In claiming that play is the highest level of preschool development, he attributes to play and its dialogues the propensity for creating voluntary intentions, to form real-life plans and volitional motives (p. 103).

Despite this high evaluation of play, when he looked at children's private speech he did not allow his observation of imaginal dialogues in solitary play to influence decisively his theory of the functions of private speech. According to Vygotsky, private speech is a stage in the development of inner speech. It is speech on its way inward. He sees it as having neither the economy of speech intended for self-guidance, nor the communicative value of speech intended for a differentiated other (Kohlberg, Yaeger, & Hjertholm, 1968). Once inward, inner speech begins to drop its dialogical nature acquired from social interaction and becomes increasingly monological and elliptical—as internally speaker and listener are now presumed to be the same.

By defining inner speech as for oneself and external speech as for others, Vygotsky leaves no room for imaginal others—be they aspects of self, representations of known others, or wholly imaginary others. He assumes that the internal speaker knows what he or she is talking about and perceiving. There is no separate interlocutor or listener. But if we were to introduce a notion of the self as non-unitary, as having multiple points of view among which it alternates, dialogue would no longer be an inferior form of thought; perhaps monologue would be in many instances.

Vygotsky (1962) argues that the monologue is superior to the dialogue: "psychological investigation leaves no doubt that monologue is indeed the higher, more complicated form" (p. 144). In the imaginal dialogues of thought, self and other do not necessarily share mutual perceptions. Thus, when self and other are differentiated, one would expect internal speech to become less elliptical and be more akin to spoken and written speech (the latter being, from Vygotsky's point of view, the most elaborate form of speech). In internal speech when self and a voice, or two

voices, hold different perspectives, their views must be more fully elaborated than if one is entertaining and explicating a single view in a
monologue. Through inner dialogue, a thought can be expressed by an
imaginal other or by the self, questioned or furthered by another. Dialogue intensifies the way in which language carries us toward what we
are going to understand, but as yet have not. "Thought germinates in
speech" between others, says Merleau-Ponty (1973, p. 131), and is this
not also true for the conversations of thought? Before reasoning became
synonymous with logical thought, its archaic meaning was "to engage
in conversation or discussion" (Morris, 1969, p. 1036), as in Isaiah (1:18):
"Come . . . let us reason together." This conversation could have both
actual and imaginal partners.

George Herbert Mead and Dialogicality

In George Herbert Mead's work, we find precisely this understanding
of reason as deeply dialogical. Unlike Vygotsky, he sees thought as re-
taining its roots in the dialogues of social interaction. He believed that
it is through the reflexivity of the dialogue that the self arises. For Mead,
all speech and thought are implicitly dialogical. The dialogue form establishes for the child the meaning of the self and his or her actions.
Awareness of the self, according to Mead, arises through adopting the
perspective of others toward oneself. This is achieved first through describing one's activities to another, or as though to another, and thereby
evoking the response of the other to oneself. At first the self is the reflection of others' attitudes toward it. Thus, where Piaget's example of a
child describing what she sees to her doll is meant to be expressive of
the child's pleasure in being a focus of attention, for Mead this perpetual
describing—which can strain the patience of those around children
("Now I'm putting on my hat. See me putting it on!")—marks the beginning of the child's transition to the role of the other, from which
indeed one sees and becomes aware of oneself and others. As the child
begins to take on all the roles of others toward oneself—policeman, parent, sibling, and so on, the child's own self is created. Indeed, for Mead,
the self is an organization of perspectives. "When playing at being someone else, the self comes to realize its own nature at the same time it
realizes the nature of the person whose role is being played" (Pfuetze,
1973, p. 83).

Gradually, however, the particular others in the dialogues of a child's
pretend play—the postman, the mother, the younger brother, the
teacher—begin to lose their specific identity as such dialogues move inward. The separate, differentiated characters begin to merge to become
what Mead calls a *generalized other*. It is this generalized other who expresses the attitude of the group that partners our thought in adulthood.

It is an amalgam of earlier multiplicity, which Mead believed moved thought toward abstraction and objectivity.

In the nineteenth century—which Mead himself wrote about in fine detail—generalization was widely considered to be "necessary to the advancement of knowledge," but "particularity" was seen as "indispensable to the creatures of imagination" (Thomas Babington Macaulay, 1825, quoted in Abrams, 1953, p. 316). One anonymous nineteenth-century writer, joining many of his contemporaries, equated science with:

any collection of general propositions, expressing important facts concerning extensive classes of phenomena; and the more abstract the form of expression, the more purely it represents the general fact, to the total exclusion of such individual peculiarities as are not comprised in it—the more perfect the scientific language becomes. Science is the effort of reason to overcome the multiplicity of impressions, with which nature overwhelms it, by distributing them into classes, and by devising forms of expression which comprehend in one view an infinite variety of objects and events. (quoted in Abrams, 1953, p. 317)

Mead's emphasis on the generalized other clearly echoes these statements, affirming what might be described as a "scientific" form of thought rather than a poetic one. The generalized other is "the most inclusive or widest community included in one's organization of attitudes" (Miller, 1973, p. 49). In its highest development, says Mead, this would be analogous to a community of logicians.

The development of the generalized other is the development of socialized thought, wherein particular thoughts have the capacity to be conveyed to the widest possible audience. Such a generalization of imaginal others—a homogenization, it often sounds like—seems indeed to be an important line of development. Its corollary, the fading out of the dramatis personae of thought, contradicts and obscures the development of particularized others who also participate in the dialogues of our thought.

Would it not make sense that these two developments—of particularized and generalized others—are not mutually contradictory but rather mutually dependent; that the generalized other does not always supplant particularized others, but that the form of the other (particularized or generalized) is dependent on the functions of the thought in a particular instance? If so, then for Mead to construct a developmental sequence from particularized to generalized other, his preferred telos must have again been scientific thought, indeed a scientific thought based on the model of nineteenth-century science.

This telos affects the preferred developmental sequence that developmental psychology, broadly speaking, proposes in childhood for imaginal dialogues: from presence to relative absence in adulthood; from dialogical play and thought to monological, abstract thought; from the multiple, often autonomous, personified presences in play dialogue to the single, unitary self. Such a sequence does not allow us to appreciate the way in which the dialogues of play and thought, dialogues between particular, often autonomous others or voices, help us practice and sustain a multiperspectival consciousness. When, as developmentalists, we affirm the value of dialogue, development can be seen as going in the opposite direction from the above-stated goals; that is, from one to many voices, from undefined voice to particularized other, from other as puppet to the "I" to autonomous other who can voice difference. Such dialogue can reflect social experience. It can also move beyond it, bringing new possibilities into being, which may later take root in the social world.

This short history of the treatment of imaginal dialogues in developmental theory suggests how monocular our concern has been regarding how we come to know and metabolize the complexity of any given situation. Were the nurture of dialogical capacities across the life span considered essential to such multiperspectival knowing, the imaginal dialogue of play would be listened to more closely and nurtured; attention to the self-talk of young children would be increased, helping the child to find ways of dialogue that support her or his exploration and action, in full knowledge that such dialogue will form the scaffolding of internal conversation for years to come. We would as well deeply attend to how conversation unfolds within friendships, families, and classrooms.

THE CAPACITY TO PLAY AND THE CAPACITY TO BE A FRIEND: DIFFERENTIATING AND COORDINATING THE PERSPECTIVES OF SELF AND OTHER

Our development toward genuine dialogue is gradual and unassured. It is largely dependent on our capacity to imagine the other as different from ourselves and as independent of our own needs to see him or her in certain ways. Robert Selman charts the young child's egocentric understanding of the other, where first the other is assumed to have similar feelings as the self. In the friendship of young children, the other is judged to be a friend by superficial appearance or sheer physical proximity. The other is a two-dimensional self, with no psychological characteristics of its own. A presumed dialogue at such a developmental moment may well be better described as a monologue, where the other is not imagined as different from the self.

Selman and Schultz, working with the interpersonal relations of emotionally disturbed children, have noted that interactive fantasy play is

markedly absent in the history of children whose interpersonal understanding is at primitive levels. These children do not understand that
self and other can interpret the same event differently; that is, the other
is not understood to have an interiority different from my own. They
are unable to differentiate between an unintentional act of another and
an intentional one (the action is equated with the intent). Neither do they
differentiate physical from psychological characteristics of the person
(i.e., if the person is deemed pretty then she is a good person). In short,
they are unable to differentiate and integrate the self's and the other's
points of view through an understanding of the relation between the
thoughts, perspectives, feelings, and wishes of each person (Selman &
Schultz, 1990).

This capacity to differentiate and integrate the self's and other's points
of view is at the core of dialogical capacity. As Selman and Schultz point
out, a deficit in this ability shows both in problematic interpersonal relating and in an absence of the dialogues of pretend play. Further, however, they describe how the seeds for interpersonal dialogue can be
planted in the dialogues of play. In their pair therapy work with children
who are isolated by patterns of withdrawal or aggression, they pair a
submissive, withdrawn child (self-transforming style) with a child who
is overcontrolling, sometimes downright bullying (other-transforming
style). Initially, they each cling to their own style, making impossible a
deepening of relationship. Selman and Schultz share an image from a
session with two boys where one traps the other in the up position on
the see-saw. There is no movement! In pretend play these two boys initially replicate their roles on the see-saw: Andy initiated a fantasy in
which he was the television/comicbook character "The Hulk," a large,
powerful, and fearsome mutant who is good inside, but who cannot
control his feelings to let the good direct him. Paul took a part as "Mini-
Man," a very small being of his own creation who can hide in flowers.
In the fantasy play one boy had the power to control the thoughts and
will of the other by virtue of a psychological "force field." With these
roles personified, however, each boy is as though seduced into wanting
to embody each of the available roles. Paul experiments with putting up
his force field, and then with "zapping" his partner, just as Andy relaxes
his grip on power and enjoys the submissive position of "Mini-Man."

Theoretically speaking we believe that this switching of roles in play is a key
therapeutic process, in effect a way to *share experience*. Andy was able to relax
his defenses and express the message that part of him was happy to be or even
had a need to be controlled, taken care of, told what to do. He could abandon
for the moment the tenderly held goals for which he generally fought so fiercely.
. . . And Paul, often too frightened to take the initiative in actual interactions, was
able to take steps toward assuming the control that felt too risky in real life,

despite its practical and emotional attractions. . . . When it is just play, children can dress rehearse for changing roles on the stage of real-life interaction. (Selman & Schultz, p. 171)

Here we see the interrelation between the dialogues of play and those of peer relationship. Now, rather than "inner speech" being the internalization of actual social discourse, as in Vygotsky's theory, we see the dialogues of play as the seed that travels up into the soil of potential friendship. Indeed, in the third year of work with these boys, we see them able to withstand the storm of each other's emotions, to venture into different roles with one other, and to begin to share around the deepest areas of each boy's concern: missing their absent parents, and the fear of one boy that his mother does not miss or love him.

Andy's tone is low. "That's the problem—my mother doesn't miss me." Andy relates an incident from the past weekend, when he and his parents were going to go out together. As Andy tells it, he rode off on his bike telling his mother where he'd be, but his mother forgot to call him. "And when I came back my mom had gone to bed, and my dad had gone to sleep. And I was left alone." Paul says softly, "I'm sorry." After a brief pause, he adds, "By the way Andy, if you see any raffle tickets around, I've lost mine." Rather than being put off and hurt by this sudden change of subject on Paul's part, Andy immediately picks up on the new topic. "Let's go look for them in the after school room," he says.

Are not such moments of friendship creative of our capacity to receive and hear our own pain, to be with it, and yet capable of engaging beyond it?

SUSTAINING ONE'S VOICE AMONGST OTHERS

For authentic dialogue to occur it is not enough for one to be able to differentiate one's perspective from the other and to allow the other a voice. One must also be able to maintain one's own voice amidst the fray of relationship. For instance, the most disturbing auditory hallucinations do not occur because of a confusion of perception with image, but because the ego's point of view becomes swamped by the voice(s) of the other. The other's command often becomes the self's action without benefit of reflection. Dialogical space collapses as the self becomes the instrument of the voice (Watkins, 1986). In less severe experience we witness similar imbalances in power between "inner" voices that criticize, berate, predict doom, and the often more fragile self who is the victim of these critiques and disparagements. Indeed, the psychotherapy of depression can be seen as addressing such inner abuses of power that leave other voices silenced or rendered impotent. The inner sustaining of voice in situations where the culture (family, school, wider culture) one is in has systematically discouraged it, is particularly difficult, often impossible. Carol Gilligan and her colleagues' work with adolescent girls exemplifies this.

In turning their attention to normative development in pre-adolescent and adolescent American girls, they unfortunately found that not all the changes they witnessed in girls were ideal. On the one hand,

As these girls grow older they become less dependent on external authorities, less egocentric or locked into their own experience or point of view, more differentiated from others in the sense of being able to distinguish their feelings and thoughts from those of other people, more autonomous in the sense of being able to rely on or to take responsibility for themselves, more appreciative of the complex interplay of voices and perspectives in any relationship, more aware of the diversity of human experience and the differences between societal and cultural groups.

On the other hand, they found

that this developmental progress goes hand in hand with evidence of a loss of voice, a struggle to authorize or take seriously their own experience—to listen to their own voices in conversation and respond to their feelings and thoughts—increased confusion, sometimes defensiveness, as well as evidence for the replacement of real with inauthentic or idealized relationships. If we consider responding to oneself, knowing one's feelings and thoughts, clarity, courage, openness, and free-flowing connections with others and the world as signs of psychological health, as we do, then these girls are in fact not developing, but are showing evidence of loss and struggle and signs of an impasse in their ability to act in the face of conflict. (Brown & Gilligan, 1992, p. 6)

In order to maintain the semblance of relationship these girls were struggling with "a series of disconnections that seem at once adaptive and psychologically wounding, between psyche and body, voice and desire, thoughts and feelings, self and relationship" (Brown & Gilligan, 1992, p. 7). Too often girls were found stepping away from articulating their thoughts and feelings if these would bring them into conflict with others. What was initially conscious public disavowal of thoughts and feelings became over time unconscious disclaiming. Girls then expressed that they felt confused about what they thought and felt, that they were unsure. Over time, many took themselves out of authentic relationship— with others and with themselves. They became unable to identify relational violations, and were thus more susceptible to abuse. Brown and Gilligan began to wonder if they were "witnessing the beginning of psychological splits and relational struggles well documented in the psychology of women" (1992, p. 106).

To encourage girls' resistance and resilience, Gilligan and her colleagues realized that it was not enough to help girls put into words for others their thoughts and feelings. For many, the fear of how their thoughts and feelings would be received had already metamorphosed into the girls' not listening to themselves. And so the women working with these girls tried to find ways to help the inner ear not go deaf and to revive a capacity to listen to one's selves, while at the same time building a group where the girls could experience that others can survive their voice(s): that authentic dialogue is possible, not just false or ideal-ized relations. Without such an experience of being received—to counter the culture's messages—the ear cannot reawaken and the voice cannot speak; be it in "internal" dialogue or "external" dialogue. Akin to Selman and Schultz's move toward play, Gilligan's team moved toward sup-porting the girls' diary and journal writing, their dramatic and poetic writing, and their literally claiming their voices in voice work.

Dialogue—in the ideal sense—necessitates both the capacity to deeply receive the other *and* the capacity to receive oneself; to allow the other a voice *and* to allow the self a voice.

BEING SILENCED VERSUS OPPORTUNITIES FOR DIALOGUE: VOICE, MIND, RELATIONSHIP, AND SOCIAL ACTION

Belenky, Clinchy, Goldberger, and Tarule (1986), in *Women's Ways of Knowing: The Development of Self, Voice, and Mind*, vividly describe the interpenetration of dialogical domains I am addressing, as they study different ways of women's knowing. In one group of women they stud-ied, women's silence in adulthood was linked to family experiences of neglect and abuse. These women were passive, subdued, and subordi-nate in adulthood. "The ever-present fear of volcanic eruptions and cat-astrophic events leaves children speechless and numbed, unwilling to develop their capacities for hearing and knowing" (1986, p. 159). These women experienced themselves as mindless and voiceless. Their child-hoods were not only lived in isolation from their family members and others outside the family, but most often were lived *without play*. The intersection of an absence of dialogue with an absence of play turned out to be particularly damaging for these children as they grew to wom-anhood.

In the ordinary course of development, the use of play metaphors gives way to language—a consensually validated symbol system—allowing for more precise communication of meanings between persons. Outer speech becomes increas-ingly internalized as it is transformed into inner speech. Impulsive behavior gives way to behavior that is guided by the actor's own symbolic representations of hopes, plans, and meanings. Without playing, conversing, listening to others, and drawing out their own voice, people fail to develop a sense that they can talk and think things through. (Belenky et al., 1986, p. 33)

Moreover, the world becomes a place of simple dichotomies—good/bad, big/little, win/lose—losing all subtlety and texture.

Without the imaginal dialogues of play and substantive interpersonal dialogues the child is constrained within a narrow band of reality. Both play and dialogue allow the child to visit the perspectives of others, as well as to dream of that which has not yet come into reality. "What is" and "who one is" become radically widened as one de-centers from the ego's perspective and the given. Through the metaphorizing of play one leaps past the given confines of "self" and "reality." The dialogues of play and the dialogues of social interaction are both creative of the self and libertory of the self. Through each empathic leap, through each re-embodiment of ourselves in play, we pass beyond our usual borders and exceed what has been. What "is" is surpassed by what might be, and "who" I am is replaced by my transit beyond myself—either through projection of the self or through the reception of the other. Working an issue through play—expressing it, addressing it from several perspectives, taking the role of the others in play—is translated into the dialogues of thought and those of our everyday interactions. It should come as no surprise that the complexity and subtlety of a child's play and flexibility in moving between the dramatis personae, can be seen in his or her participation in interpersonal dialogue, and in his or her capacities for reflection.

Childhoods that do not give opportunity for pretend play (that movement between dramatis personae), whose families discourage interpersonal dialogue, and whose schools limit the classroom experience to verbal exchanges that are unilateral and teacher-initiated, make it highly unlikely that children will learn the "give and take of dialogue" (Belenky et al., 1986, p. 34), giving them access to what lies beyond a narrow self which has been schooled for silence. For such children, and the adults that are generated from them, words have force only when uttered violently. They are action-oriented, and have only little insight into their own motivations. As they do not expect to be heard, they expect no response. Thus the volume of their voices is more important than the content. They do not expect conflicts to be resolved through non-violent means, because they lack verbal negotiation skills. Those who do not escape silence pass the legacy of their early homes on to their children:

Mothers who have so little sense of their own minds and voices are unable to imagine such capacities in their children. Not being fully aware of the power of words for communicating meaning, they expect their children to know what is on their minds without the benefit of words. These parents do not tell their children what they mean by "good"—much less why. Nor do they ask their children to explain themselves. . . .

We observed these mothers "backhanding" their children whenever the child asked questions, even when the questions stemmed from genuine curiosity and desire for knowledge. It was as if the questions themselves were another example of the child's "talking back" and "disrespect." Such a mother finds the curious, thinking child's questions stressful, since she does not yet see herself as an authority who has anything to say or teach. (1986, pp. 163–164)

Interestingly, these women were not aware of any experience within themselves of dialogue with a self or of having an inner voice; nor did their words express a familiarity with introspection or a sense of their own consciousness. Those women in Belenky's study who were able to emerge from silence into adulthood had the benefit of a school which encouraged the cultivation of mind and an interaction with the arts, had been able to forge significant relationships outside the home despite the prohibition not to do so, or had "created such relationships for themselves through the sheer power of their imaginations, by endowing their pets and imaginary playmates with those attributes that nourish the human potential" (1986, p. 163).

In the other ways of knowing that Belenky et al. describe—received knowing, subjective knowing, procedural knowing, and constructed knowing—intrapsychic and interpersonal dialogue are intimately related to each other, together forming a sense of the flatness or complexity and fullness of reality. For instance, in received knowing women experience others as the authority, silencing their own voices to be better able to imbibe the wisdom of others. It is not surprising that they seek to eliminate ambiguity from their worlds, and can be described themselves as literal-minded. On the other hand, subjective knowers conceive of all truth arising internally, stilling their public voice, and often turning a "deaf ear to other voices." Often distrusting words, they cover disagreement with conformity, and live in the isolation of their own thoughts and inner voices.

In what is clearly their preferred developmental telos, Belenky and her colleagues describe those who experience constructed knowing. In this way of knowing, knowledge is contextual. There are multiple viewpoints to be had, but not all are equally adequate to reveal what one is trying to understand. These knowers are familiar with listening to the inner voice or voices. Yet they know that even an inner voice may be wrong at times, for it is but one part of a whole. They are, as well, adept at patient listening to the voices of others. They have a high tolerance for internal contradiction and ambiguity.

Just as the child breaks the confines of the given through the dialogue of play, so too may the adult who can move between perspectives and systems of knowing. Liberated from subservience to external authority, to any one system of thought, and from slavish devotion to their own internal voices, these knowers have the dialogical tools to break the oppressive aspects of "reality." Strikingly, their nurture, care, and engagement with their own voices, the voices of others, and ideas broaden out to their nurture and care of aspects of the world. They understand that cultural dialogue itself can be intervened in, effected, and transformed. Such a work, however, cannot be undertaken when there is little or no awareness of the multiplicity of thought, little or no experience of practice in being an active participant in the give and take of dialogue, revealing as it does the perspectival nature of truth.

FROM CULTURES OF SILENCE TO LIBERTORY DIALOGUE: THE WORK OF PAULO FREIRE

This connection between coming to see the context one is in, gaining voice in relation to this context, and being able to creatively engage in efforts to effect culture is beautifully articulated in the work of Paulo Freire. Here silence and lack of dialogical capacity is understood to arise through oppression, which purposely creates voicelessness and obscures context in order to maintain power. Paulo Freire, the founder of the literacy movement in Brazil and a radical pedagogue, argues that, for the disenfranchised, learning to read should involve a process of becoming able to decode the cultural and socio-economic circumstances that shape your life and your thinking. Once able to decode these conditions one is then able to participate in the shaping of those circumstances. He called the first step in this empowering process "conscientization," a group process which allows one to actively engage with the structures one has previously identified with and been blind to.

In Freire's model, an "animator" helps group participants to question their day-to-day experience, their concerns and suffering, exploring the relation between daily life and the cultural dictates that suffuse it. Here words, much like play for the child, begin to open up the realm of the possible, liberating "reality" from the bonds of the given. Efforts at change are directed not foremost to the individual level, but to wider cultural change that will, in the end, affect the participants. This change becomes possible through the second step of Freire's method, "annunciation." Once a group knows how to decode the dominant paradigm and its effects—through having spoken together—then they can begin to conceive of social arrangements which are more just through the process of dialogue.

Why is this process necessary? Freire says that the dominant class attempts "by means of the power of its ideology, to make everyone believe that its ideas are the ideas of the nation" (Freire & Faundez, 1989, p. 74). A dominant paradigm operates by way of the monologue, not dialogue. It requires voicelessness on the part of the other to sustain itself. "The power of an ideology to rule," says Freire, "lies basically in the fact that it is embedded in the activities of the everyday life" (ibid., pp. 26–27).

It is through dialogue that one breaks out of the "bureaucratization" of mind, where there can be a rupture from previously established patterns. "In fact, there is no creativity without *ruptura*, without a break from the old, without conflict in which you have to make a decision" (Freire, in Horton & Freire, 1990, p. 38). For Freire, true education is not the accumulation of information, placed in the student by the teacher. True education must encourage this rupture through dialogue. Teacher and student must each be able to affect, to communicate with, and to challenge each other, rather than perpetuate domination through monological teaching methods that further disempower.

Freire is well aware of the internalization of oppression. Through the animator's questioning a participant begins to claim what she knows about the situation under discussion. Instead of being a passive recipient of the situation, the words of writing and speaking usher a transformation from object to subject. It is such a subject who can then dream a different reality than what is given. The animator is careful not to indoctrinate, to announce the problem and the solution. To do so would intensify the internalized oppression the participant is subject to, encouraging inner and outer silence and subservience. It is the radical listening, hosting, of the animator that opens a space for voice to occur— both internally and externally. As the other group members, who are similar to one, are able to speak and take hold of their situation in words, this empowering of voice is felt by those who listen, as if it were their own.

With brilliant clarity Freire connects dialogue with love:

Dialogue cannot exist, however, in the absence of profound love for the world and for women and men. The naming of the world, which is an act of creation and re-creation, is not possible if it is not infused with love. Love is at the same time the foundation of dialogue and dialogue itself. It is thus necessarily the task of responsible subjects and cannot exist in a relation of domination. Domination reveals the pathology of love: sadism in the dominator and masochism in the dominated. Because love is an act of courage, not of fear, love is commitment to others. No matter where the oppressed are found, the act of love is commitment to their cause—the cause of liberation. And this commitment, because it is loving, is dialogical. (Freire, 1970, p. 77)

DIALOGUE ACROSS DIFFERENCE: BOHM'S LARGE GROUP DIALOGUE

In Freire and Faundez' work the concept of culture is not linked to ideas of unity, but to diversity and tolerance. This shift toward the acknowledgment of diversity invites voices to speak that have been marginalized by the dominant culture and its paradigms. This movement from center to margin requires a process of dialogue that assumes difference and seeks to articulate it. Truth is not located in a particular perspective, it "is to be found in the 'becoming' of dialogue" (Faundez, in Freire & Faundez, 1989, p. 32).

David Bohm, physicist and colleague of Jiddu Krishnamurti, describes a kind of large group dialogue where it is through the difference that is present that one can begin to hear one's own assumptions. Bohm asks that, once we hear these assumptions, we try to suspend them, rather than use our characteristic defensive moves of overpowering the other voices, defending our assumptions as the truth. This acknowledgment and suspension of assumptions is done in the service of beginning to see what it is one means, and what it is the other might mean. It is through the diversity of the group that the partialness of a single mind can be grasped. The opportunity for this kind of large-group dialogue begins to release the self from such partiality, and makes possible a more complex and subtle form of thinking. De Mare, a colleague of Bohm's, says that

Dialogue has a tremendous thought potential: it is from dialogue that ideas spring to transform the mindlessness and massification that accompany social oppression, replacing it with higher levels of cultural sensitivity, intelligence, and humanity. (de Mare, Piper & Thompson, 1991, p. 17)

When we defend an assumption, says Bohm, we are at the same time "pushing out whatever is new . . . There is a great deal of violence in the opinions we are defending" (1990, p. 15). The other is not granted a full and free position in the dialogue. Through coming to see our own and others' assumptions we arrive at a place where we can begin to think together, seeing more of the totality that comprises our situation. Sampson (1993, pp. 1220, 1223) is careful to remind us that allowing others to speak is not enough, however, if they cannot be "heard in their own way, on their own terms," rather than constrained to "use the voice of those who have constructed them." Here, one is required to take a third-person point of view toward oneself, reflecting on how one's actions, attitudes, and assumptions arise from particular ideologies—and, further, how the ideologies we are identified with have affected the other, the stranger.

As is the case in imaginal dialogues, such dialogue in a large group requires the suspension of usual egoic modes of operation: judging, condemning, deeming oneself superior (or inferior). These interfere with listening deeply, with the radical entertaining of the other, which at the same moment can awaken us to where we each stand. Bohm releases thought from the confines of an individual person. To adequately think we need to invite and witness the multiplicity within the group. Without this reflective, conscious practice, the mind remains partial, blinded by the assumptions it has identified with.

CODA

In the end, I am asking that we focus on the interconnecting web of dialogue throughout life, committing to the nurture of dialogical capacities. Imaginal dialogues do not exist separately from the other domains of our lives. The present hierarchies of our culture, schools, and family— and thus of mind—do not deeply invite dialogue; neither does the voicelessness directly resulting from such hierarchies of power. Here I am trying to underscore the interpenetration of dialogues with imaginal others, with dialogues with oneself, one's neighbors, within one's community, between communities, and with the earth and its creatures.

These examples show the deep reciprocity between what I have called dialogical domains. The liberation of a potential voice through play, for instance, can be a harbinger of a substantial shift in the range of how one can be with another interpersonally. Likewise, the experience of deep interpersonal receptivity in a group can call into voice someone who has been silenced; this establishment of dialogical space is then more available in internal conversation. Such a focus on dialogue moves the psychological focus from the self and its interiority to the "between," across domains.

To nurture dialogical capacities that have liberational potential, we are pointed not only toward an illumination of psychic structures and their personified voices but toward the creation of child care contexts where the dramatic fray of play can be delighted in, to elementary schools where the leap between self and others in a small group can be practiced, to spiritual education and practice where the voices within silence can be discerned and addressed. It points us toward high schools and colleges where previously marginalized voices can be admitted to the mosaic, changing the underlying structure of education from the conveyance of dominant paradigms to one of dialogue across difference. It turns us toward the processes of non-violent communication and often of reconciliation that are needed to nurture the neighborhoods and communities—and ultimately nations—that we are homed in; and, finally, to the dialogue beyond words required between nature and humans if our actions are to finally preserve this earth.

REFERENCES

Abrams, M. L. (1953). *The mirror and the lamp: Romantic theory and the critical tradition*. New York: Norton.

Bakhtin, M. (1981). *The dialogic imagination*. Austin: University of Texas Press.

Belenky, M., Clinchy, B., Goldberger, N., &. Tarule, J. (1986). *Women's ways of knowing*. New York: Basic Books.

Bohm, D. (1996). *On dialogue*. London: Routledge.

Brown, L., & Gilligan, C. (1992). *Meeting at the crossroads*. New York: Ballantine Books.

Buber, M. (1958). *I and Thou*. New York: Scribner's.

Buber, M. (1970). *The way of man*. New York: Citadel Press.

de Mare, P., Piper, R., & Thompson, S. (1991). *Koinonia: From hate, through dialogue, to culture in the large group*. London: Karnac Books.

Freire, P. (1970). *Pedagogy of the oppressed*. New York: Seabury Press.

Freire, P., & Faundez, A. (1989). *Learning to question: A pedagogy of liberation*. New York: Continuum.

Goizueta, R. S. (1988). *Liberation, method, and dialogue: Enrique Dussel and North American theological discourse*. Atlanta, GA: Scholars Press.

Horton, M., & Freire, P. (1990). *We make the road by walking: Conversations on education and social change*. Philadelphia: Temple University Press.

Jung, C. G. (1947). Der geist der psychologie [The spirit of psychology]. *Eranos-Jahrbuch, pp. 385–490*.

Jung, C. G. (1969). The structure and dynamics of the psyche. *Collected Works* (Vol. 8). Princeton, NJ: Princeton University Press.

Kaplan, B. (1983a). A trio of trials. In R. M. Lerner (Ed.), *Developmental psychology: Historical and philosophical perspectives*. Hillsdale, NJ: Lawrence Erlbaum Associates.

Kaplan, B. (1983b). Genetic-dramatism: Old wine in new bottles. In S. Wapner & B. Kaplan (Eds.), *Toward a holistic developmental psychology* (pp. 53–71). Hillsdale, NJ: Lawrence Erlbaum Associates.

Kohlberg, L., Yaeger, J., & Hjertholm, E. (1968). Private speech: Four studies and a review of theories. *Child Development, 39*, 691–735.

Martin-Baro, I. (1994). *Writings for a liberation psychology*. Cambridge, MA: Harvard University Press.

Merleau-Ponty, M. (1973). *The prose of the world*. Evanston, IL: Northwestern University Press.

Miller, D. L. (1973). *George Herbert Mead: Self, language and world*. Chicago: University of Chicago Press.

Morris, W. (Ed.). (1969). *The American heritage dictionary of the English language*. New York: American Heritage/Houghton Mifflin.

Niebuhr, R. (1955). *The self and the dramas of history*. New York: Scribner's.

Pfuetze, P. (1973). *Self, society, existence: Human nature and dialogue in the thought of George Herbert Mead and Martin Buber*. Westport, CT: Greenwood Press.

Piaget, J. (1951). *Play, dream, and imitation in childhood*. New York: Norton.

Sampson, E. (1988). The debate on individualism: Indigenous psychologies of the individual and their role in personal and societal functioning. *American Psychologist, 43*, 1, 15–22.

Sampson, E. (1993). Identity politics: Challenges to psychology's understanding. *American Psychologist, 48*, 1219–1230.

Selman, R., & Schultz, L. (1990). *Making a friend in youth*. Chicago: University of Chicago Press.

Sivaraksa, S. (1992). *Seeds of peace: A Buddhist vision for renewing society*. Berkeley, CA: Parallax Press.

Vygotsky, L. S. (1962). *Thought and language*. Cambridge, MA: The MIT Press.

Vygotsky, L. S. (1978). *Mind in society: The development of higher psychological processes*. Cambridge, MA: Harvard University Press.

Watkins, M. (1986). *Invisible guests: The development of imaginal dialogues*. Hillsdale, NJ: Analytic Press.

Watkins, M. (1992). From individualism to the interdependence: Changing paradigms in psychotherapy. *Psychological Perspectives, 27*, 52–69.

Winnicott, D. W. (1971). *Playing and reality*. New York: Penguin Books.

Chapter 6

The Dialogical Self between Mechanism and Innovation

Hubert J. M. Hermans and Ingrid E. Josephs

The term "dialogue" is often associated with something "beautiful." It easily evokes the image of people sitting at a round table, involved in a conversation in order to reach a more or less perfect solution to a problem. Moreover, dialogue is frequently associated with a symmetrical form of communication in which the conversing partners give each other the opportunity to take turns in an open process of question and answer. In the present contribution we certainly acknowledge the potentials of dialogue for open communication and problem solving, but focus at the same time on the psychological factors which inhibit and constrain open dialogical processes. We do so on the basis of the conviction that the prospect and potentials of the dialogical mind can be realistically valued only if its underlying scripted and automated basis is acknowledged.

The purpose of this chapter is to show how dialogical processes, both between and within people, are, often unknowingly, bound to emotional restrictions and automatic repetitions which seriously limit the openness of interactions. This implies that people who see themselves as "dialogical" on a conscious level may, at the same time, rehearse rather fixed and inflexible scripts on a subconscious level. In elaborating on this thesis, we are particularly interested in the ways in which people entertain dialogical relationships with themselves in close connection with entertaining relationships with others.

THE DIALOGICAL SELF: DIFFERENT STORIES FROM DIFFERENT POSITIONS

The question of the dialogical quality of the self is closely related to the question of how internal or within-dialogues are related to external or between-dialogues. In an extensive review of philosophical and psychological literature, Blachowicz (1999) discusses two models for understanding the relationship of the "soul with itself": a reflection model and a social model. According to the reflection model, people think *about* their daily experiences from a higher, more abstract level that critically evaluates these experiences. This model assumes an asymmetrical relation between a foundation of lived experience and a higher level of conceptual judgment and reflection. Only the reflecting part of the self does the talking and therefore this talking is more monological than dialogical. One talks to oneself, not with oneself. The social model, on the other hand, assumes a two-way dialogical structure in the self. Inner conversation takes place among different *personae*. A person may adopt the role of, for example, "parent," "child," "advisor," or "victim" in relation to another such role within the self which then answers or responds to the first role. Instead of the asymmetry of the reflection model, the adherents of the social model tend to see a basic commonality between internal dialogue and social conversation between cognitively equivalent partners (Blachowicz, 1999).

In agreement with the social model, an upsurge of interest in the dialogicality of the self emerged a decade ago in psychological literature (e.g., Bertau, 1999; Gregg, 1991; Hermans, Kempen, & Van Loon, 1992; Josephs, 1998; Morin, 1995; Raggat, 2000; Richardson, Rogers, & McCarroll, 1998; Segall, 1996; Tan & Moghaddam, 1995; Tappan, 1999; Valsiner, 1997; Wertsch, 1991) and continues to be the subject of theoretical discussion and empirical research (e.g., special issues on the dialogical self in *Culture & Psychology*, September 2001, and in *Theory & Psychology*, April 2002).

Inspired by Bakhtin's (1929) metaphor of the polyphonic novel and James' conception of the self, Hermans and Kempen (1993) conceptualized the dialogical self as a dynamic multiplicity of (voiced) positions in the landscape of the mind, intertwined as this mind is with the minds of other people. In principle, each position in such a multivoiced self is able to tell a story from its own point of view and exchange stories with other positions in the self. Two basic characteristics define the dialogical self: intersubjective exchange and relative dominance. The principle of intersubjective exchange implies that one position in the self becomes involved in a process of question and answer or agreement and disagreement with another part of the self in such a way that one part of the self may become influenced and even innovated by another part. According to the principle of relative dominance, one part of the self may become dominant, temporarily or more permanently, over another part so that some parts are subordinated or silenced by other parts and, consequently, no longer able to remain an active partner in an ongoing dialogical interchange.

An illustrative example is the case study of Alice (Hermans & Kempen, 1993, chapter 6), a 28-year-old woman without any psychiatric history. As part of a research project on the multivoicedness of the self, she described two positions as important to her daily life: "my open side," which she considered as the dominant, positively tuned part of herself, and "my closed side" as her less familiar, dark side. From each position separately, she was invited to formulate a story about her past, present, and future. The results showed that Alice's memories from her open side centered around the contact with her mother, with whom she identified in a very positive way, whereas her memories from her closed position were more associated with her father, with whom she had a rather ambivalent relationship. It was observed that Alice had not only quite different memories from different positions, but also different and even opposing feelings about her present situation, particularly about the relationship with her friend. From her open side she was "always there for him," whereas from her closed side she said: "My partner and I have both had a broken relationship in the past; I don't want to lose myself again in another relationship" (p. 83). This illustration suggests that by studying and comparing memories, concerns, and goals from different positions, basic agreements, disagreements, and ambivalences can be brought to the surface.

From a therapeutic point of view, the dramatic changes in Alice's self-narrative are noteworthy. After the investigation, she was requested to write a diary during a period of three weeks and to rate her different story parts which she had formulated from the two positions (open and closed) at the end of each week on two variables: "relative dominance" ("How dominant was this aspect of your life during the past week?") and "meaningfulness" ("How meaningful was this aspect of your life during the past week?"). The data showed a "dominance reversal" (Hermans, 1996a, 1996b) within the three-week period of study. In this period in which she spontaneously increased her contact with her father, the story parts of her closed position became more dominant than the story parts of her open position, whereas the parts of the latter position receded to the background. At the same time the meaningfulness of her closed position increased strongly with a simultaneous decrease of the meaningfulness of her open position. Apparently, the increasing dominance of her otherwise negatively tuned closed position was experienced as very meaningful. In her diary Alice explained her experience in this way: "I'm becoming aware that an important part of myself is in that closed side . . . I'm also beginning to see that when I express my vulnerable parts, I get much closer to other people, and then, it goes better with me, too." These words suggest that by bringing a hitherto neglected or suppressed position to the surface, both the relationship with herself and with others were influenced in favorable ways. In other words, diversification in terms of a multiplicity of positions does not exclude the development of the dialogical self in the direction of an integrative unity.

EARLY DEVELOPMENTAL EVIDENCE OF AN EMBODIED DIALOGICAL SELF

Recognition of the self in the mirror has been used in developmental studies to determine self-awareness at a young age. Typically, investigators have used the "marked face technique" originated by Gallup (1968) and Amsterdam (1972). In this procedure the infant is unobtrusively marked with a red spot on the face and then placed in front of a mirror. Young children (typically between six months and one year) show social behavior to the mirror image and sometimes try to find the "actual" baby by looking behind the mirror. However, infants of fifteen months and older (typically those of twenty-four months) notice the anomaly in their mirror image and remove the red spot from their face. Some time after the solution of the marked-face task, children begin to identify their self-image in the mirror with a pronoun or by name, and, more generally, they start using language to identify themselves and to indicate that they are distinct from others ("I Micky," "I boy"). These observations have been used as early developmental expressions of self-recognition and self-awareness. A problem with the marked-face technique is that although very young children show social behavior toward the mirror image, such image is not very social by nature, and fits more with the "reflection model" than with the "social model" as distinguished by Blachowicz (1999). Recent developmental studies on "double touch stimulation" and "imitation" are more in agreement with the social model and may deepen our understanding of early manifestations or precursors of self-awareness from a dialogical perspective.

From birth onward and even prior to birth, children have perceptual experiences that enable them to specify their own body as an entity differentiated from the environment (Fogel, 1993; Rochat, 2000). In bringing their limbs in contact with other parts of their own body, they experience the combination of proprioception and double touch stimulation, that is, the mutual feeling of their hand touching their cheek and inversely their cheek touching their hand. At the same time, this experience enables infants to feel their own body as distinct from the body of someone else because the body of another person or object doesn't imply double touch stimulation. For Fogel (1993) double touch stimulation represents an early form of dialogical embodied activity: When an infant brings her knee to her mouth, she opens her mouth before mouth and knee touch each other as if the infant "receives" the knee. For Fogel the contact between mouth and knee, as a form of contact of the body with itself, has a basic commonality with the interactional giving and taking between mother and child. When the mother gives a toy to the infant, she brings the object into the visual field of the child in such a way that the infant has the opportunity to open her hands before receiving the toy. It is as if the mother says: "I offer you a toy, do you want it?" The infant, in turn, orients her body to the toy and, before taking it, opens her hands as if saying "Yes, I want it."

Like echoing in the auditory field, imitation in the visual field can be seen as a most rudimentary form of dialogical activity. From birth onward infants are able to imitate tongue protrusion modeled by an experimenter pausing with a still face between several trials of protrusion (Meltzoff & Moore, 1994). Elaborating on those experiments, Rochat (2000) studied tongue protrusion in a group of one- and two-month-old infants in two conditions: one in which the experimenter modeled tongue protrusion with a still face without any interaction with the infants, and another in which the experimenter combined tongue protrusion with actively engaging the infant in protoconversation. It was found that one- and two-month-olds responded differently in the two conditions. The one-month-olds tended to generate an overall increase of tongue protrusion in the still face condition compared to the communicative condition. In contrast, the two-month-olds tended to manifest the reverse: They increasingly showed tongue protrusion in the communicative condition. Apparently, infants are increasingly sensitive to the relative communicative attunement of the social partner. This is congruent with a general finding in developmental psychology that the second month of life marks the emergence of intersubjectivity, and in this period infants start to actively share experiences with social partners. For example, socially elicited smiling in face-to-face interactions with social partners starts around the sixth week of life (Rochat, Querido, & Striano, 1999).

Studies on double touch stimulation and imitation provide indications for the existence of a dialogical self long before the period in which children recognize their mirror image and start to use pronouns. At the same time, such studies indicate that dialogue is not to be identified with "verbal interaction" and already exists before there is any kind of "symbolic interaction." The crucial point is that dialogue should not be restricted to linguistic dialogue. Before linguistic capacities mature, children are able to understand and respond to intonations and behaviors by caregivers. Embodied forms of interchange in terms of question and answer can exist on a prelinguistic base.

PRIVATE AUDIENCE AND RELATIONAL SCHEMAS: THE ROBOT IN THE DIALOGUE

Despite the existence of dialogical capacities, both internal and external, and despite the existence of those capacities very early in human development, there are mechanisms at work which may seriously constrain the full development of our dialogical potentials. Recent studies in social psychology have supported the idea that dialogical processes evolve to a significant degree in mechanistic ways and are less multidirectional and more repetitive than one would expect. These constraints are a challenge to one of the central features of dialogue, its openness, as discussed in the writings of Bakhtin (1929/1973) (see also Vasil'eva, 1988). Two lines of research in particular emphasize the automatic structure of dialogues: "private audience" and "relational schemas."

In their research on interpersonal interaction, Baldwin and Holmes (1987) started from the assumption that a sense of self is experienced in relation to some audience: people who are present or imagined, specific or generalized, actual or fantasized. The guiding idea is that most people respond at different times to a range of different significant others, who often represent distinct ways of evaluating the self. Such evaluating others, termed as "private audience," can include such divergent figures as a spouse, best friend, religious leader, or colleague. In Baldwin and Holmes' study, a group of undergraduate women were asked to visualize the faces of either two acquaintances from campus or two older members of their family. Ten minutes later they read a sexually permissive story in a different context. When the participants were afterwards asked to rate the enjoyableness of the story, they tended to respond in ways that would be acceptable to their activated audiences. They were much less enthusiastic about the sexual story if they had recently been reminded of their older, supposedly more moralistic family members.

It is not likely that mechanisms such as these can be interpreted as merely reflecting some kind of consciously selected communicative strategy. Even when some audience is primed subliminally the effect remains. In one of their studies Baldwin, Carell, and Lopez (1990) invited graduate students in psychology to evaluate their own research ideas after exposures, subliminally, to slides of either the scowling, disapproving face of their professor or the approving face of a postdoctoral fellow. The students' evaluative ratings of their own research ideas tended to be lower following exposure to their professor's disapproving face than following the postdoctoral fellow's approving face. Presumably the self-evaluative process was guided by cognitive structures that were primed by the preceding perception of the expressive faces.

Significant others seem to be more influential in shaping social perception than representations of non-significant others, stereotypes, or traits. Anderson and Cole (1990) found that representations of significant others are richer (trigger more associations), more distinctive (have more unique features), and are more cognitively accessible (time required for retrieval of features) than non-significant others, stereotypes, and traits. In combination with the studies of Baldwin and colleagues, Anderson's research suggests that significant others form rich, unique, and accessible internal representations that may function as private audiences that watch or listen to the person and respond to him or her with affect-laden evaluations. At the same time, however, private audiences influence our self-evaluations beyond awareness in ways that are predictable on the basis of their moral standards.

On the basis of extensive review of the literature on social cognition, Baldwin (1992) proposed the term "relational schema" as a summary term of recent developments in this research domain. A relational schema is defined as a cognitive structure representing regularities in patterns of interpersonal relatedness. Relational schemas are seen as generalized representations of self–other relationships rather than representations of self or others in isolation. A relational schema can be described in terms of "if-then" contingencies. For example, a woman might learn in her contact with her husband that "If I get angry, then he will treat me with respect," or a man might discover, "If I work late in the evening, then my boss will smile at me and call me a good worker."

Relational schemas can become rather complex if the interaction is carried out to multiple iterations of if-then sequences. Baldwin (1992) gives the example of a teenage boy borrowing the keys to his mother's car. The goal of the boy is to borrow the car. He expects, moreover, that the goal of his mother is to make sure that he and the car are returned safely. If she seems reluctant, he knows that the required behavior is to reassure his mother that he will act in a responsible way. So he verbalizes phrases that have been successful in the past, for example, "I'll drive carefully" and "I'll be home before one!" He expects, if he proceeds this way, that his mother will give him the keys. If not, he may engage in different routines, such as expressing his urgent need for transport, complaining about the unfairness of her behavior, and so on. Along these lines multiple if-then sequences can be organized into a complete production system for guiding behavior. Such sequences, although they may be quite complex, are to a significant degree prestructured and repetitive and organize dialogical activities along conservative lines. As part of if-then sequences, questions and answers and agreements and disagreements do not develop in a "free space" with an unlimited multiplicity of possible directions, but are highly selective and predictable parts of a chain of interactional expectations.

THE DIALOGICAL SELF AND IMPRINTING
MECHANISMS IN THE BRAIN

Some theorists talk, implicitly or explicitly, about the relationship between the mental and the physical as if they are opposed categories. They tend to consider a particular phenomenon to be of a mental *or* physical nature. This is not the point of view which is taken in the present contribution. With Strawson (1999) we adopt "the principle of the necessary involvement of the mental with the non-mental": each particular mental or experiential phenomenon involves the existence of some particular non-mental, non-experiential phenomenon.

In agreement with this principle, Schore (1994) presents himself as an advocate of "social neuroscience" and "affective neuroscience" and he does so in the conviction that the frontiers of science lie in the borderland between separate scientific fields. He starts his analysis of the neurobiology of the self by referring to a thesis which Alexander Luria published in 1932: that complex functional brain systems are not ready-made at birth and do not arise spontaneously in development but are formed in the process of social contact and objective activity by the child. More than fifty years later developmental neurobiologists are discovering that particular areas in the brain are critically involved in attachment processes. Schore is particularly interested in the early post-natal growth of the orbitofrontal area, a region known to be involved in homeostatic affective regulation and attachment functions. This area is located in the right cerebral hemisphere, which is thought to be involved in the development of reciprocal interactions between mother and child. Due to its widely distributed anatomical linkages, the orbitofrontal cortex occupies a unique position between cortex and subcortex. It has connections both with hypothalamic and autonomous areas and with the brain stem neuromodulator systems. As such the orbitofrontal cortex functions as a preeminent component of the paralimbic core of the brain and plays a central adaptive role in emotional and motivational processes (see also Tucker, 1992, for a comparable view). It is Schore's central tenet that the early social environment, mediated by the primary caregiver, directly influences the evolution of structures in the brain that are responsible for the socio-emotional development of the child. In response to such influences, hormonal and neurohormonal responses are triggered leading to physiological alterations which are registered within specific areas in the infant's brain. As a result, the brain undergoes a structural maturation during a sensitive period (particularly, from the end of the first year to the middle of the second year).

In this structural maturation, the primary caregiver plays the crucial role as a psychobiological regulator who attunes herself to the child's internal state by appraising the child's emotionally expressive displays. Through "reflected appraisals" in non-verbal, pre-linguistic dialogues with the child, the caregiver selects and influences specific emotional states which the emerging self can experience. In reflecting the child's emotional states and responding to them, the caregiver also facilitates transitions from one state to another. For example, the mother responds with solace to the distressed child facilitating the transition from distress to relaxation.

In the light of pervasive influence of physiological alterations of the maturation of the brain, Schore refers to the ability of the dialogical self to occupy a "multiplicity of positions" as reflecting the emergent capacity to adaptively switch between psychobiological states that are colored by different affects. When the maturing child is able to develop a dialogical self, she is able to transcend her immediate state (e.g., distress) and to enhance "self-solace" capacities (see also Wilson & Weinstein, 1992). The mature orbitofrontal cortex, involved as it is in homeostatic regulation, is able to adjust and correct emotional responses, mediated by its capacity to shift between different limbic circuits and to make a transition between low and high arousal states in response to stressful alterations of external environmental conditions. The capacity of the orbitofrontal system to facilitate such transitions enables the dialogical self to maintain continuity across various situational contexts. As Schore extensively argues, this capacity is seriously reduced in forms of insecure attachment (pp. 373–385).

For the maturation of the orbitofrontal cortex, Schore emphasizes the importance of *empathy*. The capacity to understand the distress of another self begins with an accurate appraisal of the other's face, the "display board" of emotions and the site of the body where the self is most typically located (see also Broucek, 1991). The ability to take the perspective of a distressed other also requires the ability to shift from a neutral or positive into a negative state and to be tolerant to an experience of distress within the self. In order to offer comfort to another, the self must be able to read one's own emotional state in order to have access to a similar state of the other. This requires access to a self-comforting mechanism that can regulate a negative affective state and shift it back to a positive one.

As the preceding analysis suggests, the brain is not simply a ready-made "determining factor" which has a causal influence on our social activities and emotions. The brain not only produces a dialogical self, including its social and emotional aspects, but at the same time the dialogical self produces a brain. Early (pre-linguistic) dialogical activities leave, via repetitions and expectations, their traces in the maturing brain resulting in dialogical routines which become accessible in particular stimulus conditions. And when they are accessible the person may use them as if they are chosen in a state of "free will." However, the experience of "free will" itself emerges from a preceding history of interactions which leave their traces in a developing mind. This brings us to the relationship between intentionality and mechanism.

INTENTIONALITY AND MECHANISM AS
COMPLEMENTARY METAPHORS

In a thorough discussion of the clinical phenomenon of "dissociation," Segall (1996) argues that the psychological and psychiatric literature witnesses a continuous stream of publications on the "divided mind": Janet's (1924) concept of dissociation, Freud's topographical (1900/1972) and structural (1923/1960) divisions of the psyche, Jung's complexes (1911/1973), Perls' (1969) polarities, Tart's (1975) identity states, Hilgard's (1977) cognitive control structures, Maher's (1978) operating and mediating potentials, Ornstein's (1986) modular "multimind," and Hermans and Kempen's (1993) dialogical self (for a review on the multiplicity of the self, see also Rowan & Cooper, 1999).

Given the pervasive interest of theorists in the multiplicity of personality and self both in normality and abnormality, Segall is concerned about the question of whether "dissociation" can be understood on the basis of the metaphor of mechanism or the metaphor of agency (intentionality). He gives the example of a woman who, telling her therapist about her experiences of childhood abuse, spontaneously slips into the present progressive tense as she narrates her account. She then speaks in a small, high-pitched voice and childlike intonations. Later in the conversation, she resumes her normal way of speaking.

In his discussion of this case, Segall poses the question of whether the client is (mechanistically) "age-regressed" to childhood, with an autonomous child in herself speaking, or whether this is a complex performance by an (intentional) adult who is trying to deal with her past. Or to put the question in other terms, is the affect which is being expressed damned-up, pent-up affect created in the past which is being (mechanically) released, or is it new affect being generated in the present as part of a (intentionally driven) process occurring between the client and the therapist? In an attempt to answer these questions, Segall discusses Sarbin's explanation of dissociative identity disorder (DID) as a form of role-taking (Coe & Sarbin, 1991; Sarbin, 1995). For Sarbin dissociation is a skill and therefore he prefers to use the term "self-deception" rather than the mechanistic sounding term "dissociation" in order to describe the process of ego state generation and/or enactment. However, such an explanation would deny or neglect, in Segall's view, the apparent self-defense as an almost automatic response to being out of control of an unbearable situation. How then to reconcile Sarbin's criticisms of a mechanistic and authorless dissociation with the experience of dissociated control that seems so patently self-evident to DID patients?

It is Segall's central thesis that a satisfactory explanation of the phenomenon of dissociation can neither be given by an exclusive use of a mechanistic metaphor nor by an agentic one. He proposes to broaden the theoretical scope in order to explain the variety of symptoms of DID, some of which are more agentic and some of which are more automatic in nature. DID implies processes by which automatically entered states (e.g., as a defensive reaction to a traumatic event), if repeated, may become linked together over time and evolve into phenomena with a more agentic character (see also Braun & Sacks' 1985 model of DID etiology). In order to clarify his point of view, Segall compares the process of dissociation with the process of breathing. Breathing has an automatic, involuntary, and unconscious aspect, but conscious intent can alter its rhythm and depth. Actors, singers, swimmers, yogis, and expectant mothers learn to use modifications of breathing for specific purposes, but that does not make breathing an entirely intentional performance.

Along these lines, Segall proposes to complement Sarbin's role-theoretical explanation of dissociation with Hermans and Kempen's (1993) multivocal dialogical self. As authorial selves, the different I-positions in the dialogical self each function in agentic ways, whereas the process of switching between the different positions is not always or usually directed by an agent. A change in situation may automatically bring the person into another state of mind, but being in that state the person may perform intentionally driven acts. In a less extreme way, this may also happen in normal functioning when a particular remark by another person may cause somebody to burst automatically into anger, but being in that state the person may speak words and make plans in intentional ways. In the case of dissociation the switch into another state may even take place beyond awareness of the patient, but being in that state the person may be the author of a well-organized story.

Segall goes on to argue that even the switches between the positions are not entirely of a mechanistic kind. Switches may be mechanistic on one level but intentional on another level. Any biological system can be analyzed at different levels. As Hofstadter (1979) has argued, reductionistic/mechanical descriptions of biological systems and holistic/intentional models need to be combined in order to permit a more complete understanding of such systems. Whereas the process of switching positions is mechanistic at a lower level, there may be extra meaning in the switches as they reflect changing organismic conditions and promote socio-biological adaptation on a higher level. The change of positions in the case of dissociation may be an automatic switch on the lower level of functioning as it "just happens" and may even feel as "meaningless." On a higher level, however, such changes or switches may represent meaningful adaptations of the organism in order to survive.

The central idea in Segall's analysis is that something valuable is lost if dissociation is viewed as only a mechanistic process or as only an intentional transaction. Both metaphors need to be coordinated and synthesized in order to produce an enriched conception of the phenomenon in question. This implies that mechanistic metaphors and agentic metaphors, valuable as they may be as separate approaches, have to be brought together in a larger integrative theoretical framework in order to arrive at a more complete understanding of the functioning or dysfunctioning self.

INNOVATIVE DIALOGUES IN A SCRIPTED MIND

Some of the most influential theorists in social sciences and related disciplines have thought about the problem of innovation in self and identity. William James (1890) was concerned about the question of how the mind can appropriate a "new thought in the new present" (pp. 340–341) as part of the question how he could deal with the existence of both continuity and discontinuity in the process of thinking. Mead (1934), another influential theorist of the self, was well aware of the problems that would have been raised if he had restricted the social process to the internalization of the attitude of the other within the self (the generalized other). In that case the self would simply be a copy of external social roles and societal institutions. Therefore, Mead (1934) introduced the distinction between *I* and *Me*, that enabled him to locate the conventional aspects of the self in the *Me* and the innovative potentials in the *I*: "The novelty comes in the action of the "I," but the structure, the form of the self is one which is conventional" (p. 209).

As a theorist on dialogical processes *par excellence*, Bakhtin was interested in the innovative qualities of language as being used in the utterances produced by living people in interaction. His view on the relationship between language and innovation is concisely summarized by Morris (1994):

Language exists on that creative borderzone or boundary between human consciousnesses, between a self and another. It is this responsive interaction between speakers, between self and other, that constitutes the capacity to produce new meaning. (p. 5)

For a more extensive discussion of these theorists in relation to the concept of innovation, see Hermans (1999).

In contrast to the theoretical interest in the innovation of the self on the part of the founding theorists, actual empirical research on the self has often focused on the regularities and repetitive aspects of self and dialogue. As we have argued in this chapter, the dialogical self is open and closed at the same time. It is open to the extent that dialogical relationships, both internal and external, have the potential to engender new meanings as part of a process of negotiation and exchange of knowledge and information. Dialogue can develop in multidirectional ways by the dynamics of question and answer and by the tension between agreement and disagreement. At the same time the dialogical self closes itself off from innovation by the extensive use of conservative routines, as exemplified by the often unconsciously working private audiences, relational schemas, and if-then sequences. Moreover, many dialogues have a beginning but are not elaborated in any detail because they are stuck in globalized expectations, having the quality of "almost dialogues" (Lewis, 2002). Although there is evidence for the existence of early prelinguistic dialogues of a creative type (Fogel, 2002), neurobiological evidence shows that our brain is scripted at a very early age, as we have seen in this discussion. Not only early dialogues are considerably restricted (e.g., persistent withdrawal in some form of insecure attachment); also more flexible forms of dialogical selves are scripted at an early age (e.g., the shift from distress to self-solace). In the dysfunctional case of dissociation, dialogues that a patient may entertain with the social environment from one particular position are defensively split off from dialogues from another position and, as we have seen, some of the processes involved in this splitting can be understood from the perspective of a mechanical metaphor. However, at the same time it should be acknowledged that, even in the case of dysfunction, a full picture can only be achieved when agentic explanations are also taken into account, suggesting more intentionality in the dialogical activities of dissociated individuals than one would expect on the basis of a clinical-pathological description of this dysfunction.

Certainly, not all dialogical processes are scripted to the same extent. Mead (1934) gives a useful clue by referring to some domains and attitudes that may facilitate the openness and innovation of dialogical activities: The values of the *I*, he says, are found "in the immediate attitude of the artist, the inventor, the scientist in his discovery, in general in the action of the 'I' which cannot be calculated and which involves a reconstruction of the society, and so of the 'me' which belongs to that society" (p. 214). Indeed, there are at least three domains where innovation of the dialogical self is facilitated: play, art, and science. The attitudes reflected by the playful mind, esthetic and artistic perception, and committed exploration are expected to foster innovative dialogue, notwithstanding the fact that such activities have also their scripted aspects.

Altogether, the workings of the dialogical self suggest that we, as human beings, are typically "in-betweeners": We function in mechanical and scripted ways, but at the same time we are able to transcend any stabilized societal or psychological reality, due to the sensitivity of our mind for the unexpected, our desire for the exploration of the unknown, and our persistent urge to transform our society and ourselves to a higher level of functioning. However, any dialogue, starting in an open way, may inadvertently and unconsciously pass into a mechanistic process. Although mechanistic dialogical routines may in many cases enhance the efficiency of our interactions, we pay the price of a reduced openness. For future empirical research, an important task is to explore the possibilities for open and innovative dialogue in a scripted mind. A full appreciation and understanding of our dialogical potentials requires a simultaneous awareness that in the midst of our creativity we are scripted more than we think.

REFERENCES

Amsterdam, B. (1972). Mirror self-image reactions before age two. *Developmental Psychobiology, 5*, 297–305.

Andersen, S. M., & Cole, S. W. (1990). "Do I know you?" The role of significant others in general social perception. *Journal of Personality and Social Psychology, 59*, 384–399.

Bakhtin, M. (1929/1973). *Problems of Dostoevsky's poetics*, 2nd ed. (R. W. Rotsel, Trans.). Ann Arbor, MI: Ardis.

Baldwin, M. W. (1992). Relational schemas and the processing of social information. *Psychological Bullletin, 112*, 461–484.

Baldwin, M. W., Carrell, S. E., & Lopez, D. F. (1990). Priming relationship schemas: My advisor and the pope are watching me from the back of my mind. *Journal of Experimental Social Psychology, 26*, 435–454.

Baldwin, M. W., & Holmes, J. G. (1987). Salient private audiences and awareness of the self. *Journal of Personality and Social Psychology, 53*, 1087–1098.

Bertau, M. (1999). Spuren des Gesprächs in innerer Sprache. Versuch einer Analyse der dialogischen Anteile des lauten Denkens. *Zeitschrift für Sprache & Kognition, 18* (1/2), 4–19.

Blachowicz, J. (1999). The dialogue of the soul with itself. In S. Gallagher & J. Shear (Eds.), *Models of the self* (pp. 177–200). Thorverton, UK: Imprint Academic.

Braun, B., & Sachs, R. (1985). The development of multiple personality disorder: Predisposing, precipitating and perpetuating factors. In R. Kluft (Ed.), *Childhood antecedents of multiple personality* (pp. 38–64). Washington, DC: American Psychiatric Press.

Broucek, F. J. (1991). *Shame and the self*. New York: Guilford Press.

Coe, W. C., & Sarbin, T. R. (1991). Role theory: Hypnosis from a dramaturgical and narrational perspective. In S. J. Lynn & J. W. Rhue (Eds.), *Theories of hypnosis: Current models and perspectives* (pp. 303–323). New York: Guilford.

Fogel, A. (1993). *Developing through relationships: Origins of communication, self, and culture*. Hertfordshire, UK: Harvester Wheatsheaf.

Freud, S. (1900/1972). *The interpretation of dreams*. New York: Avon.

Freud, S. (1923/1960). *The ego and the id*. New York: Norton.

Gallup, G. G. (1968). Mirror image stimulation. *Psychological Bulletin, 70*, 782–793.

Gregg, G. S. (1991). *Self-representation: Life narrative studies in identity and ideology*. Westport, CT: Greenwood Press.

Hermans, H.J.M. (1996a). Voicing the self: From information processing to dialogical interchange. *Psychological Bulletin, 119*, 31–50.

Hermans, H.J.M. (1996b). Opposites in a dialogical self: Constructs as characters. *The Journal of Constructivist Psychology, 9,* 1–26.

Hermans, H.J.M. (1999). Dialogical thinking and self-innovation. *Culture & Psychology, 5,* 67–87.

Hermans, H.J.M., & Kempen, H.J.G. (1993). *The dialogical self: Meaning as movement.* San Diego, CA: Academic Press.

Hermans, H.J.M., Kempen, H.J.G., & Van Loon, R.J.P. (1992). The dialogical self: Beyond individualism and rationalism. *American Psychologist, 47,* 23–33.

Hilgard, E. (1977). *Divided consciousness: Multiple controls in human thought and action.* New York: John Wiley.

Hofstadter, D. R. (1979). *Gödel, Escher, Bach: An eternal golden braid.* New York: Basic Books.

James, W. (1890). *The principles of psychology* (Vol. 1). London: Macmillan.

Janet, P. (1924). *The major symptoms of hysteria: Fifteen lectures given in the medical school of Harvard University,* 2nd ed. New York: Macmillan.

Josephs, I. E. (1998). Constructing one's self in the city of the silent: Dialogue, symbols, and the role of "as if" in self-development. *Human Development, 41,* 180–195.

Jung, C. G. (1911/1973). On the doctrine of complexes. In *Experimental researches* (pp. 598–604). Princeton, NJ: Princeton University Press.

Lewis, M. D. (2002). The dialogical brain. *Theory & Psychology, 12,* 175–190.

Maher, A. (1978). *Experiencing.* New York: Brunner/Mazel.

Mead, G. H. (1934). *Mind, self, and society.* Chicago: University of Chicago Press.

Meltzoff, A. N., & Moore, M. K. (1994). Imitation, memory, and the representation of persons. *Infant Behavior and Development, 17,* 83–99.

Morin, A. (1995). Characteristics of an effective internal dialogue in the acquisition of self-information. *Imagination, Cognition and personality, 15,* 45–58.

Morris, P. (1994). *The Bakhtin reader: Selected writings of Bakhtin, Medvedev, Voloshinov.* London: Arnold.

Ornstein, R. (1986). *Multiminds: A new way to look at human behavior.* Boston: Houghton Mifflin.

Perls, F. S. (1969). *Gestalt therapy verbatim.* Moab, UT: Real People Press.

Raggatt, P.T.F. (2000). Mapping the dialogical self: Towards a rationale and method of assessment. *European Journal of Personality, 14,* 65–90.

Richardson, F. C., Rogers, A., & McCarroll, J. (1998). Toward a dialogical self. *American Behavioral Scientist, 41,* 496–515.

Rochat, P. (2000). Emerging co-awareness. Presentation at the International Conference on Infant Studies. Brighton, UK, July.

Rochat, P., Querido, J. G., & Striano, T. (1999). Emerging sensitivity to the timing and structure of protoconversation in early infancy. *Developmental Psychology, 35,* 950–957.

Rowan, J., & Cooper, M. (1999). *The plural self: Multiplicity in everyday life.* London: Sage.

Sarbin, T. R. (1995). On the belief that one body may be host to two or more personalities. *International Journal of Clinical and Experimental Hypnosis, 13,* 163–183.

Schore, A. N. (1994). *Affect regulation and the origin of the self: The neurobiology of emotional development.* Hillsdale, NJ: Lawrence Erlbaum Associates.

Segall, S. R. (1996). Metaphors of agency and mechanism in dissociation. *Dissociation, 9,* 154–150.

Strawson, G. (1999). The self. In S. Gallagher & J. Shear (Eds.), *Models of the self* (pp. 1–24). Thorverton, UK: Imprint Academic.

Tan, S.-L., & Moghaddam, F. M. (1995). Reflexive positioning and culture. *Journal for the Theory of Social Behavior, 25,* 387–400

Tappan, M. B. (1999). Authoring a moral self: A dialogical perspective. *Journal of Constructivist Psychology, 12,* 117–131.

Tart, C. T. (1975). *States of consciousness.* New York: Dutton.

Tucker, D. M. (1992). Developing emotions and cortical networks. In M. R. Gunnar & C. A. Nelson (Eds.), *Minnesota symposium on child psychology, Vol. 24: Developmental behavioral neuroscience* (pp. 75–128). Hillsdale, NJ: Erlbaum.

Valsiner, J. (1997). Dialogical models of psychological processes: Capturing dynamics of development. *Polish Quarterly of Developmental Psychology, 3,* 155–160.

Vasil'eva, I. I. (1988). The importance of M. M. Bakhtin's idea of dialogue and dialogic relations for the psychology of communication. *Soviet Psychology, 26,* 17–31.

Wertsch, J. V. (1991). *Voices of the mind: A sociocultural approach to mediated action.* London: Harvester Wheatsheaf.

Wilson, A., & Weinstein, L. (1992). An investigation into some implications for psychoanalysis of Vygotsky's perspective on the origin of mind, Part 1. *Journal of the American Psychoanalytic Association, 40,* 524–576.

Part III

Dialogicality and Culture

Chapter 7

Culture as a Semiosphere: On the Role of Culture in the Culture–Individual Relationship

Aaro Toomela

A dialogue can be conceptualized at different levels. We can restrict this concept to the interaction of two human beings, but in psychology a broader view on dialogue is usually assumed. Nevertheless, very often it is not clear what a dialogue is or who or what the participants of a dialogue are. Intuitively, it seems to be clear that whoever the participants of a dialogue are, they should be different from each other in some respect. If this is the case, then the next question is how the participants differ. When we analyze a specific dialogue between two humans, for example, then the differences are probably also specific to those participants. Such idiosyncratic characteristics would be interesting only for understanding the process underlying that specific dialogue. There is a possibility, however, that a broader view on human dialogues may reveal universal principles, which apply to all human minds.

In this chapter, I propose that one broad kind of human dialogue is a dialogue between an individual human mind and culture. It should be made clear from the beginning that I do not view culture and an individual human mind as things that can exist independently of one another. Rather, they constitute each other and depend on each other. This does not mean, however, that they cannot be distinguished. An individual mind and culture each bring into a dialogue—that is, into their mutually constituting co-existence—something qualitatively different.

The following analysis is dedicated to the question of what the specific qualities of culture are that make human minds possible. This kind of analysis is meaningful only when the notion of culture is defined. Before giving a definition of culture, however, some theoretical background should be presented. Definitions have a purpose, and different approaches can be identified as to how definitions of culture are created. A definition of culture becomes more meaningful and clearer when the specific purpose and approach are made explicit. In addition, the main goal of this chapter is to search for explanations of psychic phenomena. The definition of culture discussed below should have explanatory power.

Quite often in psychology, the notion of explanation implies the assumption of a sequential cause–effect structure. However, my approach to psychology is evolutionary in perspective. According to this approach, a different kind of explanation is assumed. Thus, a short description of explanation in an evolutionary framework is given before turning to the main subject of this chapter.

WHERE, HOW, AND FOR WHAT PURPOSE TO SEARCH FOR A DEFINITION OF CULTURE

The concept of culture has been defined in hundreds of ways. Considering this, we would expect hot debates about the "right" definition. However, instead of fights (or at least communication) there seems to be a kind of compartmentalization in the utilization of the concept. Theoretically, rather contradictory definitions of culture are used in parallel in different domains of the social and behavioral sciences. Different (and contradictory) views of culture can be found in developmental psychology (Best & Ruther, 1994), cross-cultural psychology (Berry, Poortinga, Segall, & Dasen, 1992; Kagitçibasi & Berry, 1989; Segall, 1986) as well as in anthropology (Rubel & Rosman, 1994) and archaeology (Watson, 1995).

Different definitions allow a researcher or theoretician to choose the definition that best suits his or her purpose. Several authors have found such a practice reasonable (e.g., Jahoda, 1995; Triandis, 1994). Thus, in proceeding with a specific definition of culture, a purpose (why, where, and for what the definition is used) should be identified. What I am trying to achieve in this chapter is to get closer to an understanding and explanation of an individual human mind. Culture, as understood here, is a notion necessary for understanding the human mind. Thus, my enterprise belongs to the field of cultural psychology.

Despite the large number of different definitions of culture, two general approaches can be differentiated in the field of cultural psychology (Tomasello, 1996). One wing of cultural psychology is sociological, emphasizing the distributed and collective nature of human cognition. The other approach is more psychologically oriented and takes distributed and individual characteristics of culture and psyche as distinguishable and complementary. In addition, a third approach can be found in studies of relationships between culture and psychology where theory is left in the background. Rather, an operational definition of culture is taken without explanation or deeper analysis.

Many papers published in the *Journal of Cross-Cultural Psychology*, for example, characterize the latter approach. In the first five numbers of the 1999 issue, thirty-four empirical articles were published. From those papers 73% defined culture operationally as a characteristic of a country, and an additional 12% connected culture with nation or ethnicity. The line of thinking in such "cross-country psychology" is usually inductive. First some systematic and statistically reliable difference between countries or nations is found. Next, it is argued that this difference "explains" some aspects of individuals' cognitive, emotional, and/or social functioning. That kind of linking of culture and psychology is called "theory." In cross-country psychology patterns of differences are identified but usually not explained. The differences just exist. The principle, known from the beginning of empirical psychology, that description in psychology or any other science is only a prerequisite for explanation (Wundt, 1897), is forgotten in this kind of approach. Cross-country psychology is potentially very valuable because it identifies phenomena that should be explained. For the present purposes little can be found in this approach, however.

The first, that is, sociological approach is also inappropriate for the present purposes because according to that approach it is not possible to separate individuals from their socio-cultural environments (Tomasello, 1996). Without analytically distinguishing qualitatively different stable aspects of a process, that is, it's structure, only superficial dynamics can be described, but again, no true explanation can be achieved. Thus, what is left is the "psychologically oriented wing" of cultural psychology where I suggest explanations of the individual human mind can be achieved. I have used the notion of explanation in the discussion above several times. My understanding of explanation differs from the usual cause–effect treatment of explanation and will be characterized next.

Understanding of Explanation from the Perspective of Evolutionary Psychology

In psychology, all major scholars from the first half of the twentieth century explicitly analyzed the question of what general principles should be followed in creating an explanation of psychological phenomena. On a theoretical level, many of those scholars—James Mark Baldwin, William James, Kurt Koffka, Wolfgang Köhler, Lev Vygotsky, Max Wertheimer, Wilhelm Wundt—were evolutionary psychologists in that respect. It is a separate question, however, whether or not the principles proposed in theoretical analyses were followed in empirical work. Evolutionary psychology of that time should not be confused with a "modern" evolutionary psychology that is "simply psychology that is informed by the additional knowledge that evolutionary biology has to offer, in the expectation that understanding the process that designed the human mind will advance the discovery of its architecture" (Cosmides, Tooby, & Borkow 1992, p. 3).

Evolutionary psychologists were interested in explaining the emergence of novelty in psychological processes. They understood that novel forms result from rearrangement of already existing material:

The point which as evolutionists we are bound to hold fast to is that all the new forms of being that make their appearance are really nothing more than results of the redistribution of the original and unchanging materials. (James, 1890, p. 146)

Thus, for understanding novel forms it is necessary to describe that from which the novel form is created. Novel forms are not "simple sums of parts" but rather qualitatively new, "organic wholes":

By organic whole, is understood one which (a) has a certain general character or individuality, while (b) it consists of distinguishable parts each with a certain character of its own, but (c) such that they cannot exist unmodified apart from the whole, while the character of the whole is similarly dependent upon them. (Hobhouse, 1901, p. 374)

An "organic whole" is explained if two complementary aspects of it are described, the elements from which the whole is built and the relationships between the elements in that whole. In modern science this view is called *General System Theory*, which postulates that every thing or phenomenon is a system. A system, in turn "can be defined as a complex of interacting elements" (von Bertalanffy, 1968, p. 55). The only significant difference between modern system theory and an evolutionary approach to explaining phenomena is that the former tries to formalize and to express mathematically all its findings, whereas the latter usually did not go beyond "verbal theories." It should be pointed out that a formal, mathematical description of a thing or a phenomenon is meaningless without the verbal theory, which ties formulas to the external world, whereas verbal theories have explanatory power without mathematical formulas. Evolutionary psychology has one further restriction. It assumes that "evolution is a single continuous process the different phases of which are only seen in their true significance when treated as parts of the whole to which they belong" (Hobhouse, 1901, pp. v–vi).

This means that every psychological study should, in addition to a structural description of elements and their relationships, give a detailed description of the developmental history of the explained phenomenon (a brilliant analysis of why every psychological study should take evolution, that is, genesis seriously, can be found in Baldwin, 1906). The reason for that lies in the fact that elements, when united into a higher-level whole, change their properties. The traditional example, used by Gestalt psychologists and Vygotsky among others, is that of the molecule of water. The elements of water, H and O, burn or support burning, but the synthesis of these elements, H_2O, can be used for extinguishing fire. Thus, in the synthetic novel form the properties of its elements are changed. The analysis of a new-level whole gives us no hints about from which components it is built. On the other hand, the analysis of elements of the future system is also insufficient. We cannot predict the properties of water from the analysis of the properties of its elements. It might be suggested that for understanding the whole it is not necessary to describe its elements. But this is not true because the elements that enter into a synthesis have qualitatively different roles in a whole system. Otherwise it would be possible to replace elements without changing the whole. It is clear that H in the molecule of H_2O cannot be replaced by O and vice versa. Furthermore, H_3 or O_3 would not have properties of water, and the synthetic product would not be able to exist at all. Thus, quality of elements is one of the determinants of the whole. In addition, it is possible to build different systems from the same elements. If we just mix H and O we get a very inflammable gas. Water results only when specific H-O-H relationships between elements are created.

In sum, evolutionary psychology explains psyche by describing the components or elements of psychological processes and the relationships between those elements. The only way to distinguish "true" and not "fictitious" elements of a system is to describe mind in evolution, in genesis. "Organic wholes" or systems and the genesis of those wholes can be characterized by several additional principles. Some of those characteristics are described in relevant places in the following analysis. A full description of evolutionary psychology can be achieved through the synthesis of the following work: Wundt (1897), Baldwin (1906), Hobhouse (1901), Vygotsky (1994). General System Theory is fully described in von Bertalanffy (1968).

DEFINITION OF CULTURE

Now it becomes possible to propose a definition of culture that should help to explain the human mind. This definition is directly developed on the basis of Vygotsky's theory. Vygotsky himself did not give an explicit definition of culture. Nevertheless, different analyses have led to sufficiently similar conclusions regarding how culture should be defined in a Vygotskian theory. Van der Veer (1996) analyzed the concept of culture in Vygotsky's theory and concluded that for Vygotsky the word "culture" is equivalent to the concepts or word meanings existing in that culture. A different line of analysis led me (Toomela, 1996a) to a similar definition: "culture is socially shared information that is coded in symbols" (p. 298). Symbols, as understood here, must have four complementary characteristics (Toomela, 1996b): First, a symbol must be an object, behavioral act, or phenomenon that can be directly perceived through sense organs. Otherwise it would be impossible to use symbols for communication. Second, the meaning of symbols must be shared by organisms, that is, a meaning of a symbol must be conventional. Third, symbols refer to objects, events, and phenomena. Finally, it must be possible to use a symbol either in ways or in contexts that are different from ways or contexts of utilization of symbol referents.

This definition relates culture to the study of symbols. Such an approach makes it interdisciplinary—symbolic processes are specifically studied in semiotics. The Tartu-Moscow school of semiotics, founded by Yuri Lotman, has approached the phenomenon of culture from a semiotic perspective. In that perspective, culture can be understood as a *semiosphere*, an abstract "space" or continuum that is filled with different types of semiotic formations at different levels of organization. Realization of communicative processes and creation of novel information is possible only within that space (Lotman, 1992a). Several ideas developed by Lotman have been illuminating for a better understanding of semiotic mechanisms of culture. Thus, the semiotic background of the definition of culture is also elaborated in the following discussion.

For a better understanding of the following analysis, some linkages of the Vygotskian definition of culture with the earlier theoretical background might be useful. Culture is understood here as a distinguishable element of an individual-culture "organic whole." Culture has a qualitatively specific role in this whole. This role can be understood by an analysis of the properties of that element. The relationship between the elements, culture and individual, can be conceptualized as a "dialogue."

One additional definition is necessary here. The qualitatively specific role of culture is relational; it has meaning with respect to an individual. Thus, a definition of what "individual" means should be also given. In the context of the theoretical line of thinking developed in this chapter, individual should be understood in psychological terms as an individual mind or personality. Personality can be defined here as proposed by Allport (1937): "Personality is the dynamic organization within the individual of those psychophysical systems that determine his unique adjustments to his environment" (p. 48).

Thus, personality—an individual mind—is a unique system of elements that are both mental and neural, constrained by laws of the nervous system and, in addition, by laws characterizing psyche. Personality is active and dynamic; personality is constantly evolving and changing. Personality, as understood here, does not "determine adjustment" unidirectionally. Rather, determination in this context means a quality of an individual which constrains how and why an individual acts (in a broad sense, both behaviorally and intrapsychologically) in a specific environment. One very important quality of that kind of constraint can be found in another definition of personality that should be understood as complementary rather than replacing the first one: "personality in the individual is the capacity for society, fellowship, communion" (Richmond, 1900, p. 21).

This definition places an individual and culture into a unified whole in exactly the sense advocated in this chapter:

We shall not be exaggerating the intimacy of union between the individual and the collective mind if we note, as an instance of it, the dependence of the individual mind on what is, in fact, the content of language. Language is the creation, the expression of the collective intelligence. It is not merely the means of communication between mind and mind; it is the storehouse of common ideas, the record of the collective perception and experience of the society among which it circulates. Language is in the intellectual region . . . a hard fact, an undeniable result of the collective action of individual minds; evidence, accordingly, of the intellectual communion of individual persons with another. (Richmond, 1900, p. 27)

Now we can go further and define more exactly what is meant by "dialogue" in this context. Dialogue is not simply some back-and-forth sharing of meanings. Rather, dialogue is the process of emergence of new meanings in the synthesis of its participants into a hierarchically higher-level form. Every participant brings into the process of a dialogue something qualitatively different. The result of interaction is the emergence of a novel synthesis where both/all of the participants have changed their properties. Some confusion may arise when we imagine a dialogue between two persons—they have a conversation and then lose their contact. It may seem that a synthesis is broken into elements again. But this is true only from a superficial perspective. First of all, in such a conversation the relationship between elements is psychological, it emerges in the minds of the participants. When in an individual-culture dialogue an individual loses the physical contact with culture, the already emerged whole will not disappear. Rather, it remains in the memory of an individual.

To understand precisely the processes involved in a dialogue of two persons, for example, the individual mental processes must be analyzed too. At one level dialogue can be analyzed with regard to its participants and their specific relationship. It is important that each participant is a system as well. Systems can be divided into their elements, each of which has a qualitatively different role in the organic whole. Memory is one element of a system of personality. Its role is preservation—it guarantees temporal stability of a person. This does not mean, however, that personality is just a "container" of products of a dialogue. Personality is a system, and memory is just one of its components. What is preserved in memory depends on the input and how this input is processed by other elements of personality—perception, emotions, and thinking, that is, in terms of Vygotsky (1926), by the "internal organization of experience" in the first place (organization—*organizacija*—should be understood here as a verb, not as a noun [A. T.]. A person is psychologically active in a dialogue; the "content" of a dialogue is reorganized in the process of internalization in a unique—personal—way. This uniqueness is uniqueness of personalities involved in a dialogue. For this reason the same dialogue may have very different consequences for each of its participants.

Understanding of "dialogue" in the sense I proposed is an elaboration of Vygotsky's understanding that individual and culture are related through social cooperation:

every higher psychological function in the process of child development appears twice, first as a function of collective behavior, as an organization of a child with an environment, and after as an individual function of behavior, as an ability for action of a psychological process in strict and exact sense of that word. (Vygotsky, 1983, p. 124)

Vygotsky did not have time to accomplish the analysis of the individual–environment system from an individual perspective and to ask what exactly characterizes individuals who are capable of a social-cultural dialogue, and what specific qualities of an individual enter the dialogue and how. These questions are also beyond the scope of this chapter. But for future studies questions of how memory, thinking, perception, emotions, attention, or whatever individual characteristics of personality act in the process of a dialogue should become central in studies of dialogues. Without understanding the individual mind—personality with all its characteristics—the processes underlying a dialogue can only be superficially described rather than explained.

The definition of culture as a semiosphere does not imply a unidirectional view on the explanation of relationships between human mind and culture. Symbols, which are not used by individuals, do not have any meaning; they do not "code information." Such symbols are just material objects; they refer to nothing. Thus, symbols exist only when used by individuals. On the other hand, no single individual would be able to develop symbols, as defined above, because the emergence of qualitatively novel aspects of the human mind and culture is related to the requirement that symbol meaning must be socially shared. This brings us to the first quality of human mind–culture dialogue that can be explained with the help of the proposed definition of culture.

How Novelty Is Generated in Culture

One important aspect of culture–individual dialogue is the emergence of novelty. Van der Veer (1996; see also Martí, 1996) suggested that a semiotic notion of culture is limited because it does not explain the innovation of culture by individuals. This question will be discussed together with the problem of *reductionism*. Namely, culture should not be reduced to the level of psychological explanation (Berry et al., 1992). The problem of the generation of novelty and the threat of reductionism are closely tied because, according to the present view, only individuals introduce novelty into culture. Nevertheless, it does not follow that culture is intra-individual.

Internalization-Externalization as a Mechanism for the Generation of Novelty

Evolutionary or systems views on explanation assume that novelty emerges only by synthesis of some elements. This view is developed further in the Tartu-Moscow school of semiotics which explains how novel information can emerge. Theoretically, in order to construct qualitatively new knowledge the information must be processed by at least two different information-processing mechanisms. Novel information will be created in the interaction of the mechanisms, in the "translation"—"dialogue" in my terms—of the information from one system to another (Lotman, 1992a, 1992b, 1993; Lotman & Uspenskii, 1993).

A clear example of qualitatively novel knowledge is the knowledge about the world beyond our senses. There are two ways to acquire knowledge (see also Harré, 1972). One is to use our senses. Humans share with many animals the ability to learn from direct observation. In addition, humans have created many tools for improving and extending our senses (e.g., microscope, telescope). Qualitatively different kinds of scientific instruments are created for detecting phenomena, which we cannot observe because we lack the necessary senses. Examples of such instruments are a compass, an ammeter, but perhaps in the first place, theories. Take the theory of a solar system: no one has ever seen what a solar system "looks like." Nevertheless, the theory makes it "visible" to us.

I have proposed (Toomela, 1996a) that information about the world beyond our senses is created in the process of *internalization*, that is, in the interaction of the two mechanisms of information processing, semiotic and sensory. In general, the process can be described as follows: Changes in the environment are registered with sense organs; in parallel, the same information is "translated" into symbols. Laws of symbol utilization allow them to be combined in ways not possible with the referents of the symbols. After recombination, the novel combinations of meanings are "translated" back into sensory representations. In this way the same sensory representations acquire meanings they would never have if not supported by semiotic transformations.

To take a concrete example, it can be suggested that to understand the meaning of an ammeter, it must be seen. But this is not sufficient. A person can observe the ammeter for years and still not understand it. In order to understand what an ammeter does, information about what we see is "translated" into (usually) verbal form: dial, pointer, and other important parts of the ammeter are referred to. Then the meaning of the parts and relationships between the parts has to be explained. This explanation is the main tool of scientific knowledge, a theory (of electricity, in this case). Finally, with this theory in mind sensory information about the ammeter acquires a new meaning. Without verbal explanation, a movement of a pointer is just a movement of a little black stick on a white background. After the explanation the movement of a pointer is an indicator of electric current. Thus, verbal explanation gives novel meanings to the same sensory phenomena.

Lotman's theory suggests that novel information is generated in the interaction of different mechanisms of information processing. Thus, it is important to understand why and how the symbolic mechanism is different from the sensory one (the other possibility is that language is just a description of changes in a sensory world). Senses react to changes in the environment. But senses are limited spatially, temporally, and qualitatively. We see only what is here and now, and only what can be seen.

Language frees humans from the limitations of senses. The process of liberation of language takes place in its social utilization. First, in conversation words can be used in the absence of their referents. Referents are not necessary for the utilization of words, whereas for the action of senses they are. Thus, language is not spatially limited. Language is also not limited temporally: Words may refer not only to the present but also to the past and future. Senses do not react to events that will take place next year; words, however, may refer to such events. Finally, words are not constrained in a qualitative way. Words relate to their referents arbitrarily, and this relationship is conventional (i.e., social). There is no inherent relationship between the phonetic form of a word and its referent. This quality of word-meaning relationship allows us to give new meanings to phenomena that are identical to the senses. For example, a voltmeter and an ammeter may look identical. Differentiation of such externally identical objects is possible with the help of words. Words may also refer to analogies. Analogy is the basic mechanism of creating knowledge about a world (Harré, 1972). When we study a phenomenon whose underlying mechanisms are unknown, we must imagine them. Such imaginations must be plausible, reasonable, and possible. To achieve this, an analogy is created. It is assumed that the phenomenon under study is similar to some other phenomenon about which we know a good deal. It is important to note that this method of analogies cannot be based on direct sensory information when a world inaccessible to the senses is studied—senses do not inform a person that there is a world beyond them.

Thus, novelty emerges when sensory information is semiotically processed. This process is individual because sensory experiences are personal. We do not see what the other person sees, we do not feel what the other person feels because our senses do not react to changes in the eyes and skin of the other person (of course, we can *know* what the other person sees or feels, but this knowledge is achieved by analogy, not by sensation).

In the beginning of cultural evolution an individual processing is necessary but not sufficient for introducing novelty into a culture—it is not yet socially shared. For becoming a part of culture, the individually created novelty must be externalized (i.e., internalized by others). Why? Because in individual use there is no force to make symbol–referent relations arbitrary and qualitatively unconstrained. The sensory world does not indicate that the relationship is arbitrary. For example, if one person calls a stone *a stone* and the other *kivi* ("a stone" in Estonian), the visual appearance of a stone as well as any other of its sensory qualities does not indicate to the persons that the relationship between the word they use and a stone could be different. In conversation, however, this possibility is immediately evident. Thus, social utilization of symbols is the mechanism that liberates words qualitatively from their referents.

The situation is different in a developed culture. Here it is not necessary to make a symbol socially shared because arbitrariness can be created by "cultural" persons themselves. A cultural person may have a dialogue with oneself. This is possible when the semiotic world has differentiated from the sensory-based organization of mind, and has become internalized. The differentiation of a semiotic mechanism is possible in social relationships where symbols are used more and more independently from their "external" (i.e., sensory-based) referents. In the process of internalization the two mechanisms first differentiate and then enter into a higher-level synthesis of a personal, semiotically mediated mind (Toomela, 1996a). Every novel experience of a person, sensory-based or semiotic, changes the sensory or semiotic element of a mediated mind. By definition, the change of an element leads to the change of the system. With the change of the system, all of its elements change. Thus, the new symbol meanings can emerge in individual minds without any social relationship when a person already has developed a mediated mind. It does not mean that social relations are not necessary for that kind of semiosis. Social relationships are absolutely necessary for the emergence of a mediated mind. But they are not necessary for the maintenance of this mind. The role of social relationships in the latter case is "historical," as a fact of development or emergence.

Stability and Change in Culture at the Level of Society

There is a cultural phenomenon that can be understood better in the theoretical context just outlined. Cultures are in some sense quite rigid in inclusion of novel information (e.g., Lotman, 1992a, 1992b, 1993; Lotman & Uspenskii, 1993). One reason for such rigidity is the social nature of symbols. Symbols are used for communication, for being understood by others. When individual novel connections emerge between a symbol and a (sensory-based) referent, then the meaning of that symbol also changes. And when such a symbol is used socially, it must be explained to others what new meanings are connected with the "old" symbol and why such change is introduced.

The reason why all externalized meanings cannot easily enter into culture does not lie so much in the fact that some time is necessary for others to understand why a new meaning instead of the old one should be connected with some symbol, or system of symbols (a scientific theory, for example). Rather, the problem lies in the complexity of the reorganization of meaning-systems. For example, when Charles Darwin created his theory of evolution and, among many other ideas, proposed that the relations of monkeys and humans should be understood in a novel way, the idea was accepted with great difficulties. In North America, and perhaps many other places in the world, there still are many who believe that the theory of evolution is wrong. It was not only the question of creating new conceptual relations in understanding the biological world. In addition, many other conceptual relations whose existence was not denied before, like statements of the Bible, were seriously challenged. Thus, it was not only necessary to demonstrate why and how monkeys and humans are "relatives," but also to demonstrate that the Bible was wrong, and common sense was wrong, and so on and so forth. Such complex reorganization of a conceptual system needs a lot of new knowledge, the ability to think, memorize, the willingness to accept the idea as possibly correct, and many other individual characteristics. Many persons do not have those capacities, due to either cognitive limitations, or irrational beliefs, or some other properties. Many others believe in authorities—the reason for that may be very rational. Modern science, for example, is so complex that it is probably impossible to become an expert in all specific fields of science. If an expert, or a few experts, are not able to accept the new idea, and the others do not have time and motives for rationally analyzing pros and cons by themselves, even a brilliant idea may be rejected. It took thousands of years, for example, to come to an agreement that the mind is a function of the brain but not of the heart, kidneys, or some other parts of the body. Maybe there are some who still do not believe it. Maybe there are some—who knows— who do not believe it any more for some very good reasons we would not be able to accept.

Thus, socialization of symbols, which liberates them from limitations of the senses, is balanced. On the one hand, socialization allows the creation of novelty. On the other hand, it does not allow every created novelty to enter into culture.

Culture Is Not Just a Play with Language

The preceding discussion revealed that symbolic information processing is based on laws different from sensory information processing. If the combinational laws of a language are sufficiently complex, every combination of symbols becomes possible. Such a flexibility of symbolic operations has led many (postmodern, in most cases) scholars to claim that language has a meaning only in itself, that it is language that *constitutes* our reality. Postmodernists disagree with a view that propositions about the world are driven or required by the particular characteristics of the world (e.g., K. Gergen, 1992, 1994; M. Gergen, 1992; Kvale, 1992a, 1992b; Løvlie, 1992; but see Polkinghorne, 1992; Shotter, 1992, for less radical views). In support of this declaration they draw attention to the idea that it is not possible to know whether a proposition about the world reflects truth or not.

Indeed, we are never able to know whether our propositions about the world are true or not. After all, there is no way to convince a person who believes that there is only her or him, and everything "outside her or him" (including postmodernists!) is just a product of her or his imagination, and that she or he is "wrong." Thus, meanings coded in symbols do not necessarily reflect reality. However, there is an illogical leap in postmodern thinking with regard to the claim that none of the propositions about the world reflect reality. Clearly, there are meanings that are not introduced by "objective reality." Fashion is one example (Lotman & Uspenskii, 1993). However, according to an evolutionary view, language would never have evolved if meanings of symbols were unrelated to the external world. According to an evolutionary perspective, everything emerges from something. Language is primarily a tool for social communication. In the beginning of language development the referents of symbols must be available to sensory perception so that it is possible to share attention on the same objects and phenomena outside those involved in the communicative act. Only later, when language is "acquired," it is possible to use language without shared attention in a sensory field. If I have only one word, *kivi*, and someone else only the word *stone*, we both must see the same stone at the same time to understand that we refer to the same thing.

Thus, language is essentially tied to the sensory world. And this is the boundary where language is connected to objective reality. Culture in general and science in particular can build plausible hypotheses about the world outside a reach of senses. And science has demonstrated that not all hypotheses are equally plausible, because scientific hypotheses must correspond to the relations in a sensory reality. In fact, all scientific ideas are in some ways tied to the sensory world. In physics and chemistry the main (shared) focus of the scientific community is on reading of measuring apparatuses—which must be available to senses. In psychology the focus is mainly on observable behaviors. And every scientific theory will be accepted in a society only when reading of apparatuses or descriptions of behaviors are logically related to theory. In addition, theories usually make predictions. If the predictions turn out to be wrong, the theory will be rejected. Thus, language does not have meaning only in itself; the reality created in language is not entirely arbitrary and/or personal, equal to the "truth" of anybody else (see also Chaiklin, 1992; Lotman & Uspenskii, 1993; Shotter, 1992, for the analysis of postmodern ideas).

In sum, according to the present view, culture is a system of signs, (i.e., a semiosphere). Similar views on culture can be found in a "postmodern discourse" (e.g., Løvlie, 1992). However, differently from many postmodernists, it is assumed here that meanings in culture are determined by both purely semiotic processes and by "indignant influences of material conditions of existence on a system of ideal imaginations of humans" (Lotman & Uspenskii, 1993, pp. 339–340).

HUMANS AND OTHER ANIMALS—IS THERE A QUALITATIVE DIFFERENCE IN MINDS?

Leading cultural psychologist Michael Cole insists, in his recent book, that culture should be kept in mind by psychologists (Cole, 1996). The main reason to do so seems to be the idea that culture is a fundamental constituent of human thought and action. Cole declares that his background is tightly related to Vygotskian thinking. Despite this claim, Cole explicitly denies the existence of any kind of qualitative hierarchy in the evolution of the human mind. This stance, however, is incompatible with Vygotsky's thinking in particular, and with evolutionary thinking in general. One basic characteristic of systems (or "organic wholes") is hierarchy: "Systems are frequently structured in a way so that their individual members again are systems of the next lower level" (von Bertalanffy, 1968, p. 74).

According to Vygotsky, hierarchy in mental evolution can be found at two levels. First, the human mind is at a qualitatively higher level than the mind of other animals. Second, hierarchically different levels of mental evolution can be found in different cultures. Some cultures are more developed than others. In almost all cases when the existence of hierarchy in mental genesis is denied, the notion of hierarchy is value-laden. This is not surprising because North American science has been pragmatic, concerned with practical consequences or values since its beginning. The editor of the first issue of the journal *Science*, for example, wrote (King, 1883):

The leading feature of American science, however, and that which most distinctively characterizes it, is its utilitarianism. True, there are in our country able investigators working in scientific fields which do not offer the promise of material reward; but notwithstanding this, it remains still true that those sciences whose principles are capable of useful application are the most zealously cultivated among us, and attract the largest number of students. (p. 1)

Thus, every discovery, every new bit of knowledge found by a scientist is or should be useful, should promise a material reward, should make life "better." This view, when imported into the realm of development or evolution, leads by analogy to the assumption that every new level of development should be "better" than the earlier one. If it is not, there is no development. This and many other limitations of pragmatism are thoroughly analyzed by James Mark Baldwin (1904). In evolutionary understanding, however, the notion of hierarchy is related to value only secondarily, if at all.

Characteristics of Hierarchy in Evolutionary Thinking

For evolutionary thinking, hierarchy is a characteristic of special structural change. In this kind of change differentiated systems become united in the hierarchically higher-level synthesis. This principle is known as *orthogenetic principle*:

it is an orthogenetic principle which states that wherever development occurs it proceeds from a state of relative globality and lack of differentiation to a state of increasing differentiation, articulation, *and hierarchic integration*. (Werner, 1978, pp. 108–109; emphasis added)

Thus, a system is organized hierarchically when it is composed of elements that are systems by themselves. The question of how to recognize when a system is hierarchical and when it is not is very important. Several characteristics can be differentiated. First, different levels of hierarchy differ qualitatively. At the higher level characteristics can be found that are absent at the next lower level. Second, the hierarchically higher-level systems "show a form of synthesis that is not accounted for by the formulations which are adequate for the phenomena at the next lower level" (Baldwin, 1906, p. 20). At the same time, "the formulations of any lower science [can be replaced by "system" in this context (A. T.) are not invalidated in the next higher, even in cases in which new formulations are necessary for the formal synthesis which characterizes the genetic mode of the higher" (Baldwin, 1906, p. 20). Similarly, in hierarchical synthesis the lower level does not disappear. It is not replaced by a higher-level. Rather, a higher-level synthesis is constrained in addition to the rules of the lower level with the rules that are specific to the higher level.

Superficially, there is a contradiction between the principles just described and the principle that elements, when united into a higher-level whole, change their properties. How can one level of organization remain unchanged when the emergence of the genetically next level of organization must be related to change in the properties of elements? Here it is important that different aspects of a system are described by different principles. There are laws that characterize functioning and existence of a level of a system. All these laws must remain among the laws that characterize the next hierarchically higher level of genesis. These laws, however, characterize the lower level of organization in general, not every particular aspect of it. The properties of elements change in particular aspects. For example, all biological organisms are physical bodies, which must exist in the limits determined by the laws of physical functioning. For the emergence of life, qualitatively new restrictions on the bodies must operate which make physical bodies in addition biological. On the other hand, when we study properties of elements which constitute a living organism, we cannot understand what life is or how it became possible. For the understanding of the latter these elements should be studied in the specific relationships they have in that organism. With the emergence of such relationships, the properties of elements change. Pure carbon in nature would be more or less hard (it depends whether it is in the form of graphite or of a diamond). Biological organisms in the architecture of which carbon is an important constituent may be very soft. We could cut a glass with a diamond but we cannot do it with our hands. I give another, psychological example. Symbols must be simultaneously physical and meaningful. When an object becomes a symbol it still remains an object. But its properties have changed. Take for example the meaning of Mount Fuji in Japanese culture. There was (and still is) a belief that the mountain is sacred and a source of secret of immortality. Male pilgrims traveled from all over the country to climb its peaks whereas women were prohibited from doing so (Guth, 1996). The mountain remains physically the same, whether considered to be sacred or not. But, in the latter case, the properties of the mountain have changed in the culture of Japan. The mountain cannot be climbed by women—the reason why, of course, is psychological, not physical.

These principles mentioned above can be used to look for hierarchy in mental genesis. Two requirements must be simultaneously met for demonstrating the presence of hierarchy in mental processes. First, we must find a mental operation (solving of a problem, memorizing, feeling, paying attention, etc.) which is organized in at least two qualitatively different ways. Let us call these organizations A and B. A and B are at hierarchically different levels when they are distributed asymmetrically in different persons or in different cultures. We must find individuals or cultures where only A is present, and we must find other individuals or cultures where A and B both are present. There should not be a single individual or culture where only B is present. In this case, A characterizes the lower level and B the higher level. To be entirely sure, the third requirement must also be met. It should be demonstrated in genetic (i.e., developmental) analysis that indeed the A type of organization is the prerequisite of the B type of organization. Unfortunately, empirical studies of the latter kind are nearly absent from modern psychology because the idea of hierarchy is rejected *a priori*. In the following discussion, evidence only for the first two requirements can be found. Correspondingly, my conclusions are only tentative.

Qualitative Hierarchical Differences between Humans and Other Animals

For nineteenth-century psychologists it was relatively clear that only humans have culture, and that humans are qualitatively at a higher level of development than other animals. Recent thinking in psychology more and more tends to universally agree that there are no qualitative differences between them (e.g., Cole, 1996). Indeed, there is increasing evidence that non-human animals use tools, are able to communicate symbolically, transmit information from generation to generation non-biologically, teach each other (see McGrew, 1998; Whiten et al., 1999, for reviews). Correspondingly, the authors attribute culture not only to humans but to other animals as well.

It is noteworthy, however, that the definition of culture in such analyses differs from the one used here. Whiten et al. (1999) have been explicit in this respect:

Culture is defined in very different ways in different academic disciplines. At one extreme, some cultural anthropologists insist on linguistic mediation, so that culture is constrained to be a uniquely human phenomenon. In the biological sciences, a more inclusive definition is accepted, . . . From this perspective, a cultural behavior is one that is transmitted repeatedly through social or observational learning to become a population-level characteristic. By this definition, cultural differences (often known as "traditions" in ethology) are well-established phenomena in the animal kingdom. (p. 682)

What is the purpose of changing a definition of culture in a way that "tradition" is made identical to "culture"? Of course, it is easier to "sell" a scientific product when something unusual is said. Many readers of *Nature* have thought that only humans have culture. And it is very intriguing to read that it is not so. But do we understand the psyche better now, after collapsing two notions, tradition and culture, into one category? My answer is no. A broad look at culture does not allow us to understand how novel knowledge, especially knowledge about a world beyond our senses, is created. A Vygotskian narrow look, however, gives us such an opportunity.

According to Vygotsky's theory (e.g., Vygotsky & Luria, 1930), the basic qualitative difference between humans and other animals is the capability of semiotically mediated thought in the former. According to him, animal and human minds are at hierarchically different levels of development. Mental processes of non-human animals work only on sensory-based mechanisms. The same mechanisms are available for humans. But for humans, in addition, it is possible to develop semiotically mediated mental operations where sensory and non-sensory (i.e., symbolic) information processing forms a higher-level synthetic whole, called *Higher Psychological Functions* by Vygotsky.

It might be important to remember here that utilization of signs is necessary but not sufficient for the emergence of semiotically mediated thought. Use of signs may be based on only sensory mechanisms as well. Simple connections between a sign and its referent, for example, may take place through sensory information processing. Similarly, in complex semiotic systems it is also possible to refer with signs to other signs. The differentiating feature is *how* signs are used. It is not sufficient to use signs for communication. The hierarchically new level of thought, where sensory operations and semiotic operations (which are differentiated from sensory operations) are united into a qualitatively new level of mental organization, differentiates humans from other animals.

We can analyze these ideas in terms of evolutionary thinking. Is there evidence for hierarchy or not? First, two kinds of mental organization are differentiated: sensory-based and semiotically mediated. This is necessary but not sufficient for hierarchy to be found. We must go further.

Is there any evidence that animals are capable of semiotically mediated thought? For example, are animals able to represent the world qualitatively beyond their senses? No. Is there any evidence that verbal-symbolic information processing exists without sensory thinking? No, again. The latter is not possible by definition, because one necessary characteristic of a symbol is that it must be an object, behavioral act, or phenomenon that can be directly perceived through sense organs. Otherwise it would be impossible to use symbols for communication. Thus, we can conclude that the human mind is at the hierarchically higher level of development.

There is no absolute restriction for other animals to become "cultural" in Vygotsky's sense. With a sufficiently developed brain it should be possible in principle. And biological evolution did not end with differentiation of humans from other animals. It is only an empirical question whether other animals are capable of semiotically mediated thought or not. Primate studies have demonstrated that apes have mental capacities many earlier scientists were not aware of. All these capacities can be explained by sensory mechanisms. There may be capacities not discovered as yet. So, in principle, some other animals may become "cultural." But here the question is not so much whether all other animals are not cultural or some—raised by humans, for example—are. Rather, the question is whether there is evidence for hierarchy in mental evolution from non-mediated to mediated thought. The evidence we have suggests that there is.

This case is a good example of characteristics of hierarchy as discussed above. James Mark Baldwin (see above) proposed that lower-level formulations characterize both lower and higher levels of organization whereas higher level is, in addition, constrained by laws and formulations which do not characterize the lower level. Symbols are perceived objects. Thus, all laws of sensory analysis apply to symbols as well. But symbols have additional characteristics—they refer to something and their meaning is socially shared. These characteristics are specific to symbols; only some of sensory objects have those.

In sum, I argued that the concept of culture should be related only to the semiosphere because in this way it is possible to understand specifically human mental operations. The broader look to culture, favored by, for example, Cole (1996), van der Veer (1996), and Martí (1996), among other cultural psychologists, loses the qualitative difference between humans and animals. Culture is not just a non-biological way of passing information over to next generations. Culture is a collective memory for information that cannot be based on sensory perception alone. Culture is also not a passive "bag" for information. Culture is a necessary environment for the development of individuals with the ability for semiotically mediated thought which, when externalized, may (but not

necessarily does—in that sense culture is an open-ended system) introduce changes to the superindividual sphere of socially shared meanings—to culture.

TRADITIONAL AND NON-TRADITIONAL CULTURES: HIERARCHICAL OR NOT HIERARCHICAL

The problem of hierarchy in the evolution of culture seems to be
solved in the social and behavioral sciences. Almost all of the scholars
agree that cultures are qualitatively different, but at the same level of
development (e.g., Berry et al., 1992; Cole, 1996; Tulviste, 1988; van der
Veer, 1996). The differentiation of the levels of cultural evolution is
claimed to stem from personal, untheoretical, and scientifically unjusti-
fied preferences. Usually it is "our" culture that is "better" than the
other—consequently "lower," "worse"—culture. So, there is no hierarchy in the evolution of culture because the differentiation of levels is
value-laden.

There are many examples of how values are attributed by a society to
a theory where no such values are proposed (cf. Chaiklin, 1992). An
evolutionary approach to psychology does not search for "better" or
"worse" levels of mental evolution. Rather, a structural, genetic hierarchy
is proposed. One hierarchical change may characterize differences between humans and other animals. A different kind of hierarchy, I propose, characterizes evolution of culture.

Hierarchy in the Development of Culture

A non-hierarchical view of culture ignores the possibility that hierarchy in some dimension does not imply hierarchy in every dimension.
When Vygotskian theory "capitalizes on abstract, de-contextualized
thinking and regards other ways of thinking as lower or less developed"
(van der Veer, 1996, p. 260) then it does not follow that the theory is
necessarily wrong. Vygotsky himself has been very clear in defining in
what dimension cultures can be viewed as hierarchical: A "primitive"
man uses symbols differently from a "cultural" man (Vygotsky & Luria,
1930). Vygotsky proposed that a word meaning develops. That development proceeds over several stages—*syncretic* concepts, *complexes*, *scientific* concepts (e.g., Vygotsky, 1996). According to his theory, all
semiotically mediated mental processes are constrained by the structure
of word meaning. So, all cultural (i.e., semiotically mediated) processes
can also be described as developing over the same stages.

According to Vygotsky, language and corresponding mediated
thought in "primitive" or "traditional" cultures is characterized by think-

ing in *complexes* whereas for a "cultural man" in addition to that, thinking in *scientific concepts* is available. Language of a "primitive man" can be described as follows (Vygotsky & Luria, 1930, present author's translation): "words of a primitive man have not differentiated from things, they still are tightly connected to the immediate sensory experience (*tshustvennym vpetchatlenijem*)" (p. 90), "language is understood and used exclusively as a direct reflection of reality (*deistvitel'nosti*)" (p. 91).

Thinking of a primitive man can be characterized congruently with language (Vygotsky & Luria, 1930, present author's translation):

Thinking, using (*pol'zujuschieesja*) this ["primitive"—A.T.] language, similarly with that language, is down to the ground concrete, pictorial and figurative, similar with it, full of details, and similarly operates with directly recollected (*vosproizvedjonnymi*) situations, points of view extracted from reality (*polozhenijami, vyhvachennymi is deistvitel'nosti*). (p. 96)

Thinking of a "cultural man," in contrast, is abstract, hierarchical, its structure is formally logical, it does not depend on the immediate reflection of reality. That kind of thinking can be called thinking with scientific concepts. It should be recalled here that "scientific" concepts are concepts with hierarchical and logical structure; they are not necessarily created in science only. According to the evolutionary view, if thinking with complexes and thinking with scientific concepts characterize hierarchically lower and higher levels of cultural evolution, respectively, we should expect to find cultures with only complex thinking and cultures with complex and scientific thinking. No cultures with only scientific thinking should exist.

There is, in fact, ample empirical evidence that this is the case. Curiously, all findings of Cole's (see Cole, 1996, for a review) cross-cultural research, for example, are in accordance with the idea that cultures can be at hierarchically higher and lower levels. Take, for example, problem solving in different cultures. It has been discovered that persons from different cultures solve logical syllogisms differently. Persons from very different cultures can solve syllogisms within the domain of everyday knowledge (like farming or fishing). However, syllogisms beyond such knowledge are hardly solved by non-literate persons (Cole, 1996; Cole & Scribner, 1974; Luria, 1974; Tulviste, 1988).

One possibility is that procedures for revealing the ability to solve syllogisms are culturally biased. When researchers have varied the contents and procedures of the particular tasks they use, it has often been found that presumably absent or underdeveloped skills reveal themselves. Often it is suggested that the ability to solve logical syllogisms is related to schooling (Cole, 1995, 1996; Tulviste, 1988). As schooling is a specific system of activity not utilized in some cultures, it would be in-correct to expect that the results of schooling, the ability to solve syllo-gisms in this case, should be attainable to all persons without such specific experiences:

> The general difficulty in relying on the results derived from experimental para-digms routinely used by psychologists for industrialized countries is that insofar as the learning and problem-solving tasks used to access cognitive processing derive from the structure and content of schooling, they are really mute with respect to cognitive processes in systems of activity organized for different pur-poses. The historical linkages between the structure of psychological tests and experimental procedures, one the one hand, and schooling, on the other, makes it logically indefensible to use such tasks as the basis of general comparisons on the relationships between different life histories and different patterns of intel-lectual development. (Cole, 1995, p. 29)

So, it is suggested that the only difference between cultures is related to specific aspects of it—to the content, but not to universal, hierarchical characteristics. As was discussed above, I propose that if we search for different levels in the evolution of a system we should expect that all types of processes possible at the developmentally lower level are pos-sible at the higher level but not vice versa. The available evidence sup-ports the idea that it is possible to differentiate two hierarchical levels, or "stages," in the development of syllogistic reasoning.

First, as we already mentioned, studies have revealed that non-literate persons are able to solve only syllogisms that are connected with their everyday activities. However, literate persons are *in addition* able to solve syllogisms outside their specific knowledge base about everyday activi-ties. Thus, there is a situation where persons from one culture are able to perform tasks attainable to persons from the other culture and in ad-dition tasks that are attainable only to persons from their own culture. Nevertheless, it is not sufficient for proposing that such observations are related to different stages of the evolution of syllogistic reasoning. Per-haps the additional ability is just more of the same kind of psychic pro-cesses. Thus, it is necessary to demonstrate that the additional ability has qualitatively different constraints on the processes within a structure—the mental structure of syllogistic reasoning.

The second line of analysis suggests that it is possible to differentiate two qualitatively different kinds of constraints on syllogistic reasoning, *content-dependent* and *content-independent*. Indeed, it can be suggested that the only constraint to syllogistic reasoning of literate persons is linguistic. The only knowledge necessary for such "advanced" syllogistic reasoning is the knowledge about a structure of language. It is possible to construct syllogisms that are not connected to specific knowledge at all! For ex-ample:

All corulany popits have crisses.

Crumps is a corulany popit.

Crumps has crisses.

Thus, even though for solving such syllogisms knowledge is necessary, and this knowledge is of a specific kind: it is metalinguistic knowledge. For some reasons, plausibly related to schooling, this knowledge is not attainable to persons from some cultures. But why? There is no reason to think that these persons do not use language. Correspondingly, language utilization is their everyday activity. Thus, the difference lies not in "what" is this everyday activity (language utilization) but "how" this activity is performed.

Several scholars have suggested that persons from "traditional" cultures rely on different mental operations than persons from industrialized cultures. Lévi-Strauss (1966), for example, suggested that persons from different cultures approach the physical world from "opposite ends"—one is supremely concrete and the other is supremely abstract. According to him, these kinds of thoughts seem to be mutually exclusive—they "have led to two distinct though equally positive sciences" (p. 269). Thus, according to this view there are two qualitatively different kinds of thought at the same "level" or "stage" of the evolution. Similar ideas have been expressed by Tulviste (1988). However, the latter also mentions that the formal or content-independent way for solving syllogisms cannot replace content-dependent ways of thinking. Both ways either co-exist or there is only one way for solving syllogisms—"empirical" (i.e., content-dependent).

Now the question emerges whether formal syllogistic reasoning can be understood as structurally (this concept is not value-laden!) more developed, at the higher stage of development. Indeed, it is the case—in content-dependent syllogistic reasoning—language is used as a tool for describing reality outside language. However, content-independent syllogistic reasoning utilizes knowledge about language itself. In other words, in the latter case there is a hierarchically higher level of language utilization—language about a world is in addition described with a language about a language. And, evolutionarily, it seems to be impossible that language about language develops either in parallel or, even less plausibly, before the language about a world.

Space limitations do not permit analysis of other examples in such detail. There are several examples of how tasks, which can be solved by "Western" people, should be modified before people from a "traditional" culture can solve them. In general, it can be said that in all such cases the modification induced an element of immediate sensory experience.

When such modifications are not possible, the performance remains poor. I will briefly discuss some relevant examples from Cole's (1996) cross-cultural research.

First, in free recall of words "traditional" people do not cluster words, and their performance does not improve significantly with repetition. Then instead of asking people to recall the items, they were asked to recall the physical locations (line of four chairs) where different categories of items were placed. If items were placed on the chairs according to their category membership, people learned rapidly and clustered their recall. So, the task in a linguistic context was performed poorly whereas the task with direct sensory support was performed much better. The pattern of findings fits exactly with a Vygotskian prediction.

Second, Cole was also successful in improving recall when instead of a list of words, information was organized as a narrative. Narratives were organized so that they were directly related to everyday experiences of participants. Lists of categorically related words were put into a context of life. Again, the manipulation of the task procedure introduced connections with a concrete world. This pattern of findings fits exactly with a Vygotskian prediction.

Third, in a classification study people were asked to sort eight cards depicting large and small, black and white, triangles and squares into two categories, and then asked to recognize them. This task was difficult. The difficulties persisted even when geometric figures were replaced with stylized drawings of men and women. This result is expectable, because the task had no concrete meaning. The finding fits exactly with a Vygotskian prediction.

Fourth, in a task where it was required to recall leaves, the performance was very good when people were asked to classify them into everyday categories according to the trees the leaves belong to. When classification rules did not relate to the "usual" way of seeing leaves, the performance was poor. The pattern of findings fits exactly with a Vygotskian prediction.

It is noteworthy that the latter study was also conducted with American/Canadian students who performed similarly poorly in all conditions. This case is a good example for demonstrating that the evolutionary higher level of mental development does not guarantee "better" performance in all tasks. Without content-specific knowledge the abstract rules are not necessarily beneficial. This is not surprising because higher-level synthesis has to subordinate to the rules of a lower level.

Fifth, "traditional" people's ability to communicate with others about objects is poor in a formal, verbal context. Speakers routinely give listeners too little information. This result is expectable, again, because words of "primitives" should, indeed, be tightly related to things they refer to.

Several other examples can be found from cross-cultural studies. The conclusion that cultures can be hierarchically different can be reached in all such cases I have found in the literature.

Hierarchically Higher Levels in Culture: Are They "Good" or "Bad"?

Evolutionarily, higher or lower levels of genesis are not unambiguously related to value of a change. In some sense it is clearly "good" to be at the higher level of mental development. Basically, what changes in the mental evolution is the number of qualitatively different ways to approach a psychological task. Every higher level of development adds possibilities for how to solve the same problem. A syllogism at one level of development, for example, can be solved only when it is related to everyday knowledge. At the higher level, an abstract, formal-logical way is added to the "psychological tool-kit" of problem solving. This might be beneficial in creating new ways for solving the same everyday tasks. I give one speculative example. Initially, humans built ships from materials which were "light." Only recently have ships been built from iron. If we look into the history of the human mind we see that iron ships emerged after thinking in "scientific concepts" became part of culture. This relationship is probably lawful. Iron is heavy, all everyday knowledge tells us that ships cannot be built from iron. When we, however, start to think "theoretically," we can discover abstract rules which explain what properties a floating object must have. And we discover that ships can be made from iron.

In some other sense, it might be "bad" to be at the higher level of mental development. If a person's goal is to do something dangerous, like constructing a more and more powerful weapon, the ability to use different ways for solving that "problem" is, of course, "bad." Thinking with scientific concepts allows humans to build neutron bombs and chemical weapons. Thus, lower or higher, primitive or cultural have only genetic, developmental meaning. The pragmatic "value" of those levels is not inherently related to the structure of them. In a (neo) Vygotskian perspective the only conclusion that can be made in this context is that genetically less complex mental structures of language are also less flexible for describing and understanding the world outside, especially the world beyond our sensory capacities.

THE PROBLEM OF UNIVERSALITY VERSUS SPECIFICITY

One of the main controversies between different notions of culture concerns the universal-specific (or *etic-emic*) dimension. Whereas some researchers claim that culture would be better viewed as a universal characteristic of all humans, others suggest that culture should be understood as specific to certain populations. Cole (1996), for example, has been explicit in that respect: "(no universal notion of a single, general, psychological characteristic called 'level of thinking,' or some surrogate, is universally appropriate)" (p. 175). Similarly, Veroff and Goldberger (1995) claimed that if the meaning and significance of a behavior or trait depends on the complex system of meanings of the culture, then the goal of finding fundamental relationships that might hold across all situations is both questionable and probably unattainable.

However, there are other voices that disagree with such a conclusion. Kagitçibasi and Berry (1989; see also Berry, 1989; Berry et al., 1992; Moll, 1995, for a similar idea), for example, suggest that cross-cultural psychology can progress only through a dialectic of the emic and etic approaches.

An Evolutionary View to the Universal and Specific Characteristics of Systems

According to an evolutionary view, psyche can be understood as an "organic whole," or a system. It is important that similar systems can be built from different elements—it is possible, for example, to create a new language the syntax of which is identical with some already existing language, but whose vocabulary (i.e., elements of a language) is entirely different. On the other hand, it is possible to build different systems from the same set of elements—vocabulary of a language, for example, allows creating infinitely many different sentences or narratives. Even though the relationships between the elements of a system may be dynamically changing, the system as a whole can at the same time be described as constrained by firm boundaries—universalities in essence. This idea has been thoroughly analyzed in Gestalt psychology. Köhler (1947), for example, differentiated "dynamic" and "topographical" factors. Dynamic factors characterize the processes of the system and topographical factors the restricting conditions to the processes:

We assume that, in all systems with which we are concerned, processes are strictly determined by factors of *some* kind. . . . To the degree to which topographical conditions are rigidly given, and not to be changed by dynamic factors, their existence means exclusion of certain forms of function, and the restriction of processes to the possibilities compatible with those conditions. (p. 64)

Koffka (1928, 1935) made a similar distinction between what he called "processes" and "conditions," respectively. The types of processes realized in a system depend on the conditions, qualitative constraints on that system. Lewin (1935) suggested that systems *as a whole* move in the direction of a state of equilibrium determined either by its internal characteristics or by its (relatively) firm *boundaries* (or "walls").

I will give an example. It is possible to represent infinitely many different objects in visual memory. However, the system of visual representations as a whole has very rigid qualitative "boundaries" (i.e., "topographical" or "conditional" characteristics). Visual systems can represent only and exclusively visual information. Touch, smell, or taste cannot be represented in a visual system because sensory mechanisms of vision do not react to those qualities of an environment.

In sum, the evolutionary theory differentiates two characteristics of systems, dynamic and topographical/conditional. When a system is described as a whole, it would be possible to find characteristics that are universal to every particular possible state of that system. If, on the other hand, the content of the system is described, large if not infinite dynamic variations within the same constraints can be found. So, universal and specific characteristics of the system can be revealed at different levels of analysis.

The Notion of Universal and Specific in Culture

The definition of culture discussed here, in essence, the definition of *universal* characteristics inherent to all cultures, is that *culture is a semiotic world*; there is no culture without "symbols." Variations can be found in the concrete utilization of symbols, in the content of culture.

Take, for example, scientific knowledge in different cultures. Scientific knowledge is expressed in symbols, usually in words. In different cultures with different languages very different words and sentences are used for describing the same knowledge. In addition, cultures differ in content: some theories are popular in one culture and practically unknown in another. Psychoanalysis, for example, was and is familiar in the Anglo-American tradition. In the communist Soviet Union, however, the theory was forbidden and almost unknown. Thus, cultures differ in languages, which are used for expressing scientific ideas as well as in the content of scientific knowledge. These aspects are specific characteristics of cultures. At the same time, however, scientific knowledge is universally stored in language.

The idea that universal and specific aspects of culture are not mutually exclusive is implicit in the works of many scholars. Rosenberg (1994), for example, suggested that culture is not a completely open-ended system but contains an element of rigidity *if described as a whole*. It has also been suggested that it is impossible to understand human development without introducing the idea of universal characteristics of cultures (Kojima, 1995; Moll, 1995; Nicolopoulou & Weintraub, 1996). Triandis (1994) proposed that all humans have, for example, language, food habits, and art. Differences can be found within these categories but not in the existence of the categories as a whole (see also Berry et al., 1992).

The idea of universal boundaries on specific differences explains why and how a hierarchically higher level of mental evolution does not guarantee better performance in every task. Several findings of a cross-cultural research are in agreement with the idea that some cultures are more developed than others (see above). At the same time, there is evidence that people from a less developed, "traditional" culture may perform better than people from more developed cultures in some tasks (e.g., Cole, 1996). The reason why it is so is that "more developed" means general "boundaries" of mental operations, but not their specific content. In principle, all language of "primitives" is figurative and cannot be differentiated from objects the words refer to. People in more developed cultures are able to use language both figuratively and independently from sensory reality. Sometimes the latter kind of language—scientific concepts, in Vygotsky's terms—is called "decontextualized." This term is misleading because scientific concepts are not out of context. Rather, they are in specific, linguistic contexts. Thus, instead of "decontextualized" the term "desensorized," liberated from connections with sensory perception, should be used.

Such general boundaries do not determine the specific content that exactly is described by language. It is self-evident (at least for me) that problems of real life cannot be solved without specific knowledge about that life. We can imagine, for example, a desert culture where people never have seen rivers, lakes, or seas. However developed their thinking in terms of general boundaries would be, they would not be able to build ships without first studying where and for what a ship will be used. People from an island culture would be much better at building ships or boats even when their level of development is lower than the desert culture. The power of a genetically—developmentally—more complex culture could be revealed only in situations where the content of knowledge is basically the same. Only in that case the availability of different ways for solving a problem would be beneficial and "superior" to those who have only one way for organizing knowledge.

RELATIONSHIP OF SEMIOTIC AND NON-SEMIOTIC WORLDS

Culture viewed as a semiosphere restricts the notion of culture to only symbols, that is, objects which refer to something else and which can be used independently of their referents. Many others relate culture also to other artifacts. Van der Veer (1996, see also Martí, 1996) suggested that the Vygotskian view of culture is limited because it does not explain the transmission of presumably non-linguistically mediated aspects of culture. A broader view is also shared by Cole (1996), who suggested that all objects which are simultaneously conceptual and material are cultural. He does not differentiate between symbolic and non-symbolic "conceptual" aspects of objects. Correspondingly, knowledge about how to use an object, independently of whether it is symbolic (refers to something else) or not, makes material objects cultural "artifacts." According to the present view, the lack of differentiation between non-semiotic ("non-linguistic") and semiotic aspects of the human mind and environment hinders the understanding of specifically human psychological and cultural processes.

The treatment of non-symbolic aspects of a world as cultural seems to stem from the general idea that all information that is transmitted over generations non-biologically is cultural. As already discussed above, non-biological transmission of knowledge over generations is not specific to humans. Correspondingly, views on culture that do not differentiate symbolic and non-symbolic aspects of a world either ignore or deny the possibility that humans and other animals may be qualitatively different. This is not the only reason why differentiation of symbolic and non-symbolic conceptual aspects of objects is useful, perhaps necessary for understanding the human mind. The other reason is that symbolic and non-symbolic ways of using objects in general or tools in particular are probably related to different psychological mechanisms.

Before going further it should be noted that it is not easy to conceptualize the differences between semiotic and non-semiotic conceptual mechanisms of object-use. This is the case because the difference is introduced by mental mechanisms; external behavior does not always indicate which of the conceptual ways underlies the action with an object. The problem is as old as the science of psychology:

it is the bane of psychology to suppose that where results are similar, processes must be the same. Psychologists are too apt to reason as geometers would, if the latter were to say that the diameter of a circle is the same thing as its semi-circumference, because, forsooth, they terminate in the same two points. (James, 1890, p. 528)

A similar problem arises in this context: It is quite difficult to understand whether a particular aspect of the (human) world is related to symbolic mechanisms or not. The main problem lies in the fact that all objects and phenomena that are available to our sensory system may become a symbol (Toomela, 1996b). Thus, objects or phenomena by themselves cannot be informative with regard to their symbolic meaning. The symbolic nature of objects can be revealed only through understanding how they are used.

There is a characteristic of culture presumably specifically related to semiotically mediated processes. In culture we should expect to find processes which give additional "non-sensory" meanings to the objects available for our senses. Such processes are observed by several scholars who have mentioned that the same objects may have very different meanings in human culture. Eckensberger (1995), for example, suggests that human actions have two dimensions. One is called "instrumental" and is related to the direct goals of the action (e.g., a hammer is used to drive a nail into a wall). The other aspect is called "subjective-functional." It means that human actions acquire meanings beyond their instrumental purposes. The latter aspect is, in essence, the semiotically mediated aspect of an action. Bornstein (1995) draws attention to the fact that the same activity may have the same as well as different meanings in similar or different contexts. It can be proposed that such a flexibility of relations between activities and meanings is mostly caused by semiotic mechanisms.

Now the question emerges: How do we differentiate symbolic and non-symbolic aspects of objects and phenomena? The only way to reveal the symbolic nature of objects is to study their utilization, to look at how they are used. There are two general analytical ways to do that. First, it is possible to study the actual utilization of objects in the surrounding world. If an object is used for referring to something else, it is a symbol. It might be recalled here that sometimes objects, instead of referring to something else, "suggest" that there is something else. Smoke, for example, does not refer to fire but rather suggests that there is also a fire. Objects which "suggest" something else can be called "signals."

Second, sometimes it is possible to defend hypotheses that an object has been a symbol or a product of activities that included semiotically mediated mental operations. This type of analysis refers to artifacts and (possibly) intentional changes introduced into nature (like hypotheses about land-use patterns in archaeology, for example; see Toth & Schick, 1993).

With these ideas in mind it is possible to reinterpret van der Veer's (1996) suggestion that there are culturally (in a broader sense) variable aspects of a world that presumably are non-linguistically mediated. Take, for example, body odor that is perceived differently in different cultures (Hannigan, 1995). It may seem that body odor, a non-linguistic phenomenon, is "part of the culture." However, Hannigan's analysis shows that body odor became a symbol and that this might be the reason why it is culturally variable. Namely, attitudes about body odors are related to the upper-class values of Eighteenth-century Europe, where aristocracy tried to delineate between the "foul" odors of the masses and the "refined scents" of themselves. So, there is historical evidence that cultural variation in attitudes toward body odor emerged because body odor acquired a symbolic meaning. It is also interesting that the "refined scent" of aristocracy/"civilized" persons is not a human scent at all. If not symbolic, then what mechanisms are responsible for an attitude that humans, to become "civilized" humans, must not smell like humans? Here it is possible to see how symbolic and non-symbolic conceptual aspects of objects differ. It is sufficient to observe the utilization of a deodorant to learn how to use it. But only the analysis of symbols, content of a culture, can explain *why* deodorants are used at all.

CONCLUSIONS

The notion of culture can be used for different purposes in different fields of social and human sciences. In this chapter I argued that a very specific, Vygotskian definition of culture is useful for explaining several characteristics special to the human mind. According to this definition, culture is socially shared information that is coded in symbols. Following the Vygotskian tradition, I proposed that the emergence and evolution of the human mind is possible only with the emergence and evolution of culture. The relationship between an individual and culture can be described as an "organic whole," where the elements constituting it can be distinguished qualitatively but not separated. Culture and individual constitute each other in their "dialogue" where they have qualitatively different—complementary—roles.

Culture, as understood here, is responsible for the differentiation of human minds from other animals. Only humans are capable of semiotically mediated thought where the same information is processed simultaneously by sensory and cultural (i.e., semiotic) mechanisms. Such psychological synthesis allows creating qualitatively novel information and going beyond qualitative and quantitative limitations of senses. Following Vygotsky, I also suggested that it is possible to differentiate hierarchical levels in the evolution of culture. Higher and lower levels are differentiated only on the developmental basis; no unambiguous value is related to differences in levels of development. Higher levels of mental evolution add qualitatively different ways of solving the same problems. Thus, some cultures can be called more developed than others. This is not the only way in which cultures differ. Hierarchical levels are connected with *how the mind operates*; in addition to that there are differences between cultures in *what* (i.e., in the content of culture). The former is related to the *etic* and the latter to the *emic* aspects of culture.

In sum, I fully agree with Cole (1996) that psychologists should keep culture in mind because culture is a fundamental constituent of human thought and action. It can be said that the human mind is a result of continuous dialogue between an individual and culture. The fact that views expressed in this chapter are sometimes remarkably different from views of other cultural psychologists should remind us that dialogue is extremely worthwhile in the field of cultural psychology.

ACKNOWLEDGEMENTS

This research was supported by the Estonian Science Foundation Grant No. 3988. The author is grateful to John W. Berry, Michael Bond, and Ingrid Josephs for their constructive comments on previous versions of this manuscript.

REFERENCES

Allport, G. W. (1937). *Personality: A psychological interpretation*. New York: Henry Holt and Company.

Baldwin, J. M. (1904). The limits of pragmatism. *Psychological Review, 11,* 30–60.

Baldwin, J. M. (1906). *Thought and things: A study of the development and meaning of thought or genetic logic*. London: Swan Sonneschein & Co.

Berry, J. W. (1989). Imposed etics-emics-derived etics: The operationalization of a compelling idea. *International Journal of Psychology, 24,* 721–735.

Berry, J. W., Poortinga, Y. H., Segall, M. H., & Dasen, P. R. (1992). *Cross-cultural psychology: Research and application*. Cambridge: Cambridge University Press.

Best, D. L., & Ruther, N. M. (1994). Cross-cultural themes in developmental psychology: An examination of texts, handbooks and reviews. *Journal of Cross-Cultural Psychology, 25,* 54–77.

Bornstein, M. H. (1995). Form and function: Implications for studies of culture and human development. *Culture and Psychology, 1,* 123–137.

Chaiklin, S. (1992). From theory to practice and back again: What does postmodern philosophy contribute to psychological science? In S. Kvale (Ed.), *Psychology and postmodernism* (pp. 194–208). London: Sage.

Cole, M. (1995). Culture and cognitive development: From cross-cultural research to creating systems of cultural mediation. *Culture and Psychology, 1,* 25–54.

Cole, M. (1996). *Cultural psychology: A once and future discipline*. Cambridge, MA: The Belknap Press of Harvard University Press.

Cole, M., & Scribner, S. (1974). *Culture and thought: A psychological introduction*. New York: Wiley.

Cosmides, L., Tooby, J., & Barkow, J. H. (1992). Introduction: Evolutionary psychology and conceptual integration. In J. H. Barkow, L. Cosmides, & J. Tooby (Eds.), *The adapted mind: Evolutionary psychology and the generation of culture* (pp. 3–15). New York: Oxford University Press.

Eckensberger, L. H. (1995). Activity or action: Two different roads towards an integration of culture in psychology? *Culture and Psychology, 1,* 67–80.

Gergen, K. J. (1992). Toward a postmodern psychology. In S. Kvale (Ed.), *Psychology and postmodernism* (pp. 17–30). London: Sage.

Gergen, K. J. (1994). Exploring the postmodern: Perils or potentials? *American Psychologist, 49,* 412–416.

Gergen, M. (1992). From mod-masculinity to post-mod macho: A feminist replay. In S. Kvale (Ed.), *Psychology and postmodernism* (pp. 183–193). London: Sage.

Guth, C. (1996). *Art of Edo Japan: The artists and the city 1615–1868*. New York: Harry N. Abrams.

Hannigan, T. P. (1995). Body odor: The international student and cross-cultural communication. *Culture and Psychology, 1*, 497–503.

Harré, R. (1972). *The philosophies of science: An introductory survey*. Oxford: Oxford University Press.

Hobhouse, L. T. (1901). *Mind in evolution*. London: Macmillan.

Jahoda, G. (1995). The ancestry model. *Culture and Psychology, 1*, 11–24.

James, W. (1890). *The principles of psychology*. New York: Dover Publications.

Kagitçibasi, C., & Berry, J. V. (1989). Cross-cultural psychology: Current research and trends. *Annual Review of Psychology, 40*, 493–531.

King, M. (1883). The future of American science. *Science, 1* (1), 1–3.

Koffka, K. (1928). *The growth of the mind. An introduction to child-psychology*. London: Kegan Paul, Trench, Trubner & Co.

Koffka, K. (1935). *Principles of Gestalt psychology*. London: Routledge & Kegan Paul.

Köhler, W. (1947). *Gestalt psychology: An introduction to new concepts in modern psychology*. New York: Mentor Books.

Kojima, H. (1995). Form and function as categories of comparison. *Culture and Psychology, 1*, 139–145.

Kvale, S. (1992a). Introduction: From the archaeology of the psyche to the architecture of cultural landscapes. In S. Kvale (Ed.), *Psychology and postmodernism* (pp. 1–16). London: Sage.

Kvale, S. (1992b). Postmodern psychology: A contradiction in terms? In S. Kvale (Ed.), *Psychology and postmodernism* (pp. 31–57). London: Sage.

Lévi-Strauss, C. (1966). *The savage mind*. London: Weidenfeld and Nicholson.

Lewin, K. (1935). *A dynamic theory of personality: Selected papers*. New York: McGraw-Hill.

Lotman, Y. M. (1992a). O semiosfere. In N. Abashina (Ed.), *Y. M. Lotman: Izbrannyje stat'i. Tom 1* (pp. 11–24). Tallinn: Aleksandra.

Lotman, Y. M. (1992b). Pamjat' v kul'turologicheskom osveschenii. In N. Abashina (Ed.), *Y. M. Lotman. Izbrannyje stat'i. Tom 1* (pp. 200–202). Tallinn: Aleksandra.

Lotman, Y. M. (1993). Kul'tura kak subjekt i sama sebe ob'jekt. (Originally published in 1989.) In N. Abashina (Ed.), *Y. M. Lotman. Izbrannyje stat'i. Tom 3* (pp. 368–375). Tallinn: Aleksandra.

Lotman, Y. M., & Uspenskii, B. A. (1993). O semioticheskom mekhanizme kul'tury. (Originally published in 1971.) In N. Abashina (Ed.), *Y. M. Lotman. Izbrannyje stat'i. Tom 3* (pp. 326–344). Tallinn: Aleksandra.

Løvlie, L. (1992). Postmodernism and psychology. In S. Kvale (Ed.), *Psychology and postmodernism* (pp. 119–134). London: Sage.

Luria, A. R. (1974). *Ob istoricheskom razvitii poznavatel'nykh processov. Eksperimental'no-psikhologicheskoje issledovanije*. Moscow: Nauka.

Martí, E. (1996). Individuals create culture: Comments on van der Veer's "The concept of culture in Vygotsky's thinking." *Culture and Psychology, 2*, 265–272.

McGrew, W. C. (1998). Culture in nonhuman primates? *Annual Review of Anthropology, 27,* 301–328.

Moll, I. (1995). Cultural people and cultural contexts: Comments on Cole (1995) and Wertsch (1995). *Culture and Psychology, 1,* 361–371.

Nicolopoulou, A., & Weintraub, J. (1996). On liberty, cultural relativism and development: A commentary on van der Veer's "The concept of culture in Vygotsky's thinking." *Culture and Psychology, 2,* 273–283.

Polkinghorne, D. E. (1992). Postmodern epistemology of practice. In S. Kvale (Ed.), *Psychology and postmodernism* (pp. 146–165). London: Sage.

Richmond, W. (1900). *An essay on personality as a philosophical principle.* London: Edward Arnold.

Rosenberg, M. (1994). Pattern, process and hierarchy in the evolution of culture. *Journal of Anthropological Archaeology, 13,* 307–340.

Rubel, P., & Rosman, A. (1994). The past and the future of anthropology. *Journal of Anthropological Research, 50,* 335–343.

Segall, M. H. (1986). Culture and behavior: Psychology in global perspective. *Annual Review of Psychology, 37,* 523–564.

Shotter, J. (1992). "Getting in touch": The meta-methodology of a postmodern science of mental life. In S. Kvale (Ed.), *Psychology and postmodernism* (pp. 58–73). London: Sage.

Tomasello, M. (1996). The child's contribution to culture: A commentary on Toomela. *Culture and Psychology, 2,* 307–318.

Toomela, A. (1996a). How culture transforms mind: A process of internalization. *Culture and Psychology, 2,* 285–305.

Toomela, A. (1996b). What characterizes language that can be internalized: A reply to Tomasello. *Culture and Psychology, 2,* 319–322.

Toth, N., & Schick, K. (1993). Early stone industries and inferences regarding language and cognition. In K. R. Gibson & T. Ingold (Eds.), *Tools, language and cognition in human evolution* (pp. 346–362). Cambridge: Cambridge University Press.

Triandis, H. C. (1994). *Culture and social behavior.* New York: McGraw-Hill.

Tulviste, P. (1988). *Kul'turno-istoricheskoje razvitije verbal'nogo myshlenija.* Tallinn: Valgus.

van der Veer, R. (1996). The concept of culture in Vygotsky's thinking. *Culture and Psychology, 2,* 247–263.

Veroff, J. B., & Goldberger, N. R. (1995). What's in a name? The case for "intercultural." In N. R. Goldberger & J. B. Veroff (Eds.), *The culture and psychology reader.* New York: New York University Press.

von Bertalanffy, L. (1968). *General systems theory: Foundations, development, applications.* New York: George Braziller.

Vygotsky, L. S. (1926). *Pedagogicheskaja psikhologija. Kratkii kurs.* Moscow: Rabotnik Prosveschenija.

Vygotsky, L. S. (1983). K voprosu o kompensatornykh processah v razvitii umstvenno otstalogo rebjonka. (Originally written in 1931.) In A. V. Zaporozhec (Ed.), *L. S. Vygotsky: Sobranije sochinenii. Tom 5. Osnovy defektologii* (pp. 115–136). Moscow: Pedagogika.

Vygotsky, L. S. (1994). The problem of the cultural development of the child.

(Originally published in 1929.) In R. van der Veer & J. Valsiner (Eds.), *The Vygotsky reader* (pp. 57–72). Oxford: Blackwell.

Vygotsky, L. S. (1996). *Myshlenije i rech.* [Thinking and speech.] (Originally published in 1934.) Moscow: Labirint.

Vygotsky, L. S., & Luria, A. R. (1930). *Etjudy po istorii povedenija. Obezjana. Primitiv. Rebjonok.* Moscow-Leningrad: Gosudarstvennoje Izdatel'stvo.

Watson, P. J. (1995). Archaeology, anthropology, and the culture concept. *American Anthropologist, 97,* 683–694.

Werner, H. (1978). The concept of development from a comparative and organismic point of view. In S. S. Barten & M. B. Franklin (Eds.), *Developmental process: Heinz Werner's selected writings, Volume 1: General theory and perceptual experience* (pp. 107–130). New York: International Universities Press.

Whiten, A., Goodall, J., McGrew, W. C., Nishida, T., Reynolds, V., Sugiyama, Y., Tutin, C. E. G., Wrangham, R. W., & Boesch, C. (1999). Cultures in chimpanzees. *Nature, 399,* 682–685.

Wundt, W. (1897). *Outlines of psychology.* Leipzig: Wilhelm Engelman.

Chapter 8

The Different Facets of "Culture": A Commentary on Toomela

Gustav Jahoda

The case for treating culture as a semiosphere has been put forward by Aaro Toomela in a stimulating and provocative manner. It is hardly surprising that it should be controversial, since the term "culture" is a polysemous one that has given rise to numerous debates. Writers of various theoretical orientations sought and are still seeking to interpret it according to their preferred framework. Among these one might single out two contrasting approaches. There are, first, those which deal with "culture-in-general" and regard culture as a symbolic and quasi-linguistic system; second, others concentrate on cultural variations according to time and place. Although these are by no means mutually exclusive, it is not easy to clarify their relationship. Hence it takes a courageous person to attempt to deal with them simultaneously, as Toomela has done.

In doing so he may be regarded as following in the footsteps of Lévi-Strauss, who had been influenced by both Roman Jakobson, the linguist, and Franz Boas, the first cultural anthropologist in the modern sense. This dual inheritance pervades his writings, but is not without its tensions. For instance, taking from Jakobson the notion of binary opposition, which Lévi-Strauss regarded as a consequence of the structure of our brains, he opposed "culture" to "nature." However, this simple dichotomy sometimes underwent a slippage even in his own usage, and others conceived of them as interdependent. Thus Boesch argued that natural objects cannot be sharply distinguished from cultural ones, since their meaning is usually culturally determined. As he put it (Boesch, 1991, p. 21): " 'Nature' is no antipode to 'culture'; nature, as we experience it, is already culture."

The way in which Lévi-Strauss tried to get the best of both worlds will be briefly illustrated. Fundamental for him were incest taboos, which he saw as straddling nature and culture: such a taboo is natural since it is found in every society, yet cultural in so far as what is defined as incest varies culturally. The taboo was seen as intimately connected to kinship systems, where sex is the natural aspect and the cultural one a system of communication whereby groups of men become respectively wife-givers and wife-receivers. Myth and ritual symbolism were said to be derived from universal attributes of the human mind, cultural forms being mere transformations of the same constituents. The basis of his analyses rested on the assumption that cultural phenomena such as kinship, totemism, or myths are analogous in their structure to language and function as codes, as Leach (1976) explained in his aptly named book *Culture and Communication*.

Brilliantly innovative as the Lévi-Straussian analysis was generally conceded to be, it was not without its critics. Here, for instance, is what Mary Douglas (1973, p. 95) wrote about his approach to symbolism:

Given the materials for analysis (any limited cultural field), given the techniques of analysis (selection of pairs of contrasted elements)—there is no possibility of an analysist going forth to display the structures underlying symbolic behavior and coming home discountenanced. He will succeed, because he takes with him a tool designed for revealing structures and because the general hypothesis only requires him to reveal them.

There are thus different opinions about the extent to which Lévi-Strauss has succeeded in welding together two disparate strands. Moreover, many developments have taken place since then in both cultural and linguistic theories. Therefore, it would be better to discuss the two aspects of Toomela's thesis separately.

ON DEFINITIONS OF "CULTURE"

Culture or civilization, taken in its wide ethnographic sense, is that complex whole which includes knowledge, belief, art, morals, law, custom, and any other capabilities and habits acquired by man as a member of society. The condition of culture among the various societies of mankind, in so far as it is capable of being investigated on general principles, is a subject apt for the study of laws of human thought and action. (Tylor, 1958, p. 1)

This classical definition by Edward Tylor, often known as "the father of anthropology," already brings out some salient issues that have recurred. First, he used the term "culture" in the singular and in fact never seems to have used the plural. However, this does not mean that he ignored variations, since he referred to "conditions of culture." Moreover, he viewed culture as being *acquired* from the social environment. Lastly, he was well aware of the relevance of culture for understanding human psychology and thought that it could be inferred from the characters of social institutions.

During the first half of the twentieth century, behaviorism was dominant in anthropology as well as psychology. Hence definitions of culture tended to stress learned behavior such as customs, beliefs, values, or in short, ways of life transmitted through the generations. However, it appears, from Kroeber and Kluckhohn's (1952) famous monograph, that already during the 1940s references to symbolism could be found in some definitions, as illustrated below:

Bain (1942): Culture is all behavior mediated by symbols.
White (1943): Culture is an organization of phenomena—material objects, bodily acts, ideas and sentiments—which consist of or is dependent upon the use of symbols. (Kroeber & Kluckhohn, 1952, p. 69)

Thereafter, and particularly as a consequence of the "cognitive revolution," definitions tended to move away from behavior and toward symbolism and meaning. This was true of Clifford Geertz (1973) who was one of the first, if not *the* first, to refer to semiotics in this context:

The concept of culture I espouse . . . is essentially a semiotic one. Believing, with Max Weber, that man is an animal suspended in webs of siginificance he himself has spun, I take culture to be those webs, and the analysis of it therefore not an experimental science in search of law but an interpretative one in search of meaning. (p. 5)

Drawing on this approach, Rohner (1984) suggested that a definition of culture suitable for cross-cultural psychology would be "a symbolic meaning system." Later Obeyesekere (1990), while agreeing with Geertz "that human beings construct their own symbolic worlds—what we call culture" (p. 101), commented shrewdly that "in reading Geertz I see webs everywhere but never the spider at work" (p. 285). Obeyesekere himself sought to show how those webs are spun, regarding this as a key task for the human sciences.

Geertz's claim that culture can only be studied hermeneutically is not universally accepted. For instance, Triandis (1996) reviewed a considerable number of definitions of culture, concluding that what all these have in common is the view that culture consists of *shared* elements. Hence he proposed a quantitative method for identifying what he called "cultural syndromes," consisting of patterns of shared beliefs, values, and so on, at a given historical epoch in a given geographic location. According to him cultures could then be described in terms of particular clusters of syndromes.

With this background one can now turn to the discussion of the nature of culture offered by Toomela. He rightly criticizes the tendency on the part of many cross-cultural psychologists to ignore theoretical issues concerning culture and to bypass them by simply equating cultures with nations. There is now also wide agreement that there can be no single authoritative definition of culture, but rather that one's definition will be related to a theoretical position and a particular purpose. In Toomela's case that purpose is "to get closer to an understanding and explanation of an individual human mind." He declares that he was inspired by Vygotsky, for whom culture was said to be equivalent to the concepts or word meanings existing in that culture. Toomela's own formulation regards culture as "socially shared information that is coded in symbols." As argued by Marková, this definition is closer to Lotman than to Vygotsky.

Although it will be evident from what has been said earlier that Toomela's definition is by no means novel, having been anticipated several times, it is a perfectly good one provided it is not claimed that it is the only defensible one. But for the present writer there are problems in understanding some of the conditions laid down by Toomela for something to function as a symbol. The reason is that the discussion is kept at a high level of abstraction, with no concrete illustrations, and therefore it is hard to grasp what he means. For instance, the first and third conditions are as follows:

> A symbol must be an object, behavioral act, or phenomenon that can
> be directly perceived through sense organs. Symbols refer to objects,
> events, or phenomena.

In the light of these postulates, consider an example of symbolism given in the *Oxford English Dictionary*, namely, "white is a symbol of purity." It is not at all clear that this would be a legitimate instance of a symbol by the above criteria. Another question that arises is whether or not material aspects of culture are intended to be included in the definition. If a symbol can be an object, then a church as a symbol of Christianity would be part of culture. Yet in another passage it is stated that "the concept of culture should be related only to the semiosphere," in which case a church would presumably be excluded.

Yet while there remain uncertainties, in general Toomela's definition in terms of shared symbols is, as has been indicated, similar to several others mostly derived from Geertz. It is perhaps worth noting that among those who took their inspiration from Geertz were also postmodernists who deny that any explanation is possible; and some of whom even want to drop the term "culture" altogether as reeking of colonialism and racism (cf. e.g., Abu-Lughod, 1991).

ON THE RELATIONSHIP BETWEEN AN INDIVIDUAL AND CULTURE

This relationship can be conceptualized in three main ways. One is that culture is *outside* and "above" the individual, as typified by Kroeber's (1917) early characterization of culture as "the superorganic." Kroeber himself later abandoned this notion and it was never widely shared. Another is that culture is located only *within* individuals (plural), for unless one considers a separate culture for each individual the singular would make no sense. This is of course not to say that the elements of culture are exactly the same for all individuals, but a certain minimum of commonality must prevail. That is implicit, for instance, in Goodenough's definition put forward a generation ago and recently reiterated (Goodenough, 1999). He suggested that a culture consists of whatever it is one has to know or believe in order to operate in a manner acceptable to its members. Lastly and most commonly, culture may be viewed as both intra- and extra-individual since the other two formulations face logical difficulties. Toomela does not address this issue directly and this leads to some incoherence, as will now be shown.

Toomela postulates "a dialogue between an individual human mind and culture," adding that this does not imply that they have an independent existence; rather, "they constitute each other." Elsewhere it is said that culture is "a distinguishable element of an individual-culture 'organic whole'," but it is not explained how they can be distinguished within the individual. In fact, the individual mind is equated with personality and this in turn is defined, following a philosopher writing in 1900, as "the capacity for society"; and the same author's reference to the "union between the individual and the collective mind" is cited with approval. It may be recalled that the period was one when "group mind" theories held considerable sway. One of the last remnants of such views was propounded by McDougall (1920), and they have since been completely discredited.

Then Toomela discusses the nature of dialogue, described as a process to which each participant contributes something different and whose outcome is the creation of new meanings of a higher order. It would seem that the culture which is a participant in the dialogue is internal to the individual, since the (single) individual and culture are regarded as "a unified whole." There is here an apparent contradiction with a denial that culture is intra-individual, but this confusion is probably due to the failure to specify and distinguish different senses of "culture," as either that part of it confined to an individual or as culture more generally shared. Assuming this interpretation is correct, the question then arises as to how the alleged individual–culture dialogue is to be understood. One can certainly speak of an internal dialogue when, for instance, the pros and cons of a particular course of action are being weighed up. But how is it possible to identify one side of the dialogue with the individual and the other with culture? One possible answer would be in Freudian terms, with the Superego representing culture, and Id impulses the biological urges of the individual. The synthesis then would be some form of sublimation. However, it is unlikely that this is what Toomela had in mind since there is no mention of Freud or psychoanalysis. In any case, even though the Superego has sometimes been viewed as the embodiment of the morality enjoined by the culture, culture embraces vastly more than morality.

The way in which the issue is phrased by Toomela, namely, the doctrine of the individual mind and culture being separate and yet united, is rather like that of the Trinity—one has to take it on faith even though it makes no rational sense. However, it should be recognized that other cultural psychologists have used what might be taken to be equivalent expressions. Thus Cole and his associates (Laboratory of Comparative Human Cognition, 1983, p. 349) wrote: "mind and culture are different aspects of the same phenomenon"; and Shweder's (1990, p. 24) version is that "culture and psyche make each other up." What they mean is that there are interactions (but not dialogues) both at the population and individual levels such that among adults it would not be feasible to divide their minds into individual and cultural aspects.

On the other hand, Cole and Shweder are interested in the way elements of culture get into minds, something entirely ignored by Toomela, who proceeds as though the world consisted solely of adults. In fact, of course, culture is involved in child development from the very beginning, and the process has been extensively documented (e.g., Goodnow, 1997; Jahoda 1998; Jahoda & Lewis, 1988; Super & Harkness, 1986). A set of ideas, values, rules, and so on, drawn from those prevalent in the culture, is gradually built into the growing mind. Of course individuals do not internalize all of culture, and cultures are not monolithic. As D'Andrade (1995, p. 248) put it, culture is "particulate, socially distributed, variably internalized and variably embodied in external forms." Yet whatever comes to be internalized in the course of development becomes an integral part of the mind of the growing child. Children are of course unaware (and so, often, are parents) that they are absorbing culture. Everything seems to be "natural," rather than arbitrary and conventional. It is quite different when an adult moves into another culture, since often painful adjustments have to be made, sometimes described as "culture shock."

Toomela refers to culture change in the context of "dialogue," in a passage that reads rather strangely:

When in an individual-culture dialogue an individual loses the physical contact with culture, the already emerged whole will not disappear. Rather, it remains in the memory of the individual.

There is a curious category confusion in this passage: Individual and culture have become a "whole," but this "whole" is located in memory, which is of course part of the individual. Probably all this means is that when an individual moves to another culture, the influence of the original one will not disappear. While this would be an entirely acceptable view, it is neither new nor surprising and requires no dialogue. Elsewhere the problem of cultural innovation and change is discussed by Toomela in relation to Lotman's theory, and this will be considered later. Here it might be noted that culture change or cultural evolution (of the latter more below) are complex processes that have been extensively studied (e.g., Ingold, 1986). There was a time when anthropologists regarded "primitive" societies as static, but it has come to be recognized that change is ever-present. Its rate has greatly accelerated over the past century with increasing globalization, but there are also resistances and not every part of a culture changes at the same rate. Relatively superficial features such as new commodities and technology tend to be accepted readily, while traditional beliefs are often little affected (cf. Jahoda, 1968).

While cultural changes take place at the macro level, with numerous, often subtle influences persisting over time, what is mostly experienced at the level of individuals is not a sudden transformation but a gradual and sometimes almost imperceptible change. Toomela treats the phenomenon in an unusual way, stating that "only individuals introduce novelty into culture. Nevertheless it does not follow that culture is intra-individual." Subsequently, this notion is elaborated in connection with the assumed "beginning of cultural evolution." At that (mythical?) stage "an individual processing is necessary but not sufficient for introducing novelty into a culture—it is not yet socially shared. For becoming a part of culture, the individually created novelty must be externalized, i.e., internalized by others." In that sense then, surely, culture must also be intra- as well as extra-individual! Subsequently, it is claimed that in a "developed culture" it is not necessary for a symbol to be socially shared, since a "cultural person" may have a dialogue with her- or himself. Taken together, these two sets of assertions appear to imply that humans early in cultural evolution used symbols but were not "cultural," which seems a rather strange position.

Then, following Lotman, Toomela asserts that cultures tend to be resistant to novel information and explains this as follows:

Symbols are used for communication . . . When individual novel connections emerge between a symbol and a (sensory-based) referent, then the meaning of that symbol also changes. And when such a symbol is used socially, it must be explained to others what new meanings are connected with the "old" symbol and why such changes are introduced.

A number of questions immediately arise; for instance, how does the new meaning emerge and who does the explaining? The concrete example provided is that of the reception of Darwinism. The reluctance to adopt the new ideas is attributed to "cognitive limitations or . . . irrational beliefs or . . . other properties." Supposing that this were the case (though the reluctance of many scientists to embrace Darwinism cannot be simply dubbed irrational), where exactly does "culture" come in, and in what sense can it be said to be "rigid"? Furthermore, Toomela here appears to more or less equate culture with science, and somewhat later does so quite explicitly when he states that both "can build plausible hypotheses about the world outside the reach of the senses"; this is hard to understand, since no examples of culture-building hypotheses are provided. Do cultural hypotheses, like scientific ones, have to correspond to sensory reality? If not, what is meant by "hypothesis" in this context?

Once again one is puzzled by the seeming elasticity of the concepts, which renders the arguments confusing. It would be best to distinguish between culture change in the broad sense and the acceptance or otherwise of scientific concepts by the general public that has been intensively studied by Moscovici and his school under the rubric of "social representations" (Moscovici, 1981). With regard to the wider aspects of culture change there is the question, not addressed by Toomela, as to why certain innovations are accepted and others are not. This has been extensively discussed by evolutionary theorists who conceive evolution in a manner very different from that of Toomela.

ON CULTURE AND EVOLUTION

Explanation in psychology, according to Toomela, must be based on developmental history. Yet, as has been shown, he focuses entirely on his version of phylogeny, altogether ignoring ontogeny. He claims that his approach is evolutionary, but astonishingly is content to dismiss current evolutionary psychology in a brief quotation which, out of context, is totally misleading. It will therefore be useful to say something briefly about evolutionary psychology in relation to culture, before going on to consider Toomela's approach.

Most of the definitions of culture in Kroeber and Kluckhohn's (1952) monograph stressed that culture is the product of learning or *nurture*, and as such is quite distinct from genetic inheritance or *nature*. So for a while it came to be taken for granted that as far as humans are concerned, genetic evolution has given way to cultural evolution in the sense of changes in acquired dispositions over time. This view has increasingly come to be challenged by those who regard it as incredible that the basic human capacity for culture has nothing to do with natural selection. They argue that the learning and transmission of culture depends on psychological mechanisms that have evolved in the course of the emergence of *homo sapiens*. This led to a number of fundamental questions regarding the relationship between biological and cultural evolution; the relationship between genetic and cultural influences on behavior; the nature of the evolved psychological dispositions and how they affect the selection of cultural traits; and so on.

Different models have been proposed and each necessarily entails a particular conception of culture (cf. Janicki & Krebs, 1998). For instance, Dawkins (1976) labeled the units of culture *memes*, claiming that like genes they are replicators influencing behavior independently and may reinforce each other or be in conflict. Durham (1991, pp. 8f.) defined cultures as "systems of symbolically encoded conceptual phenomena that are socially and historically transmitted within and between populations." While this is closely similar to Toomela's "semiotic field," their interpretations could hardly be more different. Durham's model is too complex to be summarized, but two aspects may be mentioned. He distinguished between primary values that have a genetic basis and embody evolved preferences and psychological mechanisms, and secondary values derived from collective experience and social history. While the latter is said to be mainly involved in cultural change, the former ensures that decision making in cultural selection by and large serves to enhance inclusive fitness.

There are other models, such as Boyd and Richerson's (1985) "dual inheritance" one. Among them that of Tooby and Cosmides (1992), referred to by Toomela, is one of those most heavily biased toward genetic determinism. It is therefore of some interest to indicate how they conceptualize culture, but first something must be said about their general position. According to Tooby and Cosmides, the mind consists of evolved content-specific information-processing mechanisms built into the neural architecture. Their features result from natural selection during the Pleistocene era when humans were hunters and gatherers. Hence, unlike some other Darwinian theorists, they would expect maladaptations to modern urban life. They define culture as "any mental, behavioral, or material commonalites shared across individuals" (p. 171). They then distinguish three different categories of culture, namely, *metaculture*, *evoked culture*, and *epidemiological culture*. Their summary characterization of the three types (Tooby & Cosmides, 1992, p. 121) is set out below:

Metaculture: "Mechanisms functionally organized to use cross-cultural regularities in the social and non-social environment give rise to panhuman mental contents and organization."

Evoked culture: "Alternative, functionally organized, domain-specific mechanisms are triggered by local circumstances; leads to within-group similarities and between-group differences."

Epidemiological culture: "Observers' inferential mechanisms construct representations similar to those present in others; domain-specific mechanisms influence which representations spread through a population easily and which do not."

Metaculture is universal, determined by panhuman genetic makeup; evoked culture refers to variations resulting from differing environmental conditions; epidemiological culture is a function of genetically determined ability to learn from others and transmit cultural elements, a transmission resembling the spread of illness. Unlike Durham's, the Tooby and Cosmides concept of culture is completely different from Toomela's, and evolutionary theorists themselves have many divergent views. However, all of them agree that the issues must be decided in terms of empirical evidence, such as the testing of predictions from evolutionary theory; and a good deal of that has already accumulated (e.g., Simpson & Kenrick, 1997). Moreover, all the theoretical models put forward are intended to apply to humanity as a whole rather than to particular parts of it.

The kinds of ideas about evolution discussed by Toomela have practically nothing in common with the current discussions just outlined. Rather, they date back partly to ninteenth-century *social evolutionism* which entailed the notion of a unilinear progressive development of societies occurring at an uneven rate, and partly to early (and now superseded) interpretations of Darwinism. The key statement is that "hierarchically different levels of mental evolution can be found in different cultures." The main ideas are derived from Werner, who postulated that development is a process of increasing "differentiation, articulation, and hierarchic integration," and from Vygotsky, who sometimes contrasted "the psychology of primitive man" with the "higher psychology of modern man" and compared the former to the thought of the child (cited in Scribner 1985, p. 132). Actually, Vygotsky was often somewhat ambiguous in his statements, and Toomela selects an interpretation which holds that

According to the evolutionary view, if thinking with complexes and thinking with scientific concepts characterize hierarchically lower and higher levels of cultural evolution, respectively, we should expect to find cultures with only complex thinking and cultures with complex and scientific thinking. No cultures with only scientific thinking should exist.

First of all one has to agree with the last sentence above, and might well extend it by saying that no human being with only scientific thinking *could* exist. In other words, the issue is not an empirical one, as Toomela implies, but a logical one within a developmental context. Toomela himself appears a trifle uneasy about his claims, since he seeks to assure the readers that he is not making any value judgments. However, this is hard to sustain when one calls someone's thinking "inferior." The fundamental flaw in the argument rests on repeated misuse of the concepts "mental development" and "cultural evolution." It is a flaw which, in hindsight, characterized the writings of Vygotsky and Werner. Both were influenced by Lévy-Bruhl, who had then postulated the existence of two distinct mentalities, logical and pre-logical (he recanted later). Both relied on the mainly nineteenth-century ethnographic literature available to them, which usually presented a dismal picture of the mental capacity of "primitives." It was widely believed (e.g., by Lazarus and Steinthal, philologists and founders of *Völkerpsychologie*) that so-called "primitive languages" are inferior and lack any abstractions, a view echoed by Toomela: "all language of 'primitives' is figurative and cannot be differentiated from objects the words refer to." It is now generally accepted that such a view is untenable: "It is a linguistic truism that there is no such thing as a 'primitive' language. Any existing natural language can do anything any other can do" (Steklis & Harnad, 1976, p. 445; cf. also Lieberman, 1984).

The idea of a hierarchy in the mental development of children is a perfectly reasonable way of looking at the issue. In the nineteenth century it was true that some cultures were completely devoid of science and technology. What was and remains illegitimate is to infer that adults in such cultures were mentally inferior and at the level of [European] children. While Toomela eschews direct comparison with children, he does harp on the inability of people in some cultures to master syllogisms or perform certain classification tasks; by implication he refers to them as "primitives," while Americans and Canadians are said to be at an "evolutionary higher level of development." As against that, it must be stressed that cultural evolution or culture change in the direction of "modernization" does not entail any change in basic mental potential, since there is no evidence that the brain of *homo sapiens* has undergone any changes, nor (contrary to what used to be the conventional wisdom) that it differs significantly across human groups. It is of course undeniable that the frequency of "scientific" thinking varies across cultures, but it should be remembered that in all cultures this is true only of a minority, and an inability to cope with syllogisms is widespread everywhere.

What makes the difference is access to relevant experience, notably schooling and/or technical training which can produce remarkable mental progress. One of my students came from a remote village where his family were illiterate subsistence farmers (I visited there). Had he continued to live in this setting his thinking might have been of the "primitive" kind—though even that is not to be underestimated. Many years later I met him at a conference in Cambridge to which he, having become a professor, had been invited!

Summing up: starting with a definition of culture as a semiosphere, which is fine if not particularly unusual, the chapter goes on to build up a set of alleged implications of that definition. Unfortunately, the chain of inferences is largely fallacious, drawing on old material now discredited. On the other hand, one can unreservedly agree with Toomela when he states that "Culture is a necessary environment for the development of individuals with the ability for semiotically mediated thought." But then, as Geertz (1973, p. 49) put it, "Men without culture . . . would be unworkable monstrosities."

ACKNOWLEDGMENT

Preparation of this chapter was supported by a grant from the Nuffield Foundation.

REFERENCES

Abu-Lughod, l. (1991). Writing against culture. In R. Fox (Ed.), *Recapturing anthropology: Working in the present* (pp. 137–162). Santa Fe, NM: School of American Research Press.

Boesch, E. E. (1991). *Symbolic action theory and cultural psychology*. Berlin: Springer.

Boyd, R., & Richerson, P. J. (1985). *Culture and the evolutionary process*. Chicago: University of Chicago Press.

Crawford, C., & Krebs, D. L. (1998). *Handbook of evolutionary psychology*. Mahwah, NJ: Lawrence Erlbaum.

D'Andrade, R. (1995). *The development of cognitive anthropology*. Cambridge: Cambridge University Press.

Dawkins, R. (1976). *The selfish gene*. Oxford: Oxford University Press.

Douglas, M. (1973). *Natural symbols: Explorations in cosmology*. Harmondsworth: Penguin Books.

Durham, W. H. (1991). *Coevolution*. Stanford, CA: Stanford University Press.

Geertz, C. (1973). *The interpretation of cultures*. London: Hutchinson.

Goodenough, W. H. (1999). Outline of a framework for a theory of cultural evolution. *Cross Cultural Research, 33*, 84–107.

Goodnow, J. J. (1997). Parenting and the transmission and internalization of values: From socio-cultural perspectives to within-family analyses. In J. E. Grusec & L. Kuczynski (Eds.), *Parenting and children's internalization of values* (pp. 333–361). New York: Wiley.

Ingold, T. (1986). *Evolution and social life*. Cambridge: Cambridge University Press.

Jahoda, G. (1968). Scientific training and the persistence of traditional beliefs among West African university students. *Nature, 200* (5274), 1356.

Jahoda, G. (1998). Cultural influences on development. In A. Campbell & S. Muncer (Eds.), *The social child* (pp. 85–109). Hove: Psychology Press.

Jahoda, G., & Lewis, I. M. (Eds.) (1988). *Acquiring culture: Cross-cultural studies in child development*. London: Croom Helm.

Janicki, M. G., & Krebs, D. L. (1998). Evolutionary approaches to culture. In C. Crawford & D. L. Krebs (Eds.), *Handbook of evolutionary psychology* (pp. 163–207). Mahwah, NJ: Lawrence Erlbaum.

Kroeber, A. L. (1917). The superorganic. *American Anthropologist, 119*, 163–213.

Kroeber, A. L., & Kluckhohn, C. (1952). *Culture: A critical review of concepts and definitions*. Cambridge, MA: Peabody Museum.

Laboratory of Comparative Human Cognition (1983). Culture and cognitive development. In P. H. Mussen (Ed.), *Handbook of child psychology* (4th ed., Vol. 1). New York: Wiley.

Leach, E. (1976). *Culture and communication*. Cambridge: Cambridge University Press.

Lieberman, P. (1984). *The biology and evolution of language*. Cambridge, MA: Harvard University Press.

McDougall, W. (1920). *The group mind*. Cambridge: Cambridge University Press.

Moscovici, S. (1981). On social representations. In J. Forgas (Ed.), *Social cognition* (pp. 181–209). London: Academic Press.

Obeyesekere, G. (1990). *The work of culture: Symbolic transformation in psychoanalysis and anthropology*. Chicago: University of Chicago Press.

Rohner, R. (1984). Toward a conception of culture for cross-cultural psychology. *Journal of Cross-Cultural Psychology, 15*, 111–138.

Scribner, S. (1985). Vygotsky's uses of history. In J. V. Wertsch (Ed.), *Culture, communication, and cognition: Vygotskian perspectives* (pp. 119–145). Cambridge: Cambridge University Press.

Shweder, R. A. (1990). Cultural psychology—What is it? In J. W. Stigler, R. A. Shweder, & G. Herdt (Eds.), *Cultural psychology*. Cambridge: Cambridge University Press.

Simpson, J. A., & Kenrick, D. T. (Eds.) (1997). *Evolutionary social psychology*. Mahwah, NJ: Lawrence Erlbaum.

Steklis, H. D., & Harnad, S. R. (1976). From hand to mouth: Some critical stages in the evolution of language. In S. H. Harnad, H. D. Steklis, & J. Lancaster (Eds.), *Origins and evolution of language and speech* (Vol. 280, pp. 445–455). New York: Annals of the New York Academy of Sciences.

Super, C. M., & Harkness, S. (1986). The developmental niche: A conceptualization at the interface of child and culture. *International Journal of Behavioral Development, 9*, 545–569.

Tooby, J., & Cosmides, L. (1992). The psychological foundations of culture. In J. H. Barkow, L. Cosmides, & J. Tooby (Eds.), *The adapted mind: Evolutionary psychology and the generation of culture* (pp. 19–136). New York: Oxford University Press.

Triandis, H. C. (1996). The psychological measurement of cultural syndromes. *American Psychologist, 51*, 407–415.

Tylor, E. B. (1958). *Primitive culture*. New York: Harper & Brothers.

Chapter 9

Myths and Minds: Implicit Guidance for Human Conduct

Sumedha Gupta and Jaan Valsiner

> Mythology offers the student with a situation which at first sight appears contradictory. On the one hand it would seem that in the course of a myth anything is likely to happen. There is no logic, no continuity. Any characteristic can be attributed to any subject; every conceivable relation can be found. With myth, everything becomes possible. But on the other hand, this apparent arbitrariness is belied by the astonishing similarity between myths collected in widely different regions. (Lévi-Strauss, 1963, p. 208)

Human beings live in their self-constructed meaningful worlds, which are created by themselves through semiotic devices of various levels of complexity and forms of organization. Macro-level semiotic devices through which human meaningful worlds are organized are termed here *macroscopic semiotic complexes*—myths, songs, rituals, historical narratives, fiction, sports and war games, and so on. Because they are maintained through communication between persons, these macroscopic complexes have only relative stability, and are subject to transformations and re-organizations over extended periods of time. It is interesting to find out how one type of macroscopic complex—that of orally transmitted cultural narratives (myths)—creates one of the bases for personal, internalized self-regulation. The pervasiveness of telling stories is a human characteristic, ranging from myths to gossip. The hearers of such stories are able to relate to the narrative—often despite the unrealistic features of the tale—and, in the process, reconstruct some belief about the world and themselves on its basis.

MACROSCOPIC SEMIOTIC COMPLEXES

A macroscopic semiotic complex is a textured narrative setting that embeds a multitude of general cultural meanings in specific contextual locations. These complexes are oriented toward providing guidance for personal interpretations of the world in various socially expected directions. The guidance such complexes of meaning provide is grounded within the global feelings that a person exemplifies about the world *at large*. These feelings are not directly describable through speech. Instead, they can be generic, ill-defined, in other words, "nebulous." Yet their nebulosity is not an obstacle for their functioning as cultural guidance devices. Rather, just the opposite is the case—vague, ill-defined general terms allow for a wide range of uses under very varied circumstances.

For example, feeling "depressed"—even if it can be labeled as such—cannot be specified in terms of *strictly* defined tracts of personal action. Rather, the feeling, thus labeled, colors almost any situation the person is in, and can be taken as a general orientation to any new situation. The feeling of "danger" can overwhelm the person in a setting without any specifiable external cues for such a designation, and can lead the person to specific expectations colored by that feeling. Macroscopic complexes work by interrelating with ubiquitous human affect. The multitude of meanings entailing such complexes help to structure the potential form the feeling field takes in any given situation, charting out the possible modes of action related to the feelings-full meanings. At the same time, the multitude of meanings within the complex are reorganized and defined through this ongoing relationship.

These macroscopic complexes, then, may generally function as markers, demarcating the boundaries of "zones of promoted action" (ZPA) existing within the personal semiotic field of the individual's relation with the world (Valsiner, 1998). The marking of these boundaries operates as a guidance device, setting the immediate future direction which human understanding and its affective tone might take. Figure 9.1 illustrates a way in which myths may serve as prospective boundary maintainers for human experiencing.

While entering into the personal worlds of an individual person through the reception of communicative messages (at time t1), these complexes function to maintain ongoing experiencing of the boundaries at some later time (t2). Macroscopic semiotic complexes operate with a focus toward a range of expected future encounters of the person with the world. The richly textured nature of these complexes allows an adaptive flexibility for dealing with a complex and changeable environment.

Such macroscopic complexes are expected to work through a process of actively relating to the complex and establishing intrapsychological counterpart models within different personal sense systems. The process

Figure 9.1
Constraining of Personal Experiencing through Myth

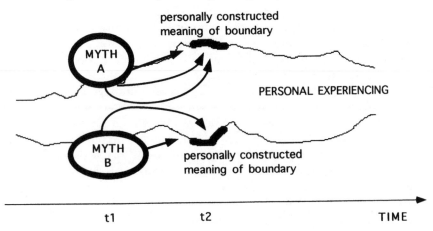

of actively relating to and establishing internal personalized versions of the complex involves, in the terminology of Ernst Boesch, dynamic relations between *myth* and *fantasm*. According to Boesch, the myth is a

collectively accepted means of explanation, justification, and exhortation, which might be expressed in the form of myth-stories, but also mythemes ... isolated themes relating to the underlying myth ... a myth-story specifies ... pattern of imaginary situations, while a mytheme corresponds to specific themes related to the myth or the myth story. (Boesch, 1991, p. 124)

Fantasms, on the other hand, are the personal counterpart of myths and function as the unique fabric of meaning individuals construct as private models. In the words of Boesch, a fantasm

concerns the nature of the anticipated ego-world relationship of the individual. ... The personal contents the individual gives to a term like "happiness" would constitute a fantasm, as would subjective meaning given to the term "self-realization" or "order." (Boesch, 1991, p. 124)

Myths thus constitute complex social inputs for the establishment and functioning of fantasms. Yet, of course, the latter are not direct replicas of the former but are their personal transformations. Myths then belong to the realm of collective culture, while fantasms exist in the realm of personal culture.

Collective Culture and Personal Culture

The role of myths in persons' psychological constructions occurs through a dialogical process with the social suggestions and meanings encoded in these holistic semiotic complexes. As is the case for the relationship between myth and fantasm, collective and personal culture constitute two interrelated psychological arenas. Collective culture entails communally shared meanings, social norms, and everyday life practices. Collective culture thus is inherently heterogeneous. It consists of different types of structures. The latter can be located semi-permanently in the environment (e.g., culturally meaningful architectural spaces, styles of objects, fashions, etc.) or constitute transitory aspects of a person's encounters with others (e.g., some allusions made by persons in public places, overheard by another person). These structures can also appear in the form of local social norms within a group (that need not generalize beyond that group), advertisements, conduct practices, and so on. Using collective culture as the basis, individual persons construct their personally idiosyncratic semiotic system of symbols, practices, and personal rules. This personal culture is contextually rich and entails both mundane as well as profound systems of action. An important societal symbol or art object, for example, can take on intense private meaning for an individual, one that is psychologically powerful enough to organize affective and action responses that transcend what would be deemed "normal" or acceptable social practice. Personal culture, then, is related to the collective meaning but expands beyond it as well, making the unique personal essence a qualitatively different semiotic system.

Myth-stories constitute an interesting, notably interrelated phenomenon in the collective culture—they exist within the interpersonal realm, yet their existence is dependent upon the individual actions (of re-telling the stories) by persons to one another and thus entail direct personalization of the story meaning inserted into the interpersonal realm. A story-teller is involved in the personal externalization of the internally reconstructed myth. Myths thus exist in the "collective memory" of a social unit only through being internalized by persons, and externalized into the social realm by these persons, in modified forms.

MECHANISMS INVOLVED IN INDIVIDUALS' CONSTRUCTION OF CULTURAL PROCESSES

As Obeyesekere asserts, any employed ontology cannot be final by the very nature of the "historicity of our being" (Obeyesekere, 1990 p. 105). Such historicity entails a dynamic relationship between individual psychological functioning and the meaning-rich environment of those individuals. The dynamic connection posited to exist between individuals and society—represented by the bi-directional relationship between personal and collective culture—provides a way in which we can try to make sense of the role of myths in persons' psychological constructions (Gupta, 1995).

Cultural processes always operate through the domains of individuals (Boesch, 1991; Valsiner, 1998). A major unsolved problem in developmental psychology, however, is the specification of how such involvement by persons is constituted. We see two component systems that play a role: semiotic autoregulation by the person, and the social provision of manifold input for that regulation.

Semiotic Regulation

Semiotic regulators are signs and symbols operating on one another, and on a person's conduct, in various forms of hierarchical order (Valsiner, 1998). Through regulators, specific meaning*ful* settings can be instantly created (e.g., moments of worry) as well as overcome by circumvention strategies (Josephs & Valsiner, 1998; Gupta, 1998). This process of personal-cultural construction of meanings *and* their immediate semiotic autoregulation is a necessary part of the ongoing flow of experiencing an existence that is in constant dynamic change. Semiotic regulation is an inevitable solution for the uncertainty of relations with the immediate transforming environment, where, as discussed briefly in Figure 9.1, all adaptation is oriented toward the immediate next future state (Bergson, 1911).

Ongoing semiotic self-regulation is necessarily microscopic in its character, since it takes place within the infinitely small present moment of experiencing the immediate past and projected future in the present (see Valsiner, 1998, p. 243, for C. S. Peirce's scheme of relating past and future in the present). The present, in other words, is the infinitely small moment of experiencing the connection of the movement-into-past and movement-from-the-projected future back to the present. This transitory nature of human experience creates permanent uncertainty, for which semiotic construction provides a relative stability. This process of semiotic autoregulation is of an instantaneous, episodic character. The constructed mediating devices are heterogeneous and temporary, yet, the *process* in which they participate—the creation of relative stability over time—is universal and helps entail maintenance of the status quo.

The collective-cultural resources (for example, macroscopic semiotic complexes) used for such microscopic regulation are necessarily general, and transportable between different immediate contexts. As maintained above, these complexes create a basis for personal, internalized self-regulation through the active construction of meaning systems. The process of bringing such materials into the episodic here-and-now contexts, thus, is inherently dialogical in its nature.

Forms of Dialogicality

Although all internalization and externalization self-regulatory processes can be assumed to work through dialogical mechanisms, it is rarely clarified in which ways such mechanisms work (Josephs, Valsiner, & Surgan, 1999). In the most general form, dialogicality entails construction of inclusive separation between a meaning (*a*) and its opposites (*non-a*). Thanks to such a distinction, a relationship between these opposites can be established. That relationship in its time-flow is the "dialogue" from which novel ways of understanding may emerge.

When viewed in these general terms, it is irrelevant whether the "dialogue" is seen taking place between persons (inter-individually), between social institutions (e.g., opposition between ideologies), in the person's subjective world (intrapersonally), or in the message that is being internalized and externalized (e.g., duality-based tension between signs, or between a sign and its countersign or absence). Here we are interested in the latter kind of dialogicality—as it may be present in a story or implied by the story. In the latter case, one form of the dialogical relationship set up is between the signs used in the myth-story and their background collective-cultural meanings. The "foreground" (of the myth-story) seems to be monological in its manifest content and, as such, is available to out-of-context readers. Its functional contrast is with its "hidden" counterpart in the implied meaning system of the in-context collective group (i.e., the "background").

Inside the myth, there exist guidelines for differential openness and constriction to interpretation of the general message (cf. Levi-Strauss, 1987). The field of accepted suggested meaning-making is given by the story at the manifest level. Yet the *moral* of the given part of the message exists only through the dialogue with the non-manifest implications of the message (i.e., versions of actions or feelings that could be there, but are not claimed). In the case of myth-stories, then, dialogicality is moved to the background, while the narrative monologicality is displayed at the manifest level. Hence myths and fairy tales are relatively robust in their manifest content (and easily translatable from one language to another—in gross contrast with poetry—as noted by Lévi-Strauss, 1963, p. 210). Yet that translatability does not include the "hidden counterpart" of the manifest story, which is available in the internalized personal subjectivities of the persons who tell and re-tell the stories.

Solidity and Flexibility of Myths

As discussed above, myths are constantly reconstructed in the minds of individual persons and in the process of narration, yet, the basic set of meanings (or social representations) which they carry remains robust. In essence, the existing corpus of textual versions of the "same" myth is regularly heterogeneous. When one story is being told, there are actually many different stories that persons reconstruct. Thus, for example, while the same community sometimes creates a series of myths on the same theme, and all of the created versions are similarly meaningful as generic cultural texts (Lévi-Strauss, 1983a), they need not be understood by different persons in similar ways when the details are in question (Menon & Shweder, 1994). This of course has been a problem for folklorists attempting to reconstruct the generic form of a folk story from its different versions recorded in the field. In the present framework, however, this dual characteristic of myths' flexibility and solidity provides an avenue for highlighting the emergence of novelty and understanding the process of personal and collective cultural evolution.

Different myth versions are the results of constructive personal externalization processes. The set of personally externalized versions of a myth generates the variety of versions that can be viewed as mutually transformable texts. This transformability is afforded by the co-constructive nature of each act of re-telling the story. The act of re-telling the story introduces modifications into it, thus creating variability within the generic theme (Bartlett, 1920). Myths, thus, are constantly being modified by their use. This guarantees heterogeneity in the set of myths of generally similar theme, which also importantly amounts to redundancy (i.e., presentation of the same suggestion in multiple ways).

This redundancy of social messages and meaning, itself born out of reconstruction and the transformability of macroscopic complexes, may play a prominent role in the types of stability found across development; a stability due possibly to the solidity of meaning constructed from essentially similar messages coming from multiple, different sources. At the same time, heterogeneity in the set of myths of similar theme provides avenues for ongoing change and novelty in meaning and psychological functioning.

Myths and Counter-Myths

Clearly, stories can be told in many ways, and myth-stories are usually simple stories in which some of the events transcend everyday life practices (i.e., those of quick and unusual transformations of characters—see Bühler, 1930, p. 101 on fairy tales). This contrast might be important by itself—fairy tales and myths create some domains of actively promoted imagination, while bypassing other possible domains of thought. When one comes to the role of myths and fairy tales as organizers of human psychological functions, their role in provoking specific forms of imagination is crucial: "fairy-tales serve as introduction to the wonderland of reality. The individual has his fancies, and the race has its myths—both handmaids to thought." (Baldwin, 1915, p. 23).

Rapid and varied changes in the image content are exaggerated in myth tales, whereas the simultaneous combination of ideas is within the domain of ignored possibilities or is left to the readers' or listeners' purview. A fairy tale or a myth-story avoids complicated descriptions or narrative styles, and replaces complications by exaggerating temporal transformations that go unexplained within the story.

Myths, then, may be seen as providing one means to explore an ephemeral reality: a reality in which plausible and concrete human experiences occur within the foundation of a world of imagination. Yet, as discussed earlier, that world of imagination is worked out on materials that are projected into the past. Thus, the constructive act of human imagination ("as-if" kind of thinking and feeling) is elucidated on narrative contents that supposedly belong to the past, and yet, functionally, are utilized in the making of the immediate future at the present moment.

The set of similar myth-stories constructed and circulating in a society can be inherently ambiguous. Aside from normative themes of the "generic" myth, there are its opposites (or "counter-myths"—Ramanujan, 1991) that make the realm of myths filled with dialogical tensions. Thus, dialogicality applies both within a myth (as reflected by different tensions implied in a given myth-story, with its foreground/background distinctions) as well as between different myths (e.g., a "main myth" and its "counter-myth" as being opposites within the same collective culture). Construction of myths and counter-myths occupies a central role in the social organization of human lives. The purpose of myth and counter-myth construction is

to provide a logical model capable of overcoming a contradiction (an impossible achievement if . . . the contradiction is real), a theoretically infinite number of states will be generated, each one slightly different from the others. Thus, myth grows spiral-wise until the intellectual impulse which has produced it is exhausted. Its *growth* is a continuous process, whereas its *structure* remains discontinuous. If this is the case, we should assume that it closely corresponds, in the realm of spoken word, to a crystal in the realm of physical matter. . . . Myth is an intermediary entity between a statistical aggregate of molecules and the molecular structure itself. (Lévi-Strauss, 1963, p. 229)

The functionality of the story, then, is in the repeated insertion of semiotic material that "gives man . . . the illusion that he can understand the universe and that he *does* understand the universe" (Lévi-Strauss, 1978, p. 17).

Myths can be analyzed into relationships and combinations of relations, as they reflect the duality of *langue* and *parole* along the lines specified by Ferdinand de Saussure. As Lévi-Strauss asserts:

The true constituent units of a myth are not the isolated relations but *bundles of such relations*, and it is only as bundles that these relations can be put to use and combined so as to produce a meaning. Relations pertaining to the same bundle may appear diachronically at remote intervals, but when we have succeeded in grouping them together we have recognized our myth according to a time referent of a new nature, . . . namely a two-dimensional time referent that is simultaneously diachronic and synchronic, and which accordingly integrates the characteristics of *langue* on the one hand, and those of the *parole* on the other. (Lévi-Strauss, 1963, pp. 211–212)

For folklorists interested in the comparison of different versions of the same generic myth, or contrasting different myths, the main focus of interest in this analysis concentrates on the *langue* side of the tension in the *langue-parole* integrated duality. Most of Lévi-Strauss' analyses of myths have followed that line. The binary oppositions that are useful for charting out the structure of the myth are actually united opposites between which continuous tension can be posited to exist.

In myths, then, we can observe a unity of monological manifest narrative with the implied background dialogicality. Thus, on the one hand, myths can be narrated as epic sequences of events. Yet, as discussed earlier, the meanings promoted by these events depend upon the implicit dialogicality that the myth evokes. Myths can be viewed similarly to symphonies (see Lévi-Strauss, 1978) where the holistic personal orientation to it sets the stage for getting or not getting pleasure from the musical experience. It is the total message structure of the myth that can be interpretable (and that can function in internalization), rather than some specific sequential sub-part of the message as it unfolds.

A CONCRETE EXAMPLE: KILLER WOMAN AND ORIGIN OF TOBACCO

As discussed earlier, of particular interest to our work is understanding the process by which myths, as macroscopic semiotic complexes, help to create the ongoing development of personal meaning. Through analysis of a specific tale, some of the mechanics of this process, elaborated on above, are highlighted. Examples of dialogicality, tension, and areas of openness and constraint, in myth structure is given. Delineation of the integrated functioning of these various factors, while an ongoing goal, is not within the scope of the following first example. The aim of the following example is to provide an analysis illustrating these ideas and further, to set the foundation allowing for ongoing exploration.

At times, even contemporary politicians (such as a president of a country—the United States) may declare different substances—such as tobacco—to be "poisons." Here we analyze a myth on the origin of tobacco as narrated within the Toba-Pilaga ethnic group in South America, which was reported by Lévi-Strauss (1983a, pp. 99–100). Let us consider the unfolding of this story in a stepwise manner:

Step 1. One day a woman and her husband went to catch parakeets. . . . The man climbed a tree containing several nests and threw down thirty or so fledglings to his wife. *He noticed that she gobbled them up. Seized with fear,* he caught hold of a larger bird and, as he threw it down, called out "Here comes a fledgling, but look out, it can fly."

Commentary: First mentioning of a tension—anticipated change of the woman into an aggressive animal.

Step 2. The woman ran after the bird, and the man took advantage of the situation to climb down and run away: *he was afraid she might eat him, too. But his wife went after him, caught up with him, and killed him.* Then she cut off his head, which she put in a bag, and feasted on the rest of his body until her stomach was full.

Commentary: Wife's aggression is confirmed, yet without transformation into an animal.

Step 3. She had scarcely returned to the village when she felt thirsty. Before going to the drinking pool, which was some distance away, *she forbade her five children to touch the bag.* But *the youngest immediately looked inside* and called the others, who recognized their father. The whole village was now informed, and everybody took fright and ran away, *except the children.* When the mother, on her return, was surprised to find the village empty, *they explained that the villagers had left after insulting them,* having fled through shame at their own spitefulness.

Commentary: Children's triggering of curiosity depicted through the mother's forbidding—which leads to the youngest child's exploration. Children mislead the mother as to the reasons for the empty village.

Step 4. The woman was indignant and, wishing *to avenge her children,* went after the villagers. She caught up with them, killed a number of them, and devoured the bodies there and then. The same process was reported several times. Terrified by these bloody comings and goings, the children wanted to escape. "Do not try to run away," said the mother, "lest I eat you too." The children implored her. "No, don't be afraid," she replied. No one was able to kill her, and the rumor soon spread that she was a jaguar-woman.

Commentary: Contradictory traits of the mother are illustrated: Violence and aggression along with maternal empathy. The woman uses her aggression to avenge the children (who had lied to her, in self-protection). The transformation of the woman into animal is mentioned for the first time.

Step 5. The children secretly dug a pit, which they covered with branches. They took flight when their mother announced to them that their turn had now come to be eaten. She rushed after them and fell into the trap. The children went to ask for help from Carancho (the culture hero, a species of falcon . . . simultaneously a bird of prey and a carrion-eater) who advised them to hollow out a tree trunk . . . and hide inside with him. *The jaguar-woman tried to tear the tree with her claws,* but they remained caught in the wood, so that Carancho was able to come out and kill her. Her corpse was burned on a woodpile. *Four or five days later a plant sprang up from the ashes. This was the first appearance of tobacco.*

Commentary: Children try to trick their mother and have her killed, after the mother announced their turn. The turn to the wisdom and power of Carancho coincides with the first explicit mentioning of the woman as a "jaguar-woman." Tobacco is created, its existence emerging from and presumably due to the jaguar-woman's remains.

This story played a role in Lévi-Strauss's structural analysis of myths, but we can give it an alternative analysis. There are dialogical tensions (within the myth) created in the course of the unfolding story, as well as the guidance of the tension from the myth to the present-day world of the teller and listeners.

Intrastory Dialogicality

Types of dialogicality evoked via the narrative entail (1) a repeated *ambiguity of the fear and trust of close kinpersons:* Man suddenly confronted by his wife's "abnormal" conduct, detecting her "appetite," and becoming uncertain about his fate; Children being assured by the mother not to be afraid, after being promised to be eaten up if they tried to escape; (2) *Ambiguity of self-defensive lies* for the powerless: Children "explained that the villagers had left after insulting them, having fled through shame at their own spitefulness"; (3) *Ambiguity of power of the ordinary in contrast with non-ordinary figures* (Carancho) in counteracting the "jaguarwoman." These tensions are promoted by minimalistic narrative methods:

"He noticed that she gobbled them up. Seized with fear . . ."

"The woman was indignant and, *wishing to avenge her children,* went after the villagers."

"Terrified by these bloody comings and goings, the children wanted to escape."

"They took flight when their mother announced to them that their turn had now come to be eaten."

This is paralleled by the gradual transformation of the image of the woman = mother = killer into the "jaguar-woman": "rumor soon spread that she was a jaguar-woman" → "The jaguar-woman tried to tear the tree *with her claws,* but they remained caught in the wood."

Each of these moments within the story build up tensions about what is being said and what is (not yet) said:

WOMAN hunting birds ← → [possibly eating up the husband]

WOMAN killer of husband ← → [still trusted mother by children]

WOMAN killer of everybody ← → [hope for surviving her]

WOMAN as a jaguar ← → [power of cultural heroes to catch a jaguar]

At each junction, the manifest content evokes the possible counteraction that is utilized in the next step.

The Tension with the Present

The ending of the story—the *point* of the emergence of tobacco—comes as a turn which, in and by itself, is not connected with the story itself. If the last sentence were not present, the inner tensions of the story could be sufficient for leading to a *moral*: for example, uncertainty of aggression in people, even close kin, need for early diagnostic signs and deception strategies; alignment with recognized "powerful others" to overcome the evil forces.

Yet it is exactly the last sentence of the story that links it with the recipients' present. The listeners to that story would probably not experience the horrors of an encounter with a "jaguar-woman" in their everyday worlds, yet seeing tobacco plants in everyday life can be a recurrent experience. The connection made with tobacco is thus set to evoke some personal rethinking of the story, and its *moral*, at times when the persons encounter tobacco.

Tobacco as an Inherently Ambiguous Cultural Object

A good demonstration of the foreground/background dialogicality in the case of this myth-story is the obvious counterclaim—based on the manifest content of the story—that the story has no linkages with tobacco at all. Indeed, the final part of the story could be easily eliminated (forgotten or untold), and the story becomes an example of stories about "jaguar-women."

Nevertheless, this would amount to a translation of the foreground/ background dialogue into that of the foreground only. In the case of the mythology of indigenous peoples, as Lévi-Strauss' analysis shows, tobacco in the South American indigenous folklore has been a substance of great ambiguity. First, it is food (e.g., expressions like "eat the cigar"), yet it is a food that might also be a deadly poison (Lévi-Strauss, 1983b, pp. 59 and 66). Furthermore, tobacco was involved in various magic rituals and healing ceremonies of the Central American societies prior to their Spanish conquest. With Middle America's Indians, tobacco came near to the symbolic power of curing all ills, being used also as power-generating talisman in war rituals, and protecting pregnant women from falling under the influence of witchcraft (see Thompson, 1970, chapter 4).

The ambiguity of the narrated myth gives rise to a new ambiguity—tobacco sprouts and grows in ways as to become a new substance of inherent ambiguity, which reflects the tensions generated by the oppositions depicted in the myth (i.e., wife/mother ← → Jaguar-woman). The binary opposition in the case of tobacco—food ← → poison—constitutes a relation of tension that can give rise to various narrative trajectories when the story is re-told. As Lévi-Strauss pointed out, tobacco

seems perpetually to oscillate between two states: that of being a supreme food and that of being a deadly poison. Furthermore, in between these two states can be found a whole series of intermediary forms, and it is particularly difficult to gauge the transitions from one to another since they depend on minute, and often imperceptible, differences relating to the quality of the commodity, the time of the harvest, the quantity consumed or the time which elapses before consumption. (Lévi-Strauss, 1983b, p. 67)

Our alternative "entrance point" into the generation of these "intermediary forms" in which any story about tobacco (or any other meaningfully "fielded" commodity—see Bühler, 1990) can be told. When the *langue*-focused side of the meaning of tobacco is given in terms of the schemes of oppositions derived by Lévi-Strauss (see Figure 9.2), then the generative process for the story-teller (re-maker of the myth) has a wide field of possibilities of how to evoke the binary contrasts and which forms of tension to suggest.

The person situates oneself in the field of binary contrast (TOBACCO: wholesome versus poisonous—Figure 9.2A), and by such positioning sets up a basis for the construction of a story (in which the actual mentioning of tobacco may be only in the end). If the meaning of tobacco were to be accepted in a unipolar side (wholesome—strong and good or dangerous—poisonous only), the stories that could be told from these two opposite perspectives cannot resemble the myth-story we have looked at. The stories told from such monological standpoints would either be some version of the glorification (e.g., a mythical hero who does good for people, unfortunately dies, and tobacco emerges on his or her gravesite to continue the good nutritional function), or denunciation (e.g., of women—or men—who are always aggressive and homicidal). However, the dialogical potency of the given myth-story is in its maintenance of ambiguous tension: the functional relationship between the

Figure 9.2
Schematic Depiction of the Meaning of TOBACCO in South American
Indigenous Mythology (A) (from Lévi-Strauss, 1983b, p. 66) and Its
Elaboration (B)

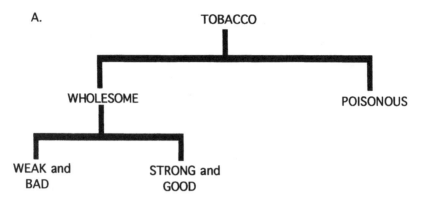

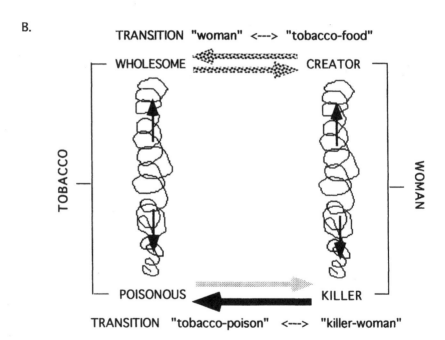

binary contrast wholesome ← → poisonous is that of a dynamic process
of uncertain kind, described in Figure 9.2B, that modifies Lévi-Strauss'
scheme for our purposes.

What this modification entails is the perspective of the (hypothetical)
story-teller who re-creates the myth on the basis of interpersonally rec-

ognized basic tensions inherent in the oppositions: *woman = life creator/life extinguisher* and *tobacco = wholesome/poisonous*. The two oppositions are represented as the opposites constantly moving "in" and "out" of each other, and the transition from one opposition to the other (i.e., the "leap" to the tobacco origin notion) is a switch of content, based on the same tension. In the myth-story presented, the dominance of the KILLER (woman) over CREATOR (woman) leads to the transition to POISONOUS (tobacco), and the story about woman's transformation is turned into contemporary everyday discourse about tobacco being in tension between poisonous and wholesome (food).

The story-teller is involved in construction of a *bricolage* (Lévi-Strauss, 1966, pp. 16-26), based on the availability of the story details (at the immediate moment) and the state of the oppositional tension. These tensions, once created, are maintained through their transfer into another binary oppositional tension that is part and parcel of everyday life. For persons who hear the "jaguar-woman" story, the drama of the killings and final capture of the killer remains remote from their everyday life, but growing, drying, and consuming tobacco is an activity that is easily encountered. Hence the *moral* of the story is encoded into the ambiguity of the everyday substance.

CONCLUSION: PERSONALIZING CULTURAL TENSIONS THROUGH MYTH-STORIES

We have seen that the positioning of story structure and meaning can be understood through the notion of the unity of opposites and the added conceptual insights into dialogicality and meaning-making it provides. Myths as texts are not products collected by folklorists, but communicative messages created in live interaction situations. These situations are episodes in which the story-teller emphasizes different characters in accordance with specific goal orientations. Thus,

The narrator performs for his audience, he entertains, making use of the comic and the tragic, for didactic gain. Stock characters are marched out by the teller of the myth to dramatic effect in order to underline a particular moral lesson. There is the knowledgeable, but diabolical and mad buffoon (the creator of all culture); there is the promiscuous and perfumed wandering hunter, the promiscuous and perfumed wife; there is the good gardener and the quarrelsome brothers. Consistently, the tales tell of characters whose out-of-control behavior leads to their own unhappiness and personal disaster and sometimes to danger for others. The quarrels of two brothers transform themselves into poisonous snakes; the wanderers never find peace; the greed for too much knowledge leads to the needless death of an old grandmother. (Overing, 1988, p. 179)

In the dramatic telling of the story, the build-up of the tension can proceed along different lines. The narrator can build up a manifest dramatization which calls for creation of the contrast with the opposites. Myths are known for the presence of all possible kinds of horrors utilized in them (Girard, 1986). Many versions of myths like the one described above can be created on the basis of narratives with linked oppositions (male/female, lying/truth, human/animal, birth/death, etc). The storyteller "works through" the appropriate oppositional tensions in the process of telling the story, the listener—in the process of listening. The psychological relevance of the stories, in terms of providing guidance for personal interpretations of the world and its semiotic regulation, may be in experiencing the underlying binary tensions rather than in the manifest content of the story. The manifest content may be easily forgotten, disbelieved, and so on, while the story's tension as a story is maintained through the binary contrasts. It is the flexibility inherent in these oppositional tensions which may allow negotiation of story content and thus heterogeneity of personal constructed meanings.

The main idea expressed in this chapter—the unity of foreground of the action of story-telling, and the collective-culturally implied background of the myth-story—leads to the central role of the *experiencing person* in the activity of ultimate sense-making and action directives. The latter is indeed embedded in distinct, situated activity contexts, in which the person is a more (or less) central (or peripheral) participant. Yet the locus of meaning-making is within the interpersonally constituted *personal* subjectivity of the individual. The person–context relationship is another example of the continuous tension between subjectivity and intersubjectivity, which cannot be reduced to an agentless version of "fusion" between the person and the situated activity experience. It is exactly through creation of fantasms from myth-stories and other macroscopic semiotic complexes that persons can create meaning, transcend the given context, and anticipate future experiencing.

NOTE

A preliminary version of this chapter was presented at the *Second Conference on Socio-Cultural Studies*, Geneva, September 14, 1996, as part of the symposium *Psychological Tools and Semiotic Mediation* (Michael Cole and Alfred Lang, co-conveners).

REFERENCES

Baldwin, J. M. (1915). *Genetic theory of reality*. New York: G. Putnam's Sons.
Bartlett, F. C. (1920). Some experiments on the reproduction of folk-stories. *Folk-Lore, 31*, 30–47.

Bergson, H. (1911). *Creative evolution*. New York: Holt.

Boesch, E. E. (1991). *Symbolic action theory and cultural psychology*. New York: Springer.

Bühler, K. (1930). *The mental development of the child*. New York: Harcourt, Brace & Co.

Bühler, K. (1990). *Theory of language*. Amsterdam: John Benjamin.

Girard, R. (1986). What is a myth? In Y. Freccero (Ed.), *The scapegoat* (pp. 24–44). Baltimore, MD: Johns Hopkins University Press.

Gupta, S. (1995). The role of myths in psychological meaning construction. Poster presented at the European Conference on Developmental Psychology, Krakow, August.

Gupta, S. (1998). Unpublished doctoral dissertation, University of North Carolina at Chapel Hill.

Josephs, I. E., & Valsiner, J. (1998). How does autodialogue work? Miracles of meaning maintenance and circumvention strategies. *Social Psychology Quarterly*, 61, (1), 68–83.

Josephs, I. E., Valsiner, J., & Surgan, S. (1999). The process of meaning construction: Dissecting the flow of semiotic activity. In J. Brandtstädter & R. Lerner (Eds.), *Action and self-development* (pp. 257–282). Thousand Oaks, CA: Sage.

Lévi-Strauss, C. (1963). The structural study of myth. In C. Lévi-Strauss, *Structural anthropology* (pp. 206–231). New York: Basic Books.

Lévi-Strauss, C. (1966). *The savage mind*. Chicago: University of Chicago Press.

Lévi-Strauss, C. (1978). *Myth and meaning: Cracking the code of culture*. New York: Schocken Books.

Lévi-Strauss, C. (1983a). *The raw and the cooked: Introduction to a science of mythology* (Vol. 1). Chicago: University of Chicago Press.

Lévi-Strauss, C. (1983b). *From honey to ashes: Introduction to a science of mythology* (Vol. 2). Chicago: University of Chicago Press.

Lévi-Strauss, C. (1987). Order and disorder in oral tradition. In C. Lévi-Strauss, *Anthropology and myth* (pp. 118–123). Oxford: Basil Blackwell.

Menon, U., & Shweder, R. A. (1994). Kali's tongue: Cultural psychology and the power of "shame" in Orissa. In S. Kitayama & H. Markus (Eds.), *Emotion and culture* (pp. 237–280). Washington, DC: American Psychological Association.

Obeyesekere, G. (1990). Oedipus: The paradigm and its Hindu rebirth. In G. Obeyesekere, *The work of culture* (pp. 69–139). Chicago: University of Chicago Press.

Overing, J. (1988). Personal autonomy and the domestication of the self in Piaroa society. In G. Jahoda & I. M. Lewis (Eds.), *Acquiring culture: Cross-cultural studies in child development* (pp. 169–192). London: Croom Helm.

Ramanujan, A. K. (1991). Toward a counter-system: Women's tales. In A. Appadurai, F. J. Korom, & M. A. Mills (Eds.), *Gender, genre, and power in South Asian expressive traditions* (pp. 33–55). Philadelphia: University of Pennsylvania Press.

Thompson, J.E.S. (1970). *Maya history and religion*. Norman: University of Oklahoma Press.

Valsiner, J. (1998). *The guided mind*. Cambridge, MA: Harvard University Press.

Chapter 10

Is "Integration" the Developmental End Goal for All Immigrants? Redefining "Acculturation Strategies" from a Genetic-Dramatistic Perspective

Sunil Bhatia

In this chapter, I examine how acculturation and its related concepts are typically studied in cross-cultural psychology and offer alternative ways of thinking about them (see also Bhatia, 2002; Bhatia & Ram, 2001a, 2001b). I specifically refer here to immigrants who primarily belong to non-European/non-Caucasian diasporic communities. Diasporas distinctly attempt to maintain (real and/or imagined) connections and commitments to their homeland. Additionally, diasporic communities recognize themselves and act as a collective community. In other words, people who simply live outside their ancestral homeland cannot automatically be considered diasporas (see Tölölyan, 1996). Examples of diasporic immigrants in the United States are Armenian Americans, Japanese Americans, Latino/Chicano communities in the United States, Asian-Indian Americans, and so on. Note here that, given the increase in travel and communication technology, the term "diaspora" can be increasingly applied to contemporary immigrant communities (see Appadurai, 1996). Furthermore, U.S. state-sponsored immigration, naturalization, and citizenship laws were historically based on racist ideologies (see Mohanty, 1991, for a full discussion of this issue). Moreover, given the pervasiveness of racial prejudice in the United States, non-European/non-white immigrants have been more likely to face exclusion and discrimination than their European counterparts. Through personal and collective re-membering, tales of discrimination, hardships, and sheer exploitation are kept alive in these immigrant communities. Therefore, non-European/non-Caucasian diasporic communities bring into sharp relief the sense of constantly negotiating between here and there, past and present, homeland and host land, self and other.

Motivated by my own experiences as an immigrant, I seek to extend and elaborate on current psychological theories of acculturation so that it encompasses some of the contradictions, dialogue, conflicts, and the local specificities involved as one moves between two or more cultural spaces. First, I argue that cross-cultural psychologists working within the area of "acculturation" propose a developmental trajectory for immigrants that implicitly privileges one end point or a singular goal. The end goal is described as an "integration strategy" (Berry & Sam, 1997), and such a strategy implies that all immigrants, after living in their host cultures, should strive toward the goal of "positively" assimilating the values and ideologies of both the dominant group and their own ethnic group. Second, I argue that missing from cross-cultural psychology's discussion is how issues of power and asymmetry affect many immigrants' attempts to integrate both the values of the host culture and their own community. For example, cross-cultural psychologists definitions of "bicultural competency" and "integration strategy" implicitly assume that both host and immigrant cultures have equal status and power. Rather than describing an ideal end state of acculturation for all immigrants, I suggest that we examine how immigrants living in hybrid cultures, border lands, and diasporic locations are constantly negotiating and contesting their multiple, and often conflicting histories and subject positions. Such an inquiry shifts the focus from looking at an immigrant's acculturation as governed by singular developmental end states (e.g., integration, assimilation) to a more *process*-oriented notion of acculturation (e.g., negotiation, dialogue).

In order to accomplish my task, I draw on the theory of *Genetic-Dramatism* as developed by Bernard Kaplan (1983a, 1992), which takes as its most central point the profoundly normative and contested character of human development. The Genetic-Dramatistic perspective (henceforth described as G-D) forces us to examine not only what is considered ideal development in our theory of cultural practices but also how we go about making decisions from a developmental point of view about the nature of such an ideal or an end goal. Thus, the G-D approach prompts us to ask the following questions: How is "acculturation" defined and by whom? What is the end point or the telos of acculturation? Who is at the center and who is at the margins in the acculturation process?

I begin this discussion by examining how the concept of "acculturation strategies" as a developmental ideal has been discussed in cross-cultural psychology. Second, by drawing on the G-D perspective, I argue that cross-cultural psychology's concepts related to acculturation strategies such as "integration," "assimilation," and "biculturalism" do not fully capture the complexities associated with the construction of "hybrid" immigrant identities. Third, I contend that the notion of "development" as theorized in the G-D perspective can provide insights that will sharpen our understanding of the political and cultural intersections that shape the present-day migrant experience.

BECOMING ACCULTURATED: THE CONCEPT OF ACCULTURATION STRATEGIES

Within the field of psychology in general and cross-cultural psychology in particular, there have been several models that explain acculturation-related issues. Cross-cultural researchers have studied topics such as acculturation and acculturative stress (Berry, 1998), socialization and enculturation (Camilleri & Malewska-Peyre, 1997), intergroup relations across cultures (Gudykunst & Bond, 1997), cross-cultural differences in work values (Hofstede, 1983), individualism and collectivism across cultures (Kagiçibasi, 1997), and bicultural identity (La-Fromboise, Hardin, Coleman, & Gerton, 1998). I do not intend to undertake a comprehensive review of all the different concepts associated with the topic of acculturation within the cross-cultural psychology literature. Rather, I will engage in a selective discussion of only those concepts that are directly relevant to the goals and purposes of the chapter as outlined above.

Prominent in acculturation research is the research conducted by Berry and his colleagues (e.g., Berry, 1980, 1985, 1990, 1997; Berry & Kim, 1988; Berry & Sam, 1997; Berry, Kim, Minde, & Mok, 1987; Berry, Kim, Power, Young, & Bujaki, 1989; Berry, Wintrob, Sindell, & Mawhinney, 1982). Their prolific output and the fact that several major introductory books on psychology (see for example Halonen & Santrock, 1996; Tavris & Wade, 1997; Westen, 1997) cite them extensively indicate that their model is one of the most influential on the subject of acculturation as developed in cross-cultural psychology. Given their significant and influential presence, I turn to their notion of "acculturation strategies" which refers to the plan or the method that individuals use in responding to stress-inducing new cultural contexts.

According to Berry (1998, p. 18), acculturation strategies are essentially invoked by individuals in the service of either one's "maintenance and development of one's ethnic distinctiveness" or deciding "whether relations with other groups in the larger society are of value and are to be sought." Thus, one's acculturation strategy consists of deciding how much "cultural maintenance" one should develop versus how much "contact and participation" one must have with the host culture (Berry & Sam, 1997, p. 296). Berry and his colleagues believe that there are four possible acculturation strategies or "options" that individuals and groups can exercise when they are adapting to the new cultural contexts.

The four different acculturation strategies are integration, assimilation, separation, and marginalization. Berry and his colleagues suggest that the *assimilation* strategy occurs when the individual decides not to maintain his or her cultural identity by seeking contact in his/her daily interaction with the dominant group. When the individuals from the non-dominant group "place a value on holding on to their original culture" (Berry & Sam, 1997, p. 297), and seek no contact with the dominant group then these individuals are pursuing a *separation* strategy. When individuals express an interest in maintaining strong ties in their everyday life both with their ethnic group as well as with the dominant group, the *integration* strategy is defined. The fourth strategy is *marginalization*, in which individuals "lose cultural and psychological contact with both their traditional culture and the larger society" (Berry, 1998, p. 119). Apart from defining the acculturating process through these four terms, there are other terms that are used to define the process of making contact and adapting to a new culture. Berry uses terms such as "behavioral shifts" (Berry, 1980) or "culture shedding" (Berry & Sam, 1997) to explain the process of adaptation and acculturation in a new culture. The term "culture shedding" as defined by Berry and Sam (1997) refers to the "the unlearning of aspects of one's previous repertoire that are no longer appropriate" (p. 298).

The notion that immigrants adopt one of the four acculturation strategies is premised on several assumptions. First, there is the assumption that integration is the best, most desired and a very possible "acculturation strategy," "telos," and "end goal" among the four strategies discussed above. Additionally, this model assumes that immigrants fall into only one of the categories. In other words, as an immigrant one has either followed the integrationist or the marginalized route. In the following sections, I explore each of these assumptions in more detail from a G-D perspective and suggest ways to think about acculturation less in terms of fixed, singular developmental end products and more as *negotiated* and *contested* developmental processes. However, before I elaborate on each of these themes, a brief introduction to Kaplan's Genetic-Dramatistic theory is necessary.

WERNER'S "HYBRID" NOTION OF DEVELOPMENT: INTEGRATION AND DIFFERENTIATION

The Genetic-Dramatistic perspective is essentially a marriage between the ideas of Heinz Werner and Kenneth Burke. The term *genetic* refers to development and was defined and elaborated by Werner (1940) in his classic work, *Comparative Psychology of Mental Development*. Kaplan (1983a) notes that Werner had a "hybrid" notion of development (p. 194). Development, according to Werner, was a concept that was governed both by "postulation" and by "intuition." That is, on the one hand, Werner believed that development had a specific meaning that entered into the "ordering of empirical" and experimental facts, and at the same time he believed that one could "read" developmental facts or the sequences of development from ontogenesis, evolutionary changes and cultural changes. Much inspired by Goethe's writings, Werner (1940) formulated the now famous dictum that development is to be defined in terms of the integration and differentiation of the part–whole relationship of any system.

Reflecting on the definition, Kaplan (1966, p. 661) tells us that although the definition of development was "relatively unambiguous," it was still fraught with ambivalence. For instance, he reminds us that it was not certain whether Werner's statement about development was taken to be referring to a scientific generalization that one arrived at after conducting an empirical examination of the ontogenetic phenomenon over time, or whether development was a heuristic concept to be defined independently of the phenomenon observed.

Werner, subsequently, in association with Kaplan, modified the definition of development and the much-needed revisions led to the birth of the *orthogenetic principle* (Werner & Kaplan, 1963). The new "changed status" of the notion of development emphasized that "insofar as development occurs in a process under consideration, there is a progression from a state of relative undifferentiatedness to one of increasing differentiation and hierarchic integration" (Kaplan, 1966, p. 661). Such a definition involved two strands of thought. On the one hand, this definition implied that one had to "posit" what one meant by normative or ideal development and on the other hand, it meant that after one had a definition of development, one had to figure out whether factors such as "historical, evolutionary ontogenetic and other changes conformed to or deviated" (Kaplan, 1966, p. 662) from such a definition. This modified definition openly warned developmentalists that one should not take a phenomenon to be "exclusively" a developmental one because it occurs in ontogenesis. Additionally, the definition also implied that in every domain—whether it is culture, history, phylogenesis, or a person's career—one could see features of increasing differentiation and hierarchic differentiation over time. Basically, Kaplan (1983b) argues that the idea of the orthogenetic principle was introduced to dissociate, or as he puts it, to "disentangle," the notion that one can figure out different "levels" or "stages" of development from the "vicissitudes and contingencies" of ontogenesis or "actual existence" (p. 55). I believe that the orthogenetic principle of development as formulated by Werner and Kaplan could be seen as the starting point for what came to be later defined by Kaplan as the Genetic-Dramatistic perspective. Kaplan (1983b) notes:

Within the Wernerian framework, therefore, we have development pertaining to the ways in which agents utilized means in the service of ends. If one differentiated the generic notion of means into acts and instrumentalities, and made explicit what was tacit for Werner, viz., context or scene, we had the famous pentad of Kenneth Burke's *Grammar of Motives*: agent, act, scene agency (or instrumentality) and purpose. (p. 56)

So why was Burke's notion of the pentad so appealing to Kaplan? In the next section, I attempt to address this question and provide reasons for why Burke's dramatism was linked with Werner's orthogenetic principle.

BURKE'S DRAMATISM: DIALOGICALITY AND MULTIPLICITY

In Burke's (1969) view, the key terms of the pentad: *Act, Scene, Agent, Agency*, and *Purpose* constitute the "generating principle" that attempts to answer the question "What is involved, when we say what people are doing and why they are doing it?" (p. xv). The five terms, according to Burke, are "principles of determination" (p. 18). That is, every ratio of the pentad will direct our attention to a different quality of observation, and thus convey different meanings. The terms of the pentad are "vocabularies" that present a particular reflection of reality.

In Burke's view the terminology that is used to present a "faithful reflection of reality" will necessarily amount to a particular "selection of reality." The process of using terms that reflect and select reality will also function as a "deflection" of reality. Thus Burke argues, *"what we want is not terms that avoid ambiguity, but terms that clearly reveal the strategic spots at which ambiguities necessarily arise"* (Burke 1969, p. xvii; emphasis in the original). For instance, Burke (1966) notes that by the mere use of the term "conscious," we are led to a corresponding "terministic nomenclature" of the unconscious. Furthermore, he tells us that because we have concepts such as "development" and "progress," our terministic situation directs our attention to the corresponding concepts such as "regression" and "primitivity." Through the permutations and combinations of the internal relationships between the terms of the pentad, Burke argues that we can discern the ways in which people frame their experiences to make sense of their world. The pentad is strictly about the terms that people use to pattern or define their experiences. The dramatistic terminology defines humans as symbol-using, symbol-misusing, and symbol-making animals. Thus, inherent within Kaplan's G-D perspective is the idea that symbolic action is the key to understanding all human action including the "act" of establishing our self–other relationships through both *dialogue* and *conflict*. Putting together both Werner's genetic psychology and Burke's philosophy of dramatism, Kaplan formulated the theory of Genetic-Dramatism.

THE GENETIC-DRAMATISTIC PERSPECTIVE: CONFLICT, DIALOGUE, AND DEVELOPMENT

There is an explicit assumption in the Genetic-Dramatism (G-D) theory that both dialogue and conflicts are part and parcel of our symbolic worlds. Kaplan recognizes that it is through our symbolic acts that we define others and ourselves. By using and misusing symbols we either identify or "disidentify" ourselves with individuals, groups, nations, causes, and movements. So often we fight for how the scene or the goal should be defined, and who will do the defining. We constantly try to persuade others to see our point of view or our goals. At times we co-operate and have a dialogue and at other times we are in conflict about what are the most appropriate or ideal means and instruments one should use to attain our teloi or goals. Drawing on Burke, Kaplan (1983b, p. 68) invites us to think about how often someone has tried to persuade us that what we would call "an invasion" is actually a "protective re-action," and how political foes tell us that our "regimentation" is nothing but a "planned economy." Further, he asks us to consider how we have tried to tell others that "science is really superstition" and that "their minds are really ghosts or that their ghosts are really minds; and their mainstreams are really puddles" (Kaplan, 1983b, p. 69). All these per-suasive tactics are not merely expressed for the sake of indulging in playful linguistic jugglery, but rather through these symbolic acts we take on a certain "attitude" toward reality. In sum, these symbolic acts are pregnant with real and potential possibilities. To this effect, Kaplan (1983b, p. 67) notes:

Dramatism is a critical and self critical method for making us aware not only of the remarkable range of "worlds" we inhabit but also of the symbolic ways in which we constitute such worlds and ourselves within those worlds. . . . The dra-matistic method is often employed to show how individuals in social situations operate on each other through symbolic action. In so much of human action, individuals representing different interests struggle over how a situation shall be named because they implicitly realize that the definition of the situation de-termines how one acts toward it and in it.

Thus, from a G-D view, Kaplan believes that there is a dialectical re-lationship between the different elements of the pentad. That is, how one sees the goals influences how one interprets the scene and instruments, which in turn, determines how one sees the agent. In this vein, Kaplan (1983b, p. 65) points out that "one man's scene is another man's purpose.

One woman's agent is another woman's instrumentality. What would be taken as an instrumentality or tool by one, is constructed as scene; by still another as a goal." Symbolic action as a form of social action encompasses the political, economic, mythical, ritualistic, and scientific realms. Our language and symbols are not merely signs that are used to refer to the world around us. Instead, they enable human beings to *interpret* events, objects, persons, and groups. The symbolic orientation presents us with a view that determines how language aids us in taking a particular "perspective" toward situations.

Development, then, according to the G-D perspective "does not lurk directly in the population studied but resides fundamentally in the perspective used" (Kaplan, 1983a, p. 196). Here, of course, Kaplan is referring to the point that development resides in one's telos or the end goal that one adopts. Kaplan elaborates:

Development is rendered "visible," so to speak, if one adopts a developmental perspective. Such a perspective, I submit, involves the presumption of teloi, an ordering of teloi, and ordering of the means and modes of operation for realizing the teloi. From such a perspective development pertains to progressions of forms with respect to function or means with respect to ends. (Kaplan, 1986, p. 95)

Such a view of development implies that a self or selves are primarily engaged in a series of cultural practices, practices wherein one employs and interprets language and symbols for achieving various goals or teloi. Such symbolic activity, where one uses a sign or a symbol to express emotions and feelings or engages in persuading oneself and others, is primarily*stipulatory* in character. The idea that symbolic action bears with it a stipulatory character tells us that there will be a conflict over the interpretation of how the agent and scene *ought* to be. Here, we can begin to make connections between the G-D perspective and the concept of acculturation strategies as formulated by Berry and his colleagues. By drawing on the G-D perspective, we can discuss *why* stipulating the "integration strategy" as an ideal developmental end state of the acculturation process is a problematic concept.

INTEGRATION: THE IDEAL ACCULTURATIVE STATE

One of the explicit assumptions made by Berry and his colleagues is that the "integrationist or bicultural acculturation strategy appears to be a consistent predictor of more positive outcomes than the three alternatives of assimilation, separation, or marginalization" (Berry & Sam, 1997, p. 318). Furthermore, the concept of integration strategy is based on the assumption that we live in a multicultural society "where a large number of distinguishable ethnic groups, all cooperating within a larger system live in a mosaic like system" (Berry, 1998, p. 118). One of the assumptions inherent in the integration strategy is that all immigrants can somehow reach a developmental end point where they "positively" assimilate the values and ideologies of both the dominant, mainstream group and their own ethnic group.

The idea that an immigrant has the "choice" to internalize the value orientations of one's own ethnic group and the dominant group as well is based on the notion that the United States is a plural society. This plural, multicultural society, according to Berry, is fundamentally built around some "core values and traditional institutions but also many cultural variations are accepted as valued characteristics of the society" (Berry, 1998, p. 118). The key phrase in this quote is "but also." "But also" indirectly refers to two points: One, that there are acculturation goals that reflect the essence of the American society, and the second point suggests that there are "other" sets of values and cultural practices that exist on the side or on the boundaries that have been considered acceptable as well.

The idea that in the United States there are some practices that qualify as representing the "core" values and "others" raises a series of questions from the G-D perspective. What are the core values of the mainstream American ways of life? Which group represents these core values and which group represents the "cultural variations"? Do both the values and norms of the host culture and the acculturating individuals' immigrant group have the same kinds of privilege and power in the American society?

From the point of view of the G-D perspective, it is not clear whether the notion of "integration strategy" is formulated as a developmental goal through empirical study of the immigrant communities over time, or whether the "integration strategy" as a developmental goal is a "heuristic," "normative," culturally constituted concept that is defined independently of the "ontogenetic" phenomenon observed. As suggested before, from the G-D perspective development is not inherent in the characteristics of populations or community activities but is, rather, defined in relation to a particular *developmental perspective*. The G-D perspective forces us to re-examine not only what is considered ideal development in our theory of acculturation, but also how we go about making decisions from a developmental point of view or many developmental views about the nature of such an end point, telos, or goal. As soon as we enter into a discussion about what are considered ideal acculturation goals— what promotes development of an individual's "integration" strategy and what inhibits the development of the "integration" strategy—we have entered the realm of ethics, axiology, and morality. In essence, we are trying to define what is a "good strategy" to get acculturated and *how* ought one to get "acculturated" in a given host culture. Inevitably, a move toward discussing "what is an ideal acculturative state" is going to bring about strife and conflict for the host culture and some immigrant communities. Thus, communities and individuals belonging to different practices will invariably get divided between "our acculturation goals" and "their acculturation goals." Perhaps this is not an earth-shattering or a mind-boggling insight, but it is important to point out that within such sharp divisions, where dialogue and conflict occur simultaneously, one can witness the explicit and implicit postulation of developmental goals and end points.

From the G-D perspective, the integration model proposed by Berry and his colleagues assumes a developmental trajectory that implicitly privileges one end point or one goal. The goal is vaguely described in the idea that by adopting the integration strategy, immigrants can somehow "positively" assimilate the values and ideologies of both the dominant group and their own immigrant group. The G-D perspective helps us recognize that the acculturation processes within the United States takes on multiple developmental trajectories for different migrants. For example, consider the scenario where the migrant was part of a "powerful center" in his/her local milieu prior to migration, and after migration, he/she finds himself or herself to be a part of a minority living on the margin or multiple margins. Frankenberg and Mani (1993) allege that race, gender, and class are crucial signifiers that mark our locations and positions in the center or the margins. Through these signifiers we identify ourselves, our selfhood, and we get identified by others as well.

In other words, our identities are constructed through both identification with the larger powerful majority as well as through opposition to it. Such an acculturation process emphasizes developmental end goals that are anchored in both the politics of integration and differentiation, unity and multiplicity, development and dramatism. This peculiar combination of similarity and difference is at the heart of the acculturation process. To describe the "integration strategy" as a singular developmental end goal minimizes the inequities and injustices faced by certain non-European immigrant groups as a result of their "culture," "nationality," or "hybrid" histories. The asymmetrical relations of power and privilege between one's ethnic immigrant culture and the dominant host culture are an important part of many (though not all) immigrants' acculturation experiences, and these experiences are tightly knitted with their evolving conceptions of selfhood. The G-D approach allows us to broaden the notion of "acculturation strategies" to include developmental goals that pay attention to the conflicts and complexities involved for immigrants whose cultures are described as "hybrid," "diasporic," "mixing," and "moving."

GENETIC-DRAMATISM AND THE DEVELOPMENT OF "HYBRID" IDENTITIES

Contemporary immigrants can no longer be characterized as uprooted, alienated individuals who traverse a linear trajectory from cultural differentiation to assimilation. On the contrary, recent scholarship in anthropology and diaspora studies employs the term "transmigration" to emphasize the continuous and ongoing process through which immigrants reconstitute their "simultaneous embeddedness in more than one society" (Glick, Basch, & Blanc, 1995, p. 48). Similarly, Hermans and Kempen (1998) have argued that cultural dichotomies such as individualism and collectivism do not fully capture the complex relationship between global cultures and the construction of self (p. 1117). They note that globalization has led to a hybridization of cultural practices and meanings that:

may create such multiple identities as Mexican School girls dressed in Greek Togas dancing in the style of Isadora Duncan, a London boy of Asian origin playing for a local Bengali cricket team and at the same time supporting the Arsenal football club, Thai boxing by Moroccan girls in Amsterdam, and native Americans celebrating Mardi Gras in the United States. (p. 113)

The above examples demonstrate that acculturation processes cannot be described in terms of fixed categories that emphasize linear trajectories. Rather, as Hermans and Kempen argue, it might be more appropriate to describe cultures as constantly "moving and mixing" (p. 117). They emphasize that essentialist and monolithic concepts of culture fail to explain the challenges accompanying the acculturation process within a world where cultures are mixing and moving, where the local and the global are merging and creating new "contact zones" between different cultures. In particular, Hermans and Kempen (1998) problematize the notion of acculturation as proposed by Berry and his colleagues. They elaborate:

From the metaphor of travel, a familiar term like *acculturation* becomes complicated because it assumes an overly linear trajectory from Culture A to Culture B. Contact zones, instead permit a two-way intensification of contact and are, moreover, open to forms of communication that run across the boundaries of many groups and cultures simultaneously. (p. 117; emphasis in the original)

Hermans and Kempen's idea that the acculturation process should be seen through the metaphors of travel, translocality, and de-territorialization challenges Berry and his colleagues' idea that the acculturation process merely involves "culture shedding" or some "behavioral shift" when one moves from culture A to B. Furthermore, by suggesting that the strategy of "integration" is the end point or the telos of the individual's or the group's acculturation process, Berry and his colleagues are overlooking the painful and alienating experiences associated with "living in between" cultures. The G-D perspective can be used as a useful analytic or heuristic tool to understand the strife and conflict that many diasporic immigrants feel as a result of straddling two or three cultural spaces that seem incompatible with each other in terms of power, privileges, and ideologies. The tension between different "acculturation" goals—such as the norms of the host and immigrant cultures—with regard to a telos or multiple teloi is similar to the "strife of systems" or the tension between the "organismic" and "developmental" points of view. Kaplan (1992) argues that the "genetic" part of the G-D perspective is roughly equivalent to the developmental point of view and the "dramatistic" part is comparable to the "organismic" point of view.

THE STRIFE OF SYSTEMS IN GENETIC DRAMATISM: DEVELOPMENTAL AND ORGANISMIC PERSPECTIVES

Kaplan (1992) tells us that the organismic approach is mainly concerned with providing a comprehensive description of the various features of the organism or multiple organisms both "cross sectionally and longitudinally" (p. 436). One of the main emphases of the organismic point of view is that one must study organisms, their culture as an ecological whole, as a fully integrated system made of interdependent part–whole relationships. Further, organismic theorists believe that the part–whole relationship within a given system cannot be explained "mechanistically" in terms of the whole or the isolated parts of the system that make it a whole. The other important point that needs to be mentioned here is that organismic theorists "recognize that temporal change, on either the individual or the societal level, does not entail orthogenesis" (Kaplan, 1992, p. 437). Further, this approach adopts a mode of analysis that focuses on how the "teleological activities" of the organism regulate the emergence of novel functions and structures in the organism over time. An analysis of the new forms and functions are undertaken without disturbing or "rupturing" the wholeness of that organism. Since so much of the effort of organismic theorists is devoted toward maintaining the wholeness and integrity of an organism, they:

reject the notion that different organisms of the same logical type (e.g., different biological forms, different sociocultural entities) can be legitimately compared with each other in terms of some extra-organismic standard, and ranked developmentally more or less advanced. Each organism contains its own standards. (Kaplan, 1992, p. 436)

The developmental perspective, according to Kaplan, is similar to the organismic perspective in "almost" all ways; however, it differs on two issues. He explains that the developmental point of view:

distinguishes the concept of development from the concept of historical change ... and it assumes some extra systemic standard, in terms of which one can assess organisms of a certain logical type as being more primitive or more advanced than other organisms of the same logical type. (Kaplan, 1992, p. 437)

To put it another way, the developmental point of view is not so much concerned with actual descriptions of what happens to an organism in orthogenesis, but is rather concerned with whether or not organisms of the same logical type "measure up" or can approximate themselves to an ideal natural order or a developmental point of view. Kaplan tells us that as long as one is objectively engaged in describing how functions operate, evolve in time, and how they can be modified with respect to various conditions, the two perspectives are like "comrades-in-arms." However, the moment we begin to speak of and assess development in terms of an external standard, rather than some intrinsic "species-specific" standard, we find that the organicists and the developmentalists are locked in a battle. The strife seems to take on an unresolvable tension, especially at the level of intervention. It is often at the level of intervention that one has to make a judgment whether an organism and the practices in which it lives, is an "advance or a regression" with respect to the "trans-systemic standards."

At this point, we can make the link between the above discussion on the strife between the developmental and organismic perspectives and Berry and his colleagues' notion of acculturation strategies. To recall, Berry and his colleagues argue that the four main acculturation strategies are integration, assimilation, separation, and marginalization. This chapter is mainly concerned with problematizing the concept of the integration strategy. According to Berry and his colleagues, an immigrant adopts an integration strategy when he or she attempts to maintain cultural and psychological contact in his/her everyday interactions with both his or her ethnic group as well as the dominant group. As discussed before, the integration model implicitly privileges one developmental end point or goal. Thus, from the developmental system, an immigrant's integration of his or her ethnic/minority culture with the host culture is the norm, or the "extra-systemic" standard by which one's acculturation in the host culture is measured. Such a view does not aim to explicitly get at the "actual descriptions" of what happens to an immigrant in everyday living, but is mainly concerned with whether or not immigrants in some way "measure up" to the developmental end point of integration. The emphasis here is on achieving and measuring a developmental end state of acculturation rather than examining the developmental process of acculturation itself. By emphasizing the integration strategy as an ideal developmental end point, Berry and his colleagues are neglecting to take into account the "organismic" dimensions of the immigrant experiences. Such a dimension emphasizes immigrants' connections, contact, and participation with their own community members.

The effort to feel "whole," "united," or "related" to one's ethnic community does not imply that the immigrants are adopting a "marginal" identity or are fulfilling an *equal* part of an "integration" strategy. Rather, immigrants seek connectedness or relatedness to their community through participation in religious rituals, and other social events that enable them to feel "belongingness" with their community. Such retreats into one's community by no means suggests that the immigrant's journey form the majority culture to one's minority culture and vice versa is an undisturbed, balanced, and effortless journey. On the contrary, for most immigrants, such an acculturation process is marked by an *irreducible tension* between the incompatibilities, conflicts, and asymmetries of the immigrant's culture and host culture, homeland and adopted land, majority and minority culture, and mainstream and ethnic cultures. The G-D perspective, with its emphasis on both the developmental and organismic points of view, unity and multiplicity, dialogicality and conflict, allows us to think about the construction of diasporic immigrant identities as negotiated, contested, and in-between rather than moving toward an integrated identity that is always stable, healthy, and positive. Thus, there are several conceptual problems with describing the integration strategy as the developmental end goal in the immigrant's acculturation process.

First, Berry and his colleagues describe the integration strategy as being an end goal of an immigrant's acculturation without explaining the process by which such a goal would be achieved. Second, missing from their discussion on "integration strategy" is how issues of conflict, power, and asymmetry affect many diasporic immigrants' acculturation processes. For example, integration, at least as discussed by Berry and his colleagues, implicitly assumes that both the majority and minority cultures have equal status and power. Furthermore, it is not clear what the term "integration" exactly means. How does one know when someone is integrated or not with the host culture? Who decides whether an immigrant is pursuing a strategy of marginalization, integration, or separation? Radhakrishnan (1996), a scholar who studies immigrants living in the diaspora, suggests that the notion of multiple, hyphenated, and hybridized identities of the diaspora is a challenge to the idea that there can be some kind of a blissful marriage or integration of the cultures between the hyphen. Realizing that the whole business of understanding the diasporan identity is a tough proposition, Radhakrishnan engages in raising a series of insightful questions. He asks:

When someone speaks as an Asian-American, who is exactly speaking? If we dwell in the hypen who represents the hyphen: the Asian or the American, or can the hyphen speak for itself without creating an imbalance between the Asian and America components. . . . True, both components have status, but which has the power and the potential to read and interpret the other on its terms? If the Asian is to be Americanized, will the American submit to Asianization? (Radhakrishnan, 1996, p. 211)

Through these questions Radhakrishnan is foregrounding the point that the acculturation process is not a matter of one's individual strategy, where one has the free choice to unproblematically integrate the values of the host culture and one's own immigrant group. Although integration and bicultural competency may be worthy goals to achieve, the G-D perspective alerts us to the point that such an ideal blinds us to the complexities and contradictions of living in multiple cultural spaces. Thus, it is important to pay attention to the process of how immigrants living in the diaspora or with multiple heritages reconcile and negotiate their diverse subject positions. Chaudhary (1998) describes "hybridity" as encompassing "the fluid state of having multiple, shifting identities which are constructed and differentially privileged in response to contextual demands for alienation and allegiance" (p. 47f.). This concept of hybridity is exemplified in scholar and writer Yeps' (1998) reflections on his own identity. He defines himself as *Asianlatinoamerican*, being born in a Chinese family who lived first in Peru and then later in the United States. He believes that he has integrated all three cultures within himself. However, he does not claim his "integration" to be always harmonious or free from tension. Rather, his experience with his own multicultural identity brings him "internal and external conflicts" (p. 80). Similarly, Lavie and Swedenberg (1996) emphasize that the notion of borderland identities is not a place where one can safely create an idea of a place filled with "imaginative interminglings and happy hybridites for us to celebrate" (p. 15). Rather they use war like metaphors to suggest that borders are like "minefields, mobile territories of constant clashes," where "formations of violence" continuously signify "zones of loss, alienation" and pain. Lavie and Swedenberg (1996) clarify:

Living in the border is frequently to experience the feeling of being trapped in an impossible in-between, like cosmopolitan Franco-Maghrebis who are denied the option of identifying with either France or Algeria and are harassed both by white racist extremists and Islamist xenophobes. . . . Borders and diasporas are phenomena that blow up—both enlarge and explode—the hyphen: Arab-Jew, African-American, Franco-Maghrebi, Black-British. Avoiding the dual axes of migration between distinct territorial entities, the hyphen becomes the third space. (p. 15f.)

Lavie and Swedenberg's idea of describing hybrid identities as being in an "impossible in-between" has been discussed by several disaspora theorists. Bhabha (1994, p. 219), for example, describes the concept of hyphenated identities as made up of "incommensurable elements." Paul Gilroy (1993) makes a plea for a Black Atlantic that goes beyond rigid ethnic categories and proposes conceptions of ethnicity, race, and nationality that are complex and multilayered. Such scholarship on contemporary, traditional diasporic communities is in congruence with the spirit of the G-D perspective. The G-D perspective, along with these other bodies of research on immigrant issues, highlights the need for cross-cultural psychologists to rethink and redefine the notion that immigrants, irrespective of what histories and cultures they carry with them, can adopt a happy, balanced "bicultural or integrated" acculturation strategy in their host country. The idea of living in the borders with hyphenated identities and inhabiting a "third space" forces us to redefine acculturation as a negotiated and a contested process rather than as a moving toward a fixed, singular developmental end goal.

CONCLUSION

In sum, the G-D approach with an emphasis on development and drama provides us with alternative ways of thinking about the acculturation process. The G-D approach basically seeks to foreground the point that not all immigrants share the acculturation practices of the host culture. And, when there are no shared meanings about what constitutes a set of "core" acculturation practices, there are often conflicts about who and how one should name and define the developmental processes and end goals of acculturation. The G-D perspective is a "critical and self-critical" method that makes us aware that the world we live in is symbolically constructed. For example, symbolic action is manifested through localized power struggles, and asymmetrical relationships of privileges in our communities. These ideological struggles in our community practices are often about what is a good life, or what standards one should uphold in life. Such struggles about the norm or the "good life" have deep implications for not only how we live generally, but also how we go about discussing issues of immigration, acculturation, and selfhood. The G-D perspective enables us to explore both the politics of identity construction and multiple developmental goals. Especially, terms such as "bicultural competency" and "integration strategy" implicitly assume that both host and immigrant cultures share equal status and power. The G-D perspective, rather than describing an end state of acculturation for all immigrants, is interested in examining how immigrants living in hybrid cultures and postcolonial and diasporic locations are negotiating and, reconciling conflicting histories and incompatible subject positions. Such an inquiry foregrounds a *process*-oriented notion of acculturation (e.g., negotiation).

Furthermore, the G-D perspective allows us to add a developmental perspective to the larger study of acculturation issues. Such a perspective is unique because it urges cross-cultural psychologists to examine development from multiple end points rather than studying it by examining only ontogenetic changes. A developmental perspective enables us to see what brings about changes and transformations in a given set of community practices. Development and drama go together because communities that are undergoing transformation have to settle on questions about optimal end goals for living. Such a move automatically takes us into the realm of dialogue and conflict, unity and multiplicity. Thus, the G-D perspective emphasizes that wherever there is a developmental point of view there is continuity and transformation, dialogue and resistance, strife and integration, and division and separation. The forces that divide and integrate create a dialectical existence between unity and difference, birth and death, and integration and differentiation. It is this dialectic that Kaplan has described as the drama of human relations: a symbolic relationship based on the existence of division and merger, one and the many, the organismic and the developmental, the genetic and the dramatistic. Thus, at the core, the issues about immigrants and acculturation in our community are issues about growth and development. The G-D perspective brings us one step closer to understanding the dynamics involved in acculturation practices of immigrant communities with multiple cultures and histories.

REFERENCES

Appadurai, A. (1996). *Modernity at large: Cultural dimensions of globalization.* Minneapolis: University of Minnesota Press.

Berry, J. W. (1980). Acculturation as varieties of adaptation. In A. Padilla (Ed.), *Acculturation:Theory, models and some new findings* (pp. 9–25). Boulder, CO: Westview Press.

Berry, J. W. (1985). Psychological adaptation of foreign students in Canada. In R. Samuda & A. Wolfgang (Eds.), *Intercultural counseling* (pp. 235–248) Toronto: Hogreffe.

Berry, J. W. (1990). Cultural variations in cognitive style. In S. Wapner (Ed.), *Biopsycho-social factors in cognitive style* (pp. 289–308). Hillsdale, NJ: Erlbaum.

Berry, J. W. (1997). Immigration, acculturation and adaptation. *Applied Psychology: An International Review, 46*, 5–68.

Berry, J. W. (1998). Acculturative stress. In P. B. Organista, K. M. Cren, & G. Marin (Eds.), *Readings in ethnic psychology* (pp. 117–122). New York: Routledge.

Berry, J. W., & Kim, U. (1988). Acculturation and mental health. In P. Dasen, J. W. Berry, & N. Sartorius (Eds.), *Cross-cultural psychology and health: Towards applications* (pp. 207–236). London: Sage.

Berry, J. W., Kim., U., Minde, T., & Mok, D. (1987). Comparative studies of acculturative stress. *International Migration Review, 21*, 491–511.

Berry, J. W., Kim, U., Power, S., Young, M., & Bujaki, M. (1989). Acculturation attitudes in plural societies. *Applied Psychology, 38*, 185–206.

Berry J. W., & Sam, D. (1997). Acculturation and adaptation. In J. W. Berry, M. H. Seagull, & C. Kagitçibasi (Eds.), *Handbook of cross-cultural psychology: Social behavior and applications* (Vol. 3, pp. 291–326). Needham Heights, MA: Allyn and Bacon.

Berry, J. W., Wintrob, R., Sindell, P. S., & Mawhinney, T. A. (1982). Cultural change and psychological adaptation. In R. Rath, H. Asthana, D. Sinha, & J.B.P. Sinha (Eds.), *Diversity and unity in cross-cultral psychology* (pp. 157–170). Lisse: Swets and Zeitlinger.

Bhabha, H. (1994). *The location of culture*. New York: Routledge.

Bhatia, S. (2002). Acculturation, dialogical voices and the construction of the diasporic self. *Theory & Psychology, 12*, 53–75.

Bhatia, S., & Ram, A. (2001a). Locating the dialogical self in the age of transnational migrations, border crossings and diasporas. *Culture & Psychology, 7*, 297–310.

Bhatia, S., & Ram, A. (2001b). Rethinking "acculturation" in relation to diasporic cultures and postcolonial identities. *Human Development, 44*, 1–18.

Burke, K. (1966). *Language as symbolic action: Essays on life, literature, and method*. Berkeley: University of California Press.

Burke, K. (1969). *A grammar of motives*. Berkeley: University of California Press.

Camilleri, C., & Malewska-Peyre, H. (1997). Socialization and identity strategies. In J. W. Barry, P. R. Dasen, & T. S. Saraswathi (Eds.), *Handbook of cross-cultural psychology: Basic processes and human development* (Vol. 2, pp. 41–67). Needham Heights, MA: Allyn and Bacon.

Chaudhary, L. (1998). "We are graceful swans who can also be crows": Hybrid identities of Pakistani Muslim women. In S. D. Gupta (Ed.), *A patchwork shawl* (pp. 33–46). New Brunswick, NJ: Rutgers University Press.

Frankenberg, R., & Mani, L. (1993). Cross currents, cross talk: Race, "postcolinality" and the politics of location. *Cultural Studies, 7*, 292–311.

Gilroy, P. (1993). *The black Atlantic: Modernity and double consciousness*. Cambridge, MA: Harvard University Press.

Glick, S. N., Basch, L., & Blanc, C. S. (1995). From immigrant to transmigrant: Theorizing transnational migration. *Anthropological Quarterly, 68*, 48–63.

Gudykunst, W., & Bond, M. H. (1997). Intergroup relations. In J. W. Berry, M. H. Seagull, & C. Kagitçibasi (Eds.), *Handbook of cross-cultural psychology: Social behavior and applications* (Vol. 3, pp. 119–161). Needham Heights, MA: Allyn and Bacon.

Halonen, J. S., & Santrock, J. W. (1996). *Psychology: Contexts of behavior*. Dubuque, IA: Brown & Benchmark.

Hermans, J. M., & Kempen, H.J.G. (1998). Moving cultures: The perilous problems of cultural dichotomies in a globalizing society. *American Psychologist*, 53, 1111–1120.

Hofstede, G. (1980). *Culture's consequences: International differences in work related values*. Beverly Hills, CA: Sage.

Kagitçibasi, C. (1997). Individualism and collectivism. In J. W. Berry, M. H. Seagull, & C. Kagitçibasi (Eds.), *Handbook of cross-cultural psychology: Social behavior and applications* (Vol. 3, pp. 1–49). Needham Heights, MA: Allyn and Bacon.

Kaplan, B. (1966). The study of language in psychiatry: The comparative developmental approach and its application to symbolizations in psychopathology. In S. Arieti (Ed.), *American Handbook of Psychiatry* (Vol. 3, pp. 659–688). New York: Basic Books.

Kaplan, B. (1983a). Trio of trials: The past as prologue, prelude and pretext. In R. Lerner (Ed.), *Developmental psychology: Historical and philosophical perspectives* (pp. 184–227). Hillsdale, NJ: Erlbaum.

Kaplan, B. (1983b). Genetic-dramatism: Old wine in new bottles. In S. Wapner & B. Kaplan (Eds.), *Toward a holistic developmental psychology* (pp. 53–74). Hillsdale, NJ: Erlbaum.

Kaplan, B. (1986). Value presuppositions in developmental theories. In L. Cirillo (Ed.), *Value presuppositions in developmental theories* (pp. 89–102). Hillsdale, NJ: Lawrence Erlbaum.

Kaplan, B. (1992). Strife of systems: Tension between organismic and developmental points of view. *Theory & Psychology*, 2, 431–443.

LaFromboise, T., Hardin, L. K., Coleman, H.L.K., & Gerton, J. (1998). Psychological impact of biculturalism: Evidence and theory. In P. B. Organista, K. M. Cren, & G. Marin (Eds.), *Readings in ethnic psychology* (pp. 123–155). New York: Routledge.

Lavie, S., & Swedenberg, T. (1996). Introduction: Displacement, diaspora, and geographies of identity. In S. Lavie & T. Swedenberg (Eds.), *Displacement, diaspora and geographies of identity* (pp. 1–26). Durham, NC: Duke University Press.

Mohanty, T. M. (1991). Cartographies of struggle: Third world women and the politics of feminism. In C. T. Mohanty, A. Russo, & L. Torres (Eds.), *Third world women and the politics of feminism* (pp. 2–47). Bloomington: Indiana University Press.

Radhakrishnan, R. (1996). *Diasporic mediations: Between home and location*. Minneapolis: University of Minnesota Press.

Tavris, C., & Wade, C. (1997). *Psychology in perspective*, 2nd ed. New York: Addison-Wesley.

Tölölyan, K. (1996). Rethinking diaspora(s): Stateless power in the transnational moment. *Diaspora*, 5, 3–35.

Werner, H. (1940). *The comparative psychology of mental development*. New York: International Universities Press.

Werner, H., & Kaplan, B. (1963). *Symbol formation: An organismic-developmental approach to language*. Hilldale, NJ: Lawrence Erlbaum Associates.

Westen, D. (1997). *Psychology: Mind, brain and culture*. New York: John Wiley & Sons.

Yeps, G. (1998). My three cultures: Navigating the multicultural identity landscape. In J. N. Martin, T. K. Nakayama, & L. A. Flores (Eds.), *Readings in cultural contexts* (pp. 70–79). Mountain View, CA: Mayfield Publishing Company.

Index

About the Contributors

EMILY ABBEY is a graduate student in psychology at Clark University in Worcester, Massachusetts. She is currently interested in psychological reactions to ambiguity.

SUNIL BHATIA is Assistant Professor in the Department of Human Development at Connecticut College in New London. He is interested in studying issues related to the intersection of culture and self within the field of cultural psychology. In particular, his research analyzes how concepts such as transnationalism, hybridity, and post-colonial diasporas have important implications for reframing concepts such as culture, dialogicality, and identity in cultural psychology. His work has been published in *Culture and Psychology*, *Human Development*, *History of Psychology*, and *Theory and Psychology*.

PATRICK C. DAVIS has been an undergraduate student at Clark University in Worcester, Massachusetts.

SUMEDHA GUPTA received her Ph.D. from the University of North Carolina at Chapel Hill, working on ways in which human beings deal with worries. She has also been interested in memory development and literacy.

HUBERT J. M. HERMANS is Professor Emeritus of Psychology at the University of Nijmegen, The Netherlands. He developed a valuation theory and a self-confrontation method, an idiographic procedure for assessing a person's meaning system. His most recent work is on the multivoicedness and dialogicality of the self. Among his books are *The Dialogical Self: Meaning as Movement* (with Harry Kempen, 1993) and *Self-Narratives: The Construction of Meaning in Psychotherapy* (with Els Hermans-Jansen, 1995). He is First International Associate of the Society for Personology and President of the International Society for Dialogical Science (ISDS).

GUSTAV JAHODA, now Professor Emeritus at the University of Strathclyde in Glasgow, Scotland, was one of the pioneers of cross-cultural psychology. He carried out fieldwork on perception, cognition, and attitude change, mainly in Africa. Since his retirement he has retreated to the library, writing on theories of culture and historical topics.

INGRID E. JOSEPHS is Professor of Psychology at the University of Nijmegen, The Netherlands. Her main area of interest is the development of the self within a cultural psychological framework. She has published in *Culture & Psychology*, *Human Development*, and *Theory & Psychology*.

MARIA C.D.P. LYRA is Professor of Psychology at the Federal University of Pernambuco, Recife, Brazil. She is interested in the emergence and development of early communication between mothers and infants from a dialogical and dynamic systems perspective. She is co-editor of *Dynamics and Indeterminism in Developmental and Social Processes* (with Alan Fogel and Jaan Valsiner, 1997) and *Construction of Psychological Processes in Interpersonal Communication* (with Jaan Valsiner, 1998).

IVANA MARKOVÁ was born in Czechoslovakia and obtained her degrees in philosophy and psychology at the Charles University in Prague. Since 1967 she has lived in the United Kingdom. She is Professor of Psychology at the University of Stirling in Scotland. Her main research interests are language, thought, communication, and epistemology of social psychology, taking a cultural and historical perspective. She studies communication in the speech impaired and in social representations of democracy, responsibility, rights, and political trust in several European countries. She is the author of *Paradigms, Thought and Language* (1982), *Human Awareness* (1987), and *Dialogicality and Social Representations* (2003), and she has edited and co-edited several books on language, dialogue, and representations of disability. She is a Fellow of the British Academy and of the Royal Society of Edinburgh.

JOSEPH F. RYCHLAK is Professor Emeritus at Loyola University, Chicago. In addition to teaching for 44 years at five universities, Rychlak has distinguished himself as a psychotherapist, author, theorist, and scientific researcher. He is a fellow of both the American Psychological

Association and the American Psychological Society. He has twice been elected president of the APA Division of Theoretical and Philosophical Psychology. Rychlak is known as a rigorous humanist because he submits his nonmechanistic theoretical claims to the traditional scientific test. Among his major publications are *The Psychology of Rigorous Humanism* (1977), *Logical Learning Theory: A Human Teleology and Its Empirical Support* (1994), *In Defense of Human Consciousness* (1997), and *The Human Image in Postmodern America* (2003).

MICHELINE SOUZA is completing her doctoral work in developmental psychology at Clark University in Worcester, Massachusetts. She is working on the process of making sense of self in the context of childhood cancer and hospitalization. She is also interested in the social development of infants and in health psychology of children and adults.

AARO TOOMELA is Professor in the Department of Special Education at the University of Tartu, Estonia. His major interest is in the role of culture in human development. He is the editor of *Cultural Guidance in the Development of the Human Mind* (2003).

JAAN VALSINER, Professor of Psychology at Clark University in Worcester, Massachusetts, works on issues of cultural and developmental psychology. He has written a number of monographs, among which *Understanding Vygotsky* (with René Van der Veer, 1991), *Culture and the Development of Children's Action* (2nd ed., 1997), and *The Guided Mind* (1998) are of note. He is the founding editor of the journal *Culture and Psychology* (from 1995 on) and is editor of numerous volumes and of the book series *Advances in Child Development Within Culturally Structured Environments*.

MARY WATKINS is a core faculty member and the coordinator of community and ecological fieldwork and research in the Depth Psychology Doctoral Program at Pacifica Graduate Institute, Carpinteria, California. She is the author of *Waking Dreams* (1984) and *Invisible Guests: The Development of Imaginal Dialogues* (1986), and is co-author of *Talking with Young Children About Adoption* (with Susan Fisher, 1995). She has worked as a clinical psychologist with adults and children, and has also worked with groups around issues of peace, envisioning the future, diversity, vocation, and social justice.

Recent Titles in
Advances in Child Development Within Culturally Structured Environments
Jaan Valsiner, Series Editor

Child Development Within Culturally Structured Environments: Parental
Cognition and Adult-Child Interaction
Jaan Valsiner

Child Development Within Culturally Structured Environments: Social
Co-Construction and Environmental Guidance in Development
Jaan Valsiner

Child Development Within Culturally Structured Environments: Comparative-
Cultural and Constructivist Perspectives
Jaan Valsiner

Child Development Within Culturally Structured Environments: Construction
of Psychological Processes in Interpersonal Communication
Maria C.D.P. Lyra and Jaan Valsiner, editors

Cultural Guidance in the Development of the Human Mind
Aaro Toomela, editor